OTHER BOOKS BY DAVID ALAN JOHNSON:

The City Ablaze: The Second Great Fire of London, 29th December 1940

The London Blitz

V for Vengeance

Union: The Archives Photographs Series

The Battle of Britain: The American Factor

Germany's Spies and Saboteurs

Righteous Deception: German Officers against Hitler

Betrayal: The True Story of J. Edgar Hoover and the Nazi Saboteurs Captured during WWII

Decided on the Battlefield: Grant, Sherman, Lincoln, and the Election of 1864

Union Revisited

Battle of Wills: Ulysses S. Grant, Robert E. Lee, and the Last Year of the Civil War

Yanks in the RAF: The Story of Maverick Pilots and American Volunteers Who Joined Britain's Fight in WWII

The Last Weeks of Abraham Lincoln: A Day-by-Day Account of His Personal, Political, and Military Challenges

ADMIRAL CANARIS

How Hitler's Chief of Intelligence Betrayed the Nazis

DAVID ALAN JOHNSON

Prometheus Books

Essex, Connecticut

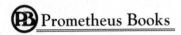
Prometheus Books

An imprint of Globe Pequot, the trade division of
The Rowman & Littlefield Publishing Group, Inc.
4501 Forbes Blvd., Ste. 200
Lanham, MD 20706
www.rowman.com

Distributed by NATIONAL BOOK NETWORK

British Library Cataloguing in Publication Information Available

Library of Congress Cataloging-in-Publication Data
Names: Johnson, David Alan, 1950– author.
Title: Admiral Canaris : how Hitler's chief of intelligence betrayed the Nazis / David Alan
    Johnson.
Other titles: How Hitler's chief of intelligence betrayed the Nazis
Description: Lanham, MD : Prometheus Books, [2024] | Includes bibliographical references. |
    Summary: "Admiral Wilhelm Canaris, Adolf Hitler's chief of military intelligence, accomplished
    something that neither President Franklin D. Roosevelt nor Prime Minister Winston Churchill
    could ever achieve—he saved the lives of hundreds of Jewish refugees and other racial and
    political undesirables by rescuing them from Nazi Germany and other Nazi-occupied countries.
    Admiral Canaris is a page-turning story of one of the most important and least likely saboteurs
    within the Third Reich"— Provided by publisher.
Identifiers: LCCN 2023044163 (print) | LCCN 2023044164 (ebook) | ISBN 9781633889989
    (cloth) | ISBN 9781633889996 (epub)
Subjects: LCSH: Canaris, Wilhelm, 1887–1945. | World War, 1939–1945—Secret service—
    Germany. | World War, 1939–1945—Jews—Rescue. | Anti-Nazi movement. | Holocaust,
    Jewish (1939–1945) | Germany. Wehrmacht. Amt Ausland/Abwehr—Officers—Biography. |
    Germany. Kriegsmarine—Officers—Biography. | Intelligence service—Germany—History—
    20th century.
Classification: LCC D810.S8 C265 2024 (print) | LCC D810.S8 (ebook) | DDC 940.54/8743
    [B]—dc23/eng/20231012
LC record available at https://lccn.loc.gov/2023044163
LC ebook record available at https://lccn.loc.gov/2023044164

To Laura; Thanks for everything.

Contents

PREFACE

Adm. Wilhelm Canaris, Adolf Hitler's chief of military intelligence, accomplished something that neither President Franklin D. Roosevelt nor Prime Minister Winston Churchill could ever achieve: he saved the lives of several hundred Jewish refugees and other racial and political "undesirables" by rescuing them from Nazi Germany and other Nazi-occupied countries. While Rabbi Stephen Wise and members of the World Jewish Congress, along with other Jewish leaders, protested Adolf Hitler's campaign against the Jews in occupied Europe, Admiral Canaris actually removed hundreds of Jews from Nazi territory right past both the Schutzstaffel (SS) and the Gestapo.

By using his rank and authority, Admiral Canaris was able to smuggle hundreds of refugees, mostly Jews but not exclusively, out of the Third Reich by disguising them as his own intelligence agents. Many other individuals, in both the United States and Britain, tried their best to rescue Jews from Hitler and the Nazis, but Admiral Canaris actually succeeded. Admiral Canaris did as much to save Jews and other prisoners from Nazi death camps as Oskar Schindler but received far less credit for what he accomplished—which includes rescuing five hundred Jews from the Netherlands by enlisting them as his own agents and smuggling them out of the country. And Oskar Schindler was not being watched by the Gestapo and the SS while was carrying out his rescue operations.

Researching this book did present its problems, mainly because information regarding the admiral's rescue efforts turned out to be so hard to find. This scarcity of information accounts for the fact that so few detailed accounts have been published about Admiral Canaris's rescue activities. In fact, one reference librarian suggested that this project should be abandoned because there is not enough information to support a book-length account of the admiral's efforts to rescue Jews and other "undesirables."

No records exist that give the exact number of Jews and other refugees whom Admiral Canaris helped to escape the Nazis. The admiral was not able to smuggle to safety every victim of the Nazis, or even everyone he wanted to save, but he did his best to assist anyone who needed help. In March 1941, the head of the Abwehr section in The Hague approached Canaris with an idea for rescuing hundreds of Jewish residents in the Netherlands. Admiral Canaris approved the plan, and the transporting of about five hundred Jews began in May. The refugees were disguised as Abwehr agents and sent to South America, officially designated as "infiltration agents," where they joined hundreds of authentic German agents operating in Argentina, Uruguay, Brazil, and nearly every other South American country. Their first stop was Spain, where they sailed to South America from Spanish ports. This was accomplished with the cooperation of Spanish dictator Francisco Franco, who had been friendly with Canaris since before the war. The admiral also encouraged sympathetic Abwehr officers to assist any Jews and refugees who were in trouble and did his best to see that Jews and "half Jews"—those with one Jewish parent—were supplied with false Abwehr identification. The fact that the Abwehr had the authority to issue its own visas, passports, and other documents made it impossible for the SS or the Gestapo to stop or even question these refugees.

In addition to Jews, the Nazis also persecuted intellectuals, Catholic priests, Polish nationalists, and anyone else they considered unsympathetic to the Hitler regime. Admiral Canaris also assisted as many of these "undesirables" as possible. The wife of the Polish military attaché to Berlin was given the necessary support to escape to Switzerland, and the archbishop of Krakow fled Poland with Canaris's help. While the Nazis waged their campaign of persecution against these "objectionables," Admiral Canaris was doing everything possible to hinder their campaign.

Wilhelm Canaris has frequently been called the mystery man of Adolf Hitler's military intelligence department. He was a career naval officer, with an outstanding war record, who rebelled against the Nazi

government. He was a product of a country that practiced institution-
alized anti-Semitism, but he also helped rescue Jews and other enemies
of the Third Reich at the risk of his own life. Although he was head of
the Abwehr, Nazi Germany's military intelligence branch, the admiral
often gave the impression of not being able to handle the routine duties
of a naval officer, let alone serve as the chief of Hitler's spy network. An
American journalist who met Admiral Canaris several years before the
war admitted that he could not see how such a dull, uninteresting, and
not-very-bright naval officer could have been appointed head of German
military intelligence. "I could not believe that this rumpled, tongue-tied,
absent-minded little man was the new chief of the Abwehr," the journalist remarked.

But Admiral Canaris's unmilitary bearing was actually a cover that
he had devised for himself, and it camouflaged a very sharp and devious
mind. He had been appointed director of the Abwehr because of his
record as a naval officer during World War I, as well as for his political
views—he was an ardent German nationalist who admired Adolf Hitler
and believed that Germany should be the equal of every other European
nation in terms of military might. When Adolf Hitler and the Nazis
came to power in the early 1930s, Canaris supported their intent to
rearm Germany and, especially, their desire to rebuild the German navy.
He often spoke out in favor of Hitler and what he had accomplished to
restore German prestige. But when the Nazis began their campaign of
assassination and terror, including the systematic murder of thousands
of Jews and other "undesirables," the admiral turned completely against
the regime. He determined to do everything possible to fight Hitler and
the Nazis.

On the day World War II began in September 1939, Admiral
Canaris said that a victory for Hitler would be catastrophic. To mislead
and misinform German generals in the field, he deliberately gave incorrect and misleading intelligence reports regarding enemy intentions—as
head of the Abwehr, Canaris had the ability to submit false information
without being detected. This not only put German forces at a military
disadvantage but also caused Hitler to lose faith in all of his intelligence
services, including loyal agents who were supplying genuine information.

Admiral Canaris also began rescuing "undesirables," individuals who had religious or political beliefs that went against the Nazi point of view, and kept them from falling into the hands of the SS and the Gestapo. Admiral Canaris was deeply disturbed by Hitler's persecutions, both on moral and religious grounds. Rescuing religious and political outcasts not only gave Canaris the satisfaction of saving lives but also helped to frustrate Hitler and his regime at the same time.

But the SS was beginning to become suspicious of Admiral Canaris as well as of his rescue activities. Border guards stopped a Jewish family at the Czech-German frontier and found thousands of American dollars in their luggage. Foreign currency was strictly regulated; the guards wanted to know exactly how they managed to acquire so many US dollars. Their explanation was that the Portuguese consul in Munich asked them to hold the money "on account." It was discovered that the consul was an associate of Admiral Canaris and was also involved in a scheme to smuggle Jews out of German-occupied countries disguised as Abwehr agents.

The Gestapo was informed of this incident. They, in turn, informed the Sicherheitsdienst (SD)—the intelligence division of the SS. The Portuguese consul, Dr. Wilhelm Schmidhuber, was arrested and beaten by the Gestapo. Under pressure, Dr. Schmidhuber began talking about Admiral Canaris and his efforts to rescue Jews. An investigation was begun to determine exactly what Canaris knew about this rescue operation, but the admiral had enough political influence to stop it. The head of the SD, Reinhard Heydrich, had also become suspicious due the fact that so many Jews had been employed as Abwehr agents. Heydrich had the idea of combining the Abwehr and the SD and assuming control of both departments. He was always on the lookout for information that could be used against Admiral Canaris and his agency. But Heydrich was assassinated by Czech agents on May 27, 1942, which left Admiral Canaris in charge of the Abwehr and free to continue with his rescue campaign.

The admiral's project for smuggling Jews out of Germany and German-occupied territory was unintentionally furthered by Hitler himself. In the summer of 1942, a sabotage operation, code-named Operation Pastorius, was launched against the aluminum and light-metals industry in the United States. Two four-man sabotage teams were sent across the Atlantic by German U-boats. One team landed in Florida; the other group came ashore on Long Island, New York. But one of the men, George Dasch, was an anti-Nazi who had made up his mind that the sabotage operation would not succeed. He went to the Federal Bureau of Investigation (FBI) and reported details of the operation to federal agents. The FBI arrested the other men before they had the chance to do any damage.

When the failure of Operation Pastorius was reported to Hitler, he blamed Admiral Canaris for the fiasco—the operation had been carried out under the auspices of the Abwehr. Hitler shouted that the lives of eight specially trained saboteurs had been wasted because of the admiral's incompetence. Admiral Canaris tried to explain that the men who had taken part in the operation were actually amateurs who had been chosen for the job because of their familiarity with America, not because of any specialized training. But Hitler was in no mood to be placated. "You should have used criminals or Jews," he shouted, going on in the same general tone for quite some time. Admiral Canaris, along with the others in the room, stood by without saying a word.

Hitler's outburst about using Jews gave Admiral Canaris an idea. He decided to take the remark literally and to interpret it as an order, a *Führerbefehl*, a special decree issued by Hitler. Whenever the admiral used his authority to assign new Jewish "agents" to the Abwehr, anyone in either the SS or the Gestapo who questioned Canaris's order would be told simply, "Orders from the Führer." At the time of Hitler's outburst, both Feldmarschall Wilhelm Keitel and Heinrich Himmler were present, which conveniently supplied Canaris with two high-ranking witnesses to the *Führerbefehl*.

But the stress of his anti-Nazi activities, including the rescue of "undesirables," was beginning to take its toll on Admiral Canaris's health. By 1943, he was physically exhausted as well as mentally drained. In January, he was asked to help prevent an elderly Jewish man from being deported to Poland, which would almost certainly mean his death. The admiral had to decline, explaining that he was "hemmed in" and would not be able to assist.

Admiral Canaris was finally dismissed as head of the Abwehr at the beginning of 1944. The Abwehr's failure to give any advance warning of the Allied landings at Anzio in January 1944 convinced Hitler that it should be abolished. Canaris was dismissed from the service on February 18, 1944. He was named director of the Economic Warfare Department, which was nothing more than a make-work desk job. Friends advised the admiral to go to Spain, where he would have the protection of Spanish dictator Franco, but the admiral did not want to leave. "I want to share the fate of Germany," he told his wife. He came closer to getting his wish than he realized at the time. Admiral Canaris was implicated in the plot to assassinate Hitler on July 20, 1944, and was hanged on April 9, 1945, less than a month before Hitler committed suicide.

Adm. Wilhelm Canaris's role in rescuing Jews has largely been overlooked, in spite of the fact that his rescue campaign was highly effective. In July 1944, he was accused by the Nazis of helping individuals who did not agree with Hitler to escape from the country, including "numerous Jews [and] persons with religious affiliations" who were threatened by the Nazis. This was one of the charges used to convict and execute him. Admiral Canaris risked his life on several occasions to help Jews and other refugees escape certain death at Auschwitz and Dachau. Just before the war in Europe came to an end, circumstances sent Admiral Canaris to his own death at a concentration camp.

CHAPTER ONE

Orders from the Führer

ADM. WILHELM CANARIS LISTENED TO THE TIRADE IN COMPLETE silence. Unwelcome news always put Adolf Hitler in a bad mood, and the news concerning Operation Pastorius had been nothing short of disastrous. Since the early morning hours of June 28, 1942, he had not heard any good news concerning the operation. It soon became apparent that everyone who had taken part in the action, all eight men, had been arrested. They had been in the United States less than two weeks when they were taken into custody and had accomplished nothing, not a single act of sabotage. Hitler had been venting his anger for at least a quarter hour over the failure of the sabotage mission, screaming and shouting and working himself up into a near frenzy.

Operation Pastorius was the code name for a sabotage mission directed against several aluminum and light-metal alloy factories in the eastern and midwestern United States. These factories supplied the US aircraft industry with most of the alloys needed for making airplanes of all types, including bombers and fighters. Two four-man teams had been sent across the Atlantic aboard German submarines; they had been assigned the task of putting these plants out of action and had been given special training on the sabotaging of light-metal factories. Four of the men landed on Long Island, New York; the other group came ashore on the coast of Florida. All eight men had lived in the United States for many years before the war and were well acquainted with American ways and customs. But one of the men, George Dasch, was an anti-Nazi who made up his mind to undermine the sabotage operation. He went to the Federal Bureau of Investigation (FBI) shortly after coming ashore and reported the details of the sabotage mission to federal agents. The FBI arrested the other seven men before they had the chance to do any damage.

Hitler had also sent for Col. Erwin von Lahousen, the head of Abwehr II, the department responsible for sabotage and sedition. Hitler wanted to scold Colonel von Lahousen for his part in the fiasco along with Admiral Canaris. Canaris was the overall chief of the Abwehr, the German military intelligence service. Feldmarschall Wilhelm Keitel, the overall commanding general of German armed forces, and Heinrich Himmler, chief of the Schutzstaffel (SS), were also present. Everyone in the room stood in silence during Hitler's outburst.

At the top of his voice, Hitler demanded an explanation for the disaster. The lives of eight highly trained saboteurs had been wasted, he said, because of the bungled expedition, and he wanted to know why Operation Pastorius had failed so dramatically. Admiral Canaris did his best to explain that the men were not trained agents or munitions experts. All eight men were amateurs who had been chosen for the Pastorius assignment because each of them had lived in the United States and was familiar with the country. But Hitler was in no mood to be placated. If eight men had to be sacrificed, he shouted, Admiral Canaris and Colonel von Lahousen should have chosen men that were unnecessary to Germany, lives that would not be missed. "You should have used criminals or Jews!" he said.[1] Admiral Canaris said nothing in response to that or anything else Hitler had to say during the rest of his outburst.

Hitler's outpouring about using Jews as agents did serve one useful purpose, at least to Admiral Canaris's way to thinking. It gave him an idea: he decided to take this offhand remark and use it as the basis for a rescue operation to smuggle Jews out of German-occupied territory. He turned it into a *Führerbefehl*, a special order issued by Hitler, and used the remark as a mandate to disguise Jews and other "undesirables" as Abwehr agents. Once these new "Abwehr recruits" had been issued their papers and identity cards, they could be assigned to duties outside the country, beyond the reach of the Gestapo and the SS. Sending Abwehr employees overseas was nothing out of the ordinary; Admiral Canaris already had many members of his agency at work abroad. Thousands of intelligence agents had been assigned to South American countries, including Argentina and Uruguay, which gave Admiral Canaris a perfect cover for his rescue operation. Smuggling Jews and other victims of the Nazi regime out of the country was a fairly simple matter. An eyewitness to the admiral's activities recalled, "Numerous Jews or half-Jews were dressed in army uniforms on Canaris' instigation, carrying official military intelligence ID cards."[2] If anyone questioned the nationality of his new agents or showed any sign of suspicion, the admiral had an answer already prepared: "Orders from the Führer."[3]

While the Nazis were waging their war against Jews, Christian clergymen, intellectuals, and anyone else they considered inconvenient, Admiral Canaris was doing his best to hinder their efforts. He used his rank and influence to save as many "undesirables" as he could from concentration camps and death chambers. Because the Abwehr had the authority to create identity cards, passports, and visas, along with any other documents that Admiral Canaris might need for his purposes, the Gestapo had no effective method to stop or even question the admiral in his rescue efforts. His standard response, "Orders from the Führer," would be enough to justify sending a growing number of agents to Switzerland or Spain, and then across the Atlantic, under the very noses of the Gestapo.

The admiral would often invoke the name of Adolf Hitler to help strengthen an argument or give his point of view added authority and prestige. During the course of a conversation with a Nazi Party member or a government official, he would nonchalantly say something like "I have also spoken about this to the Führer" or "The Führer thinks . . ." Just mentioning "the Führer" was often enough to make his point of view prevail, even though the discussion he had with Hitler may have had nothing to do with the topic under discussion and had probably been about the weather or somebody's health. It was not exactly the same thing as mentioning a *Führerbefehl*, but it had the same effect.

* * *

Wilhelm Canaris had not always been an opponent of Adolf Hitler or the Nazi Party. He had been a career officer in the German navy all of his working life and had an outstanding record as a junior officer during World War I. His background in the German naval service and his enthusiastic support for German nationalism gave no indication that he would ever become an anti-Nazi, which makes his turning against Hitler even more remarkable.

Young Willy Canaris first became interested in a naval career in 1902, when he was fifteen years old, during a trip to Greece with his parents. While the family was visiting Athens, he discovered a monument dedicated to an Adm. Constantine Kanaris, who had been one of the heroes of the Greek War of Independence. Kanaris managed to compile quite an impressive war record—he led a night attack on the Turkish fleet in the Chios Channel on June 18/19, 1822; he also destroyed several Turkish troop transports off Samos in August 1824. Wilhelm made up his mind that he wanted to be a naval hero, just like his famous—at least in Greece—ancestor. He would eventually discover that he was not related to Admiral Kanaris in any way, but this did not deter his dream of becoming a naval officer. Even after he rose to the rank of admiral himself, Wilhelm Canaris kept a portrait of Constantine Kanaris in the living room of his house in Berlin and would tell visitors that the Greek admiral was his "grandfather."[4]

When Carl Canaris, Wilhelm's father, found out that his son was interested in a career as an officer in the Imperial German Navy, he was more than slightly surprised. Carl was a manager at the Lower Rhine Smelting Works in Duisburg-Hochfeld, as well as a member of the firm's board of directors. He was a hardheaded member of the bourgeoisie and expected his children to follow his example. Willy's eldest brother, Carl August, worked his way to the top of the German steel industry and was appointed manager of the Henschel locomotive and machine works. Willy's sister Anna married an engineer named Rudolf Buck, who became the director of the giant Buderus Ironworks. The entire Canaris family was involved in either the iron and steel industry or the coal-mining business. Wilhelm was expected to become an engineer or an executive in steel manufacturing, just like his relatives. Carl Canaris was not really opposed to his son's decision to become a career naval officer; he just did not quite know what to make of Wilhelm's choice of careers.

But, then again, Willy was always a bit unusual. He read a lot—probably too much, at least according to his father's way of thinking—and tended to keep to himself instead of joining in the activities of other boys his own age. The root of his sympathies for outsiders and outcasts can be traced to this part of his life. He was bookish and precocious, traits that made him unpopular with his classmates at school. Most of Wilhelm's time was spent reading or playing by himself—he was quiet and introverted by nature and did not make friends easily. When he entered the Steinbart Gymnasium in Duisburg, he remained an outsider. Even though he was one of the best and smartest students in his class, he only had one friend. He knew what it felt like to be disliked and excluded and would feel sympathy for outcasts throughout his life. This sympathy would extend to political and religious outcasts in Hitler's Germany, along with other victims of the Nazi regime.

Although the elder Canaris did not oppose a military career for his young son, he could not understand why Wilhelm had chosen the navy. Carl Canaris was of the opinion that a career in the cavalry would be much more suitable for the son of a wealthy iron-smelting executive—much more glamourous and socially acceptable. He even went so far as to buy a horse for Wilhelm, which turned out to be a very well-received gift; the boy did go on to become an accomplished horseman. Under pressure from his father, Wilhelm finally did apply for a commission in the Bavarian 1st Heavy Cavalry Regiment. But he still had his heart set on a lifetime as a naval officer.

In September 1904, an event took place that changed the course of Wilhelm's life. On September 26, Carl Canaris died of a stroke at the age of fifty-two. Wilhelm's mother, Amélie, agreed that the cavalry could not offer the life that her son was looking for. Wilhelm was determined to go to sea; Amélie could see that. He would never be happy in the cavalry or in any other branch of the German army. She also did not see the glamour that her husband saw in the cavalry. She gave Wilhelm her permission to pursue his dream and submitted his name to the Cadet Admissions Board at the Kiel Naval Academy, to which he won acceptance.

Amélie Canaris influenced her son's life in other, subtler ways as well. She was not very much like her husband as far as temperament and disposition were concerned. Carl Canaris is usually depicted as a stiff-necked and hardheaded Prussian with a direct manner and a no-nonsense attitude toward the world in general and toward Wilhelm in particular. He did not really care if Willy wanted to join a cavalry regiment or not; Carl wanted Willy to join the cavalry, and that was that. Amélie Canaris had the opposite attitude. She was lively, cheerful, and enthusiastic. Her ancestors had been farmers from Silesia, which had become part of Prussia in the mid-1700s. But they were never Prussians at heart; they were much too calm and easygoing. Amélie was also easygoing and gentle. She treated young Wilhelm with more generosity than her husband, taking his interests to heart and sympathizing with him, while Carl tended to be stern and uncompromising. This attitude would influence Wilhelm in later years. His tendency to sympathize with outcasts and outsiders, like his mother, instead of sharing his father's hard and unforgiving attitude, would sometimes put him at odds with his superiors, especially after the Nazis came to power in the 1930s.

Because of his mother's sympathetic attitude, Wilhelm was allowed to embark upon a career as a naval officer. He entered the Naval Academy at Kiel on April 1, 1905, at age eighteen. For the next two and a half years, Midshipman Canaris endured the harsh discipline of the academy's instructors, along with all the drills aboard the training ship *Stein*, the lectures in physics, mathematics, navigation, and all of the other activities that a naval cadet had to perform on his way to becoming a naval officer. During his time aboard the *Stein*, which was a three-masted training vessel, he experienced a number of problems because of his height—he was only five feet, three inches tall. Climbing the ship's masts and rowing its whaleboat required physical strength and stamina that he did not have. But he managed to survive everything the academy inflicted upon him—drills, rope climbing, and all. With willpower and determination, as well as a better-than-average intellect, he did complete all of the academy's requirements. Midshipman Canaris passed his final examinations and was assigned to the light cruiser *Bremen* in October 1907.

The *Bremen* was a new ship, commissioned in 1904, and turned out to be a plum assignment for the young academy graduate. The cruiser's primary task was to "show the flag" along the Atlantic coast of Central and South America, to let the citizens of Brazil, Argentina, Panama, and all the other countries of the region know that the kaiser, Wilhelm II, had interests in that part of the world. Showing the flag was a peaceful way of making Germany's presence felt, but it was still a form of intimidation. Midshipman Canaris's main task was to act as the ship's linguist: he spoke English quite fluently, was fairly conversational in French, and had some understanding of Russian. He also assisted with the training of crew members when needed and gave lectures in subjects assigned by his superiors.

The officers aboard the *Bremen* liked the little midshipman and enjoyed having him in their company. Even though young Canaris was short in stature and tended to be quiet and introverted, he was also cheerful and conscientious. Every officer on board had only praise for him—in their reports, they always made it a point to mention his efficiency, his reliability, and his enthusiasm. After Canaris was commissioned as a sublieutenant on September 28, 1908, the *Bremen*'s captain had this to say about him: "He promises to be a good officer once he acquires a little more confidence and self-assurance."[5] He would go on to acquire a good deal of both and to become an excellent, if not always conventional, officer.

Sublieutenant Canaris was not your usual junior officer, even when he was twenty-one-years old. Most officers his age were interested primarily in naval matters: navigation, gunnery, tactics. While Canaris was also interested in these, he also had other things on his mind. For one thing, he read a great deal more than any of his fellow officers on a variety of subjects. Also, he had an interest in languages—something he did not share with any other officer aboard the *Bremen*. Because his ship would be steaming in waters close to Central and South America, Sublieutenant Canaris took it upon himself to learn Spanish; he had an ear for languages and managed to pick up it fairly quickly and easily. His newly acquired language was put to good use in 1909, when Sublieutenant Canaris was sent ashore to speak with senior officials in the Venezuelan government regarding German influence in the region. He spoke so effectively to the country's political leaders that the president, Vincente Gomez, awarded Canaris the Order of Bolivar, Fifth Class. Many years later, when he was a senior officer, Admiral Canaris would use his fluency in Spanish to form a special relationship with Spanish dictator Francisco Franco.

Sublieutenant Canaris enjoyed his time as a junior officer aboard the *Bremen* and also enjoyed the companionship of the other officers. But it is the lot of a junior officer to be transferred for his own professional development, and Canaris said a fond farewell to the ship and its officers in January 1910. His next assignment was to a torpedo boat squadron; he took part in the unit's North Sea maneuvers. Five months later, he was transferred to another torpedo squadron, just in time for more North Sea exercises. He made a favorable impression on the officer commanding the squadron, who recommended him for future command of a torpedo boat. But the frigid weather, along with the rough conditions connected with serving aboard the small boats, damaged his health; he developed a serious lung disorder, which made it necessary for him to leave the squadron.

As the result of his health issues, Sublieutenant Canaris was granted six month's medical leave. He was also promoted to lieutenant senior grade. In December 1911, Lieutenant Canaris received another assignment at sea, aboard another cruiser, which was much more to his liking. His new ship was the *Dresden*, which had been commissioned only two years earlier. Aboard the *Dresden*, Lieutenant Canaris sailed to the eastern Mediterranean, as well as to the gulf coast of Mexico. In July 1914, the *Dresden* received orders to evacuate the former president of Mexico, Victoriano Huerta, to another country—Mexico was in the throes of a civil war, and Huerta was persona non grata in his own country. Lieutenant Canaris was sent ashore to escort the former president to the *Dresden*—his language skills were once again put to use—and Huerta was taken to Kingston, Jamaica.[6]

Up to that point, Lieutenant Canaris's naval career had been respectable but not outstanding. He had shown himself to be intelligent and highly efficient, and his knowledge of languages had proved invaluable on two separate occasions. But he had not had the chance to show that he was anything more than a slightly above-average junior officer. At the end of August 1914, that situation changed abruptly and completely.

On the afternoon of July 31, 1914, the *Dresden*'s radio operator received an urgent message from Naval Headquarters in Berlin: "Drohende Kriegsgefahr Grossbritannien, Frankreich, Russland. Bundesgenosse Österreich-Ungarn, voraussichtlich Italien. Nicht heimhehren. Kreuzerkrieg führen gemass den Mobilmachungsbeftimmungen [Imminent danger of war Great Britain, France, Russia. Allies Austria-Hungary, probably Italy. Don't go home. Waging cruiser warfare according to the mobilization regulations]."[7] This amounted to a war warning. German cruisers were to carry out unrestricted warfare against British merchant shipping, much in the same way that submarines would attack merchantmen later in the war.

If the message was meant to be inspiring, it had just the opposite effect. Although the *Dresden* was a fairly new ship, she was low on coal and supplies. Also, she was a light cruiser, with a main armament of ten 4-inch guns. She would now be up against the Royal Navy, the largest and most powerful navy in the world—British battleships were armed with 14-inch guns. The *Dresden* was in desperate need of fuel, fresh water, food, and good luck. Her captain, Fritz Lüdecke, changed course; he could not go back to Germany. Instead, he would sail for the coast of Argentina and hunt for British shipping before enemy warships caught up with him.

Lieutenant Canaris suddenly found himself with a brand-new job: he was now the *Dresden*'s intelligence officer. Because the ship had been given the assignment of intercepting and sinking enemy shipping, it was vital to have up-to-date information on British merchant vessels in the area. But the *Dresden*'s main source of information consisted of broadcasts from radio stations in Central and South America, which were notoriously unreliable—these stations relied upon British sources, mainly British news agencies, for their data. The British were well aware that German warships were tuning into these stations and deliberately supplied them with inaccurate reports. In order to find reliable statistics regarding the movements of British shipping, German cruisers, including the *Dresden*, had to find their own contacts. Because Lieutenant Canaris was the only man on board who spoke fluent Spanish, he was given the task of finding reliable information on the British merchant fleet and its activities.

Lieutenant Canaris not only spoke and understood Spanish but also had acquired some actual experience in intelligence work when he was stationed aboard the *Bremen*. In 1908, he had been instrumental in building an intelligence network in Brazil and Argentina. The *Bremen*'s captain, Albert Hopman, had established contacts in these countries with the help of a relative, referred to simply as "Uncle Rudolf" in Hopman's diary. "We went ashore with Canaris and settled cipher matters with Uncle Rudolf," according to an entry dated November 25, 1908. Another entry, dated December 24, 1908, gives another insight into Lieutenant Canaris's intelligence activities: "Went ashore with Canaris and negotiated with Herr Georgius about V. Informant matters." A V-Mann—*Vertrauensmann*, or "trusted person"—was an informant or agent.[8]

This was a brand-new world for Lieutenant Canaris, and he loved both the work and the challenge. He discovered that he had a talent for cloak-and-dagger work as well as for subterfuge. Among the tasks he performed as intelligence officer was making contact with acquaintances, mostly businessmen who lived in Brazil and Argentina, people he met during his days aboard the *Bremen*. He also arranged for an American radio station at San Juan, Puerto Rico, to receive a report from the *Dresden* that the cruiser would be going back to Germany by way of the Azores; Lieutenant Canaris knew that this broadcast would be passed along to British intelligence by American sources.

Another misleading report sent by Lieutenant Canaris informed a Brazilian station that his ship would be heading toward Germany. Actually, the *Dresden* was steaming southward at the time, picking up coal and provisions from German freighters on her way to Montevideo, Uruguay. British intelligence did not realize that they had been duped, or at least did not find out that the *Dresden* was operating off the coast of Uruguay and Argentina, until the cruiser had sunk two British merchantmen. The *Dresden*'s captain, Fritz Lüdecke, was very happy to find out that his intelligence officer had such a knack for duplicity.

But the *Dresden*'s effect upon British shipping went beyond the sinking of the two freighters. Even though these were the only two ships sunk by the *Dresden*, British naval intelligence spread the word that a German cruiser was operating off the coast of Argentina. This warning served to keep British vessels out of Brazilian and Argentinean ports.

Word of the *Dresden*'s presence off Argentina also sent British warships to the area. Early in September, Lieutenant Canaris's contacts sent word that the cruisers HMS *Good Hope* and HMS *Monmouth*, along with the light cruiser HMS *Otranto*, were heading south to intercept the *Dresden*. Captain Lüdecke made a decision to leave the area and head for the Pacific Ocean; he had been ordered to sink British merchant shipping, not to fight with British cruisers. After entering the Pacific, the *Dresden* inadvertently made contact with the German Far East Squadron, under the command of Adm. Graf von Spee. It would turn out to be a very happy accident.

Admiral von Spee's squadron was quite an impressive group of warships, consisting of the heavy cruisers *Scharnhorst* and *Gneisenau*, the light cruisers *Nürnberg* and *Leipzig*, the auxiliary cruiser *Prinz Eitel Friedrich*, an auxiliary vessel, and eight colliers. Now the *Dresden* had joined the group as well. The British warships chasing the *Dresden* also made their way into the Pacific, right behind the German cruiser. Lieutenant Canaris's connections in Argentina and Chile kept the *Dresden*—along with the rest of Admiral von Spee's Far East Squadron—informed of the enemy's movements. On the night of October 6/7, 1914, *Dresden* sent a signal to Admiral von Spee to report that British warships were steaming to the west off Cape Horn. Another signal was sent soon afterward: "Unconfirmed report from freighter in Coronel, Chile: British cruiser squadron rumored waiting for German Far East Squadron off Easter Island."[9] The signal also mentioned that two enemy cruisers had passed to the west of Punta Arenas on the morning of October 5.

Thanks to Lieutenant Canaris, Admiral von Spee had accurate information regarding the enemy's warships, while the British commanders had no exact idea where von Spee's cruisers were headed. The reports kept coming in from contacts in Chile and were immediately sent off to Admiral von Spee. Lieutenant Canaris expanded his intelligence base by keeping in touch with the captains of German-owned merchantmen and asking them to keep a lookout for British ships. The freighter captains were more than happy to oblige and began sending their own reports to Lieutenant Canaris aboard the *Dresden*.

All of the reports gave Admiral von Spee a priceless edge: they allowed him to locate the British squadron off the Chilean port of Coronel on November 1, 1914. The German cruisers opened fire as the daylight was beginning to fade and sank HMS *Good Hope* and HMS *Monmouth*. Only the increasing darkness saved the *Otranto* and *Glasgow*. The Battle of Coronel was a complete, and completely unexpected, German victory. The Royal Navy had been the undisputed rulers of the seas up to that point. As impressive as the accuracy of the German gunners had been at Coronel, the victory would never have taken place without the brilliant intelligence work of Lt. Wilhelm Canaris.

Admiral von Spee recognized the role that Lieutenant Canaris played in the unlikely victory at Coronel and rewarded him accordingly—the young lieutenant was presented with the Iron Cross, 2nd class. Handing the British cruisers such a setback whetted the admiral's appetite for still more successes in the not-too-distant future. His immediate plans were to return to the South Atlantic and sink more British warships and merchant vessels. But unfortunately for the German cruisers, Admiral von Spee's plans excluded Lieutenant Canaris. The admiral did not bother to ask the lieutenant what his contacts knew about British activities in the South Atlantic.

The admiral received word that an armed rebellion had broken out in South Africa and also that the British fleet would be steaming there to help defend British colonists in that part of the world. If all the British warships left the South Atlantic for Africa, the main British naval base in the area, Port Stanley in the Falkland Islands, would be left unprotected. From Admiral von Spee's point of view, he now had the opportunity to remove the influence of the Royal Navy from the entire region, once and for all. All he had to do was attack Port Stanley; after what his Far East Squadron had done at Coronel, it seemed to him that the port was his for the taking. It seemed like a good scheme, at least on paper.

But the captains of Admiral von Spee's cruisers, including Captain Lüdecke of the *Dresden*, did not agree. There was no information on British defenses protecting Port Stanley, they argued; there was only a rumor that the British fleet would be departing for Africa. Before planning any sort of attack, it would be best to find out exactly what the British had left behind before they sailed off for South Africa—they certainly would not have left one of their primary naval bases undefended. Lieutenant Canaris should at least be given enough time to get in touch with his intelligence contacts and find out exactly what they knew about Port Stanley. It would be best—actually essential—not to act without acquiring some good, solid intelligence first.

But Admiral von Spee would not listen. His cruisers had just decimated a squadron of the finest warships in the world, and he intended to follow up his victory at Coronel with an attack on Port Stanley. He did not want to wait until Lieutenant Canaris supplied him with reports from his contacts, which might take weeks. On the morning of December 8, 1914, the German Far East Squadron advanced toward the Falkland Islands and found itself confronted by a full array of British warships: two battlecruisers and six cruisers. As soon as Admiral von Spee realized his predicament, he reversed course and did his best to escape the trap he had set for himself. But the British warships were faster than the German cruisers and had no trouble overtaking them. The Battle of the Falkland Islands, as it became known, was Coronel in reverse. Admiral von Spee's fleet was destroyed, one cruiser at a time, and the German Far East Squadron ceased to exist. Admiral von Spee was killed during the course of the battle, along with two of his sons. Only the *Dresden* was able to get away. Captain Lüdecke managed to outrun the British squadron, and the cruiser escaped into the darkness.

The *Dresden* found a hiding place in one of the small bays along Chile's southernmost coast. But the Chilean government sent Captain Lüdecke a message, which Lieutenant Canaris translated from Spanish: because of international neutrality laws, the *Dresden* would only be allowed to remain in Chilean waters for twenty-four hours.[10] British authorities were behind this demand; the British consul in Punta Arenas was well aware that the *Dresden* was in the vicinity of the Strait of

Magellan and also that at least seven British warships had been sent to find and sink her. But thanks to Lieutenant Canaris and his contacts in Punta Arenas, which were every bit as active as the British diplomatic staff in the town, Captain Lüdecke was kept well informed of what the enemy warships were up to. The *Dresden* always managed to keep one step ahead of the enemy. The cruiser escaped from Punta Arenas because of Lieutenant Canaris's connections—the Royal Navy squadron was headed directly for the Chilean port, but the *Dresden* had already sailed by the time the British warships arrived.

Lieutenant Canaris's man in Punta Arenas was also responsible for the *Dresden* being able to replenish her supply of coal and resume commerce raiding. A collier, *Sierra Cordoba*, was sent to rendezvous with the German cruiser based on information sent by Canaris's contact. This gave Captain Lüdecke a new lease on life. He sent a message to Berlin: "On 3 February, will try to break through to the west coast of South America with 'Sierra Cordoba.' Will attempt to continue cruiser operations in East India given availability of sufficient coal."[11]

Now that *Dresden* had her coal bunkers filled, Captain Lüdecke lost no time in leaving Chilean waters and heading for the open Pacific. The cruiser rang up full speed and made her way through the tangle of small islets on her way out to sea. Before leaving, Lieutenant Canaris instructed his contacts in Punta Arenas to circulate a report that the *Dresden* was steaming eastward, into the Atlantic; this was for the benefit of British agents in the area, who would send the misleading information on to British naval intelligence. The *Dresden* reached the open sea, finally clear of Chilean waters, on February 14.

Captain Lüdecke took the *Dresden* on a north-northwesterly course, away from the coast of Chile and into the shipping lanes. On February 27, he encountered the British freighter *Conway Castle*, a sailing vessel carrying a cargo of barley. After taking the crew off, Captain Lüdecke ordered the *Conway Castle* to be sunk by gunfire. The crew was later transferred to a Peruvian ship. It would be the last prize the *Dresden* would claim.

By early March, the *Dresden* was running low on coal and supplies again, and her engines were in dire need of a complete overhaul. Captain

Lüdecke knew that his ship was no longer in fighting trim and that she would have no chance at all of surviving a battle with British warships. He also knew that several British warships were out looking for him; radio traffic between them made him well aware that the *Dresden* was heavily outnumbered and outgunned. He did manage to escape one enemy cruiser, HMS *Kent*, but realized that his only hope of surviving was to find a neutral port and request to be interned there for the rest of the war.

Captain Lüdecke did succeed in finding sanctuary in Cumberland Bay, on the north coast of the Chilean island of Más a Tierra. But HMS *Kent* discovered *Dresden*'s hiding place and radioed for other British warships to reinforce her. HMS *Glasgow* joined the *Kent* on the morning of March 14; the two cruisers opened fire on the *Dresden*. In the course of the barrage, the German cruiser was hit repeatedly and badly damaged. Captain Lüdecke dispatched Lieutenant Canaris to the *Glasgow* by open boat; he wanted his intelligence officer to lodge a complaint. The *Dresden* was in Chilean waters, Lieutenant Canaris told the *Glasgow*'s captain. Firing on the German ship in neutral waters was a violation of international law. The *Glasgow*'s captain was not interested in the fact that the *Dresden* was in Chilean territorial waters. His orders were to sink the *Dresden*; any details about neutrality or international law would have to be settled by diplomats at a later date.[12]

The British reply was expected; Captain Lüdecke did not really expect the two enemy cruisers to cease fire and withdraw because of his objection. The protest was only a ruse to buy time. While Lieutenant Canaris was arguing with the captain of the *Glasgow*, Captain Lüdecke was making preparations to scuttle the *Dresden* and evacuate her crew to Más a Tierra. By the time Lieutenant Canaris returned to the ship, the crew had already been taken off and the demolition charges set. At 11:15 a.m., the charges blew in two cataclysmic explosions; what was left of the cruiser *Dresden* settled on the bottom of Cumberland Bay.

The ship had escaped capture by the British, but the crew now faced the prospect of indefinite internment. Lieutenant Canaris did not intend to sit out the war in the quiet confines of the island of Quiriquina, a few miles away from the mainland of Chile. He was an officer in the Imperial

German Navy and intended to rejoin the navy, and the war, as soon as he could arrange an escape from captivity. His opportunity came on the night of August 3/4, 1915.

Lieutenant Canaris made the acquaintance of a local fisherman during his time on Quiriquina and arranged for the fisherman to take him over to the mainland. As soon as he landed, he made his way to the German embassy in Santiago. The embassy staff issued him a counterfeit Chilean passport in the name of Reed Rosas. By train and by horseback, Lieutenant Canaris crossed the Andes and made his way across Argentina to Buenos Aires. From there, he sailed to Amsterdam aboard the Dutch steamer *Frisia*. He docked in the Netherlands on September 30 and finally arrived in Berlin on October 4.

When he presented himself at the German Admiralty, Wilhelm Canaris was a physical wreck. The seven-thousand-mile journey had taken its toll; he had lost a considerable amount of weight and was both physically and mentally exhausted. Canaris was never exactly the hardy and robust type to begin with. After returning from South America, he was in a seriously debilitated and rundown condition. In November, after a few weeks of recuperation, he was presented with the Iron Cross, 1st class, by the kaiser and was also promoted to *Kapitänleutnant*. He was then sent home for extended leave to recover from his weakness and fatigue; the Admiralty recognized the effect of the two-month ordeal on the young officer.

Lieutenant Canaris's first assignment after returning to duty was as an intelligence officer in Spain. German naval intelligence had established a base in Madrid shortly after the war began. The lieutenant's instructions were to keep track of Allied shipping in the Mediterranean, as well as to inform U-boats in the area of enemy ships and their movements. His fluency in Spanish, along with his natural flair for guile and deception, served him well at his new post in Madrid. He avoided making contact with the German embassy as much as possible; using his counterfeit Chilean passport, which he retained after returning from South America, and going by the name Reed Rosas made avoiding the embassy and its staff fairly easy. Only a few select people at the embassy knew anything about Lieutenant Canaris or the reason for his appearance in Madrid.

Once he had established himself in his new position, the lieutenant quietly went about his business. He acquired information about the movements of enemy ships from the dockhands at the port of Cartagena and passed all useful information—number of ships, course and speed, port of departure and destination—to the U-boat base at Pola, Croatia, on the Adriatic Sea. These reports proved invaluable to submarine commanders, who used them to track and sink several Allied ships. According to one source, "He blew up nine British ships from his base in Spain."[13] German submarines operating from Pola owed their success directly to the crafty little intelligence officer in Madrid.

In spite of his achievements, Lieutenant Canaris was not very happy with his work or his assignment. Even though he was probably the most successful German agent in Spain, "his heart was not really in it."[14] He was a naval officer. As far as he was concerned, a naval officer should serve at sea, especially in wartime. Senior officers at the German Admiralty were in complete agreement with him. The Admiralty was always looking for qualified, intelligent officers for its U-boat flotilla, which was growing both in size and efficiency, and Lieutenant Canaris was looking to get away from his intelligence job in Madrid. Their mutual need was met in October 1915, when Wilhelm Canaris was assigned to the Inspectorate of Submarines. He would be going back to sea, at long last, in a completely new environment.

Lieutenant Canaris's first assignments in the U-boat arm consisted of a wide range of training courses—and many of them. There were courses on submarine warfare, including the care and handling of torpedoes, along with instruction on handling and operating as well as supplying and provisioning a submarine. Submarine school lasted nearly two years. Lieutenant Canaris passed his final examinations on September 11, 1917, and was pronounced operational—according to his superiors, he was well qualified to command a submarine.

After several weeks of staff duty at the U-boat base at Cattaro, in Croatia—which must have seemed like several years to the paperwork-hating lieutenant—Canaris was given command of a mine-laying submarine at the end of November 1917. He performed his job so well, sowing mines in Allied shipping lanes in the Mediterranean, that he was given command of U-34 and sent to the western Mediterranean. This patrol proved to be another success: U-34 torpedoed and sank three British freighters, which earned Lieutenant Canaris special mention from his superior officers. Word of his achievements eventually reached Kaiser Wilhelm, who asked, "Is this a descendent of the national hero of the Greek War of Independence?"[15]

Because of his accomplishments with U-34, Lieutenant Canaris was given command of a new submarine, UB-128. By the time the boat had finished her sea trials and was ready for her first patrol, summer was almost over. Unfortunately for Lieutenant Canaris, the U-boat war in the Mediterranean was also coming to an end. German submarine bases in the Adriatic Sea were shut down when Austria-Hungary surrendered to the Allies in October 1918. All U-boats received a signal to return to Germany; their war in the Mediterranean was over, and their Adriatic bases were being destroyed.

On their journey back to Kiel, the crew of UB-128 received a series of distressing radio signals. From the news reports, it had become evident that the fighting was not going well. Not only had Austria-Hungary surrendered, but the military situation for Germany was growing more desperate with each passing day. Finally, on November 11, everyone on board received the news they had been dreading: Germany had surrendered, Kaiser Wilhelm had abdicated, and a republican form of government had been declared. The war was over, and a new world had begun. Not everyone knew exactly how they would fit into this new world, including Wilhelm Canaris.

The men of UB-128 found out just how foreign and alien the new Germany had become during their first day in Kiel. The governor of the port town, Gustav Noske, gave a talk to the crew to explain what had happened while they were away: a revolution had occurred, and all traces of order had been replaced by rebellion and anarchy. Lieutenant Canaris and the rest of the crew found this hard to believe, so much so that Governor Noske was asked to give another, more detailed lecture on the following day. During the course of this second talk, a policeman interrupted with an urgent message: a group of mutineers was preparing to break up the meeting and arrest the governor. Everyone was shocked by

Lt. Wilhelm Canaris (*center*) and crew members of the submarine UB-128 in the summer of 1918. After World War I, the Treaty of Versailles limited the size of the German navy and strictly prohibited submarines. *Source:* National Archives.

this interruption, but all were now also convinced that they had returned to a new and altogether frightening country. Order and authority had been replaced by mob rule and lawlessness.

The mutiny was not restricted to Kiel; it had spread throughout Germany. The port of Lübeck had also been taken over by rebel sailors earlier in November; they had taken the city and were holding their officers prisoner. Other captive towns included Dresden, Hanover, Cologne, and Breslau. They were occupied and ruled by what were known as Councils of Workers and Soldiers. In Kiel, Governor Noske managed to work with the local council and was eventually elected as its head. This helped to restore a degree of order and also led to the appointing of a naval officer as a liaison between naval headquarters and Governor Noske. That officer was Lt. Wilhelm Canaris.

Lieutenant Canaris and Gustav Noske became allies in the revolution/civil war that divided the country and reached its climax in Berlin in mid-January 1919. Two right-wing paramilitary groups, the Freikorps (army volunteers) and the Naval Brigade (navy veterans), moved against the Council of Workers and Soldiers on January 15. Lieutenant Canaris was with them during this offensive; the left-wing council offered no resistance. By the end of the day, all public squares, buildings, and other municipal property occupied by the council had been taken over by the army/navy volunteers.

The Berlin uprising had been put down, but the left-wing revolutionaries continued to occupy other cities throughout Germany. Members of both the Freikorps and the Naval Brigade took violent steps to counter the activities of these groups. They shot communists and communist sympathizers in organized executions and were not above committing acts of cold-blooded murder. Two leading communists, Rosa Luxembourg and Karl Liebknecht, were both shot by members of the Freikorps. Lieutenant Canaris may or may not have known about the two shootings—there is not enough evidence about his involvement either to convict or to acquit. He was certainly involved with the new Citizens' Defense units (*einwohnerwehren*) that guarded banks, utilities, and public buildings against communist uprisings. These units were in complete violation of the controversial Treaty of Versailles. Lieutenant Canaris also had the diplomatic ability to address the National Assembly of the Weimar Republic and come to the defense of the *einwohnerwehren*. Gustav Noske, who had become minister of defense in the Weimar Republic, was very glad to have the lieutenant on his side.

Lieutenant Canaris's influence increased with the passing of time. He became a member of the German Admiralty staff, as well as a leading advocate of rebuilding the German navy—this became Canaris's leading cause throughout the Weimar era. Because of his connections within the Admiralty, along with his association with Gustav Noske, the thirty-three-year-old naval officer became even more prominent. Gustav Noske had an idea of becoming dictator of Germany and made Lieutenant

Canaris a member of his personal staff. It looked as though the lieutenant had hitched his wagon to a rapidly rising star.

But because of political infighting, Gustav Noske lost a sizeable portion of his political power. The peace terms of the Treaty of Versailles, signed at the end of June 1919, limited the German army to one hundred thousand men; Noske disbanded both the Freikorps and the Naval Brigades and resigned as defense minister. Left- and right-wing political factions were at each other's throats. Naval officers revolted against the Councils of Workers and Soldiers; their uprising was countered by the left-wing councils, which gained the upper hand. Officers were taken prisoner by rebellious enlisted men. Lieutenant Canaris was among the officers placed under arrest and spent several days in a Berlin jail. After a series of humiliating "interrogations," he was sent back to Kiel with a demotion; he was now a naval staff officer.[16]

In spite of his demotion, Lieutenant Canaris's main focus was still the restoration of the German navy. The Versailles Treaty restricted the German navy, called the Reichsmarine during the Weimar Republic, to a very small fleet, which consisted of about a dozen warships, a dozen torpedo boats, and no submarines. One of the battleships was the *Schleswig-Holstein*, commissioned in December 1906. The Reichsmarine was meant to be a strictly defensive unit, and a very small one at that. Because this new peacetime navy had been so sharply reduced from the battle fleet that existed during the war—most of the German warships had either been handed over to the Allies or scuttled to keep them out of enemy hands—many of the navy's sailors had no ships, no assignments, and no purpose.

When Lieutenant Canaris reported to Kiel to take up his new job, he immediately saw that something had to be done about the Reichsmarine. Along with other officers, including the station commander, Canaris decided that the only acceptable course of action would be to rebuild and rearm the navy in secret. Germany would not always be controlled by the Allied powers and their damned Versailles Treaty. When the country was finally free of her current predicament, the new Germany would need a modern, blue-water fleet.

The first step toward rebuilding the navy would be to reestablish discipline among the sailors stationed at Kiel. Lieutenant Canaris quickly discovered that most of the men had none at all; they were disrespectful and surly and had no intention of either listening to officers or obeying orders. He was disheartened by what he saw but also determined to do something about the problem. The more rebellious men were dismissed, and members of the Freikorps and the Naval Brigade were recruited. Both organizations had been outlawed by the Versailles Treaty, and their members had either dispersed or gone underground. Money would also be needed. With the help of a retired captain who had access to a cache of surplus arms and ammunition at the Kiel naval arsenal, Lieutenant Canaris sold a quantity of these weapons to other countries. This was highly illegal, but as far as Canaris was concerned, any viable method that helped him reach his goal was permissible.

Every one of these activities was against the law. Expanding the navy's personnel lists went directly against the Versailles Treaty, which strictly limited the Reichsmarine to fifteen thousand officers and men. Selling government property was punishable by a prison sentence. Plotting to rebuild the German battle fleet was also prohibited by the Versailles Treaty as well as by the government in Weimar, which made Lieutenant Canaris guilty of treason. The fact that he managed to perform these clandestine activities without getting caught shows just how talented he had become at subterfuge. This ability would serve him well in the years to come, when he would use it to deceive a completely different German regime.

While he was involved in his secret plot to build a new and illegal German navy, Lieutenant Canaris received orders from Berlin that gave him a new assignment. He was ordered to report to the training ship *Berlin*, which was based at Kiel, and assume duties as the ship's executive officer. The training ship's captain was Wilfried von Loewenfeld. Lieutenant Canaris had met Lieutenant Commander von Loewenfeld during the earliest days of the Kiel mutiny. In those days, von Loewenfeld had been an advocate of upgrading the Reichsmarine to a modern battle flotilla and had even formed his own secret anti-Weimar military unit,

known as the Third Naval Brigade. In other words, his views on rebuilding the German navy coincided exactly with Canaris's.

But Lieutenant Canaris very quickly discovered that Commander
von Loewenfeld had completely changed his outlook since they had
known each other in 1918. The commander no longer wanted anything
to do with secret military groups or with the movement to build a new
and modern German navy. In fact, he seemed to be going out of his way
to show his support for the Weimar Republic as well as for the Treaty
of Versailles. The fact that Commander von Loewenfeld was cold and
unfriendly also helped to make Lieutenant Canaris's life a misery. Even
though his first cruise aboard the *Berlin* was a voyage to Spain, which he
regarded as his second home, the lieutenant could not have been unhap-
pier. He became so discouraged that he seriously considered resigning his
commission and leaving the naval service.

One incident that helped to make Canaris's time aboard the *Berlin* a
bit less depressing was meeting Reinhard Heydrich, an acquaintanceship
that would affect his life and his naval career in years to come. Heydrich
was nineteen years old in the summer of 1923, when he was assigned to
the *Berlin* as a naval cadet. Cadet Heydrich seemed to be a model officer
trainee: he always did what he was told and performed all of his duties
efficiently, which earned him excellent fitness reports from his superiors.
But his manner and his personality made him an outcast among the
ship's junior officers. He was tall, lanky, and on the awkward side physically; his manner consisted of an irritating mix of shyness and arrogance.
Also, his family background helped to separate him from the other cadets
and young officers. Both of his parents were musicians. His mother sang
opera, and his father founded the Halle Conservatory of Music. Cadet
Heydrich himself was a talented violinist. But his taste in music and his
upbringing just separated him from the other men aboard the *Berlin*.

The fact that Reinhard Heydrich was not accepted by the others is
exactly what brought him to Lieutenant Canaris's attention. "Canaris,
who had a soft spot for loners, took to the young man."[17] The two got
along very well and also had a lot in common: both of them were German nationalists and politically to the right. Heydrich frequently visited
Canaris's house and often played violin duets with the lieutenant's wife,

Erika, while Canaris cooked dinner. (Canaris married Erika Waag on November 22, 1919.) Heydrich's naval career would be cut short in 1931, when he was dismissed from the service for having an affair with a girl and refusing to marry her. Later in the year, the former naval officer would be appointed head of the newly created Sicherheitsdienst (SD), the security service of the SS. When Canaris became head of the Abwehr, German Military Intelligence, in 1935, Reinhard Heydrich would become his opponent.

But in 1923, the presence of the gawky nineteen-year-old cadet was one of the few bright spots for Lieutenant Canaris aboard the *Berlin*. The lieutenant was very disenchanted with life aboard the ship. He especially disliked Commander von Loewenfeld and his pro-Weimar political point of view. The ship's doctor noted that Lieutenant Canaris showed definite signs of fatigue and general mental exhaustion, which resulted in a pronounced lack of concentration. Canaris fully agreed with the doctor's evaluation; he realized that he was not in the best state of mind or in the best of health. And he also knew the reason behind his sudden lack of vitality: he was completely fed up with the Reichsmarine and everything that went with it. He had been promoted to the rank of lieutenant commander and should have been happy that his career was advancing exactly as he had planned. Instead, he could see no future for himself in the Reichsmarine. As far as he was concerned, the navy had nothing to offer him.

From Commander Canaris's point of view, the navy was outmoded and obsolete and was being kept that way deliberately by the Weimar Republic and the Treaty of Versailles. He wanted to rebuild and modernize the navy, to transform the fleet into a force to rival the British navy, and saw that there could be no hope of this while the Versailles Treaty was in effect. His record from the war would have been the envy of any officer in any navy, but it meant nothing to Commander von Loewenfeld or to anyone else in the Versailles-controlled Reichsmarine. In January 1924, Canaris finally decided that enough was enough and submitted his resignation. "Because I no longer feel physically equal to the demands of the service in the Reichsmarine, I request my discharge at the end of March with statutory maintenance as provided by the

Reinhard Heydrich. Wilhelm Canaris and Heydrich met when Heydrich was a young officer. The two had a lot in common and became friends. *Source:* National Archives.

WVE [Armed Forces Welfare Law]." The letter, dated January 15, 1924, was submitted to the base commander at Kiel, Adm. Ernst von Gagern. Wilhelm Canaris intended to leave the navy and go to work in the family iron-smelting business.[18]

Admiral von Gagern was not happy when he received Commander Canaris's letter of resignation. Canaris was one of the best brains in the navy, or at least one of the best brains that he had ever encountered, and he did not want to lose an officer of his ability. The admiral responded in February 1924, "I would like to keep you, your intelligence, drive, and efficiency for the navy's benefit," and he assured the thirty-seven-year-old officer that the current political situation would not last forever. He went on to say that he would try to change "our political, etc., circumstances" himself and also mentioned something about an assignment in the Far East for the disillusioned lieutenant commander.[19]

The admiral's letter certainly had its desired effect: it changed Commander Canaris's mind about leaving the navy. It was obvious that Admiral von Gagern shared the same ultimate goal as himself—they both wanted nothing less than the complete rebuilding and rearming of the German navy. Now that he had an ally—and a highly influential one—Wilhelm Canaris completely changed his point of view concerning both the navy and his naval career. His one ambition was to help remake the German navy into a formidable war fleet and to hell with the Versailles Treaty and all of its humiliations! It was beginning to look like that ambition was shared by a number of naval officers, including at least one well-connected admiral. (The admiral was also a baron. His full title was Rear Adm. Ernst Freiherr von Gagern.)

Not everyone who wanted to rearm the German military forces or hated the Versailles Treaty was a naval officer. "Down in Bavaria the young firebrand Adolf Hitler grasped the strength of the new nationalist, antidemocratic, antirebellion tide," historian William L. Shirer wrote. "He began to ride it."[20] Commander Canaris was fairly well informed about Adolf Hitler and his activities. He had heard, like everyone else in Germany, about the failed Munich Beer Hall Putsch of November 1923 and might possibly have met Hitler.[21]

Adolf Hitler and his upstart National Socialist German Worker's Party appealed to Commander Canaris, as well as to a good many other German officers. The feature that he admired most about Hitler was his disdain for the Versailles Treaty. In *Mein Kampf,* Hitler said that the treaty was "a shame and a disgrace" and an "instrument of boundless extortion and abject humiliation" that will make all of Germany shout, "Give us arms again!" Every political party and politician in Germany was against the treaty, but Hitler made it a special target of his contempt. Commander Canaris could not have agreed more with Hitler and his opinions.[22]

At this point, Canaris was probably not aware of Hitler's views concerning race and religion or his attitude toward Jews and others that he considered "undesirable"—the first edition of *Mein Kampf* would not be

Adolf Hitler (*right*) in 1930. His plan to reestablish Germany's armed forces in defiance of the Versailles Treaty brought him popular support throughout post–World War I Germany, including with Wilhelm Canaris. *Source:* National Archives.

published until July 1925. But when the commander finally did come to realize exactly what Hitler thought about Jews, Poles, and other Slavs, he did not change his mind. When Hitler first went to Vienna, he wrote, "I was repelled by the conglomeration of races which the capital showed me, repelled by this whole mixture of Czechs, Poles, Hungarians, Ruthenians, Serbs, Croats, and everywhere, the eternal mushroom of humanity—Jews and more Jews."[23]

Commander Canaris was not offended by this opinion; he was used to hearing it. German society was openly anti-Jewish and anti-Slav. People bluntly spoke their minds about their dislike of Jews, as well as their aversion to Poles and other eastern Europeans. He had been hearing remarks about Czechs, Poles, Hungarians, and Jews throughout his entire life, so it was nothing new to hear Hitler saying the same thing. Canaris would actually suggest that all Jews in Germany should wear the yellow Star of David for identification purposes—he favored resettlement of all German Jews outside Germany, and the yellow star would make pinpointing them easier. He told Propaganda Minister Josef Goebbels, "I would like to summarize that the Jews (a marked (b must be resettled. This in all circumstances, because the disadvantages for the Reich will be much greater if the present state is left to exist than the psychological burden that is associated with it."[24]

The fact that Commander Canaris agreed with Adolf Hitler's opinion of Jews and eastern Europeans makes his turning against Hitler and the Nazis all the more remarkable. In the 1920s and 1930s, he had no way of knowing that *Mein Kampf* and Hitler's rhetoric would lead to places like Auschwitz, Dachau, and—ultimately, for Wilhelm Canaris—Flossenbürg. He saw only that Hitler was a strong-willed German nationalist, like himself, who was dedicated to abolishing the Versailles Treaty and rearming the German navy. As far as Commander Canaris was concerned, everything else was beside the point.

CHAPTER TWO

Changes of Regime, Changes of Fortune

THE MORE CDR. WILHELM CANARIS THOUGHT ABOUT GERMANY'S CURrent predicament—the kaiser in exile, an unpopular republic governing the country, a well-armed and hostile France just to the west, and the hated Treaty of Versailles reducing the status of Germany to a second-rate power, at least in his mind—the more unhappy and dejected he became. By the mid-1920s, he was preoccupied with rearming Germany and rebuilding and modernizing the Reichsmarine. His thoughts were concentrated on reviving one segment of the navy in particular: the German submarine service.

Submarines had been explicitly forbidden by the Versailles Treaty, and for a very good reason. During World War I, the U-boat was Germany's most effective weapon and the bogeyman of the British merchant navy. In 1917, U-boats threatened to cut Britain's Atlantic supply line and starve her into submission. The Versailles Treaty expressly prohibited Germany from building submarines because they were so lethal. This was exactly why Commander Canaris had determined to develop a new submarine fleet for the Reichsmarine. Creating a clandestine submarine service would be the most effective method for Germany to regain her position among the world's naval powers. And compared with a battleship or a cruiser, the U-boat was fairly inexpensive to build.

After the armistice of November 1918, existing German submarines were either confiscated by the Allies or broken up for scrap. But the drawings and blueprints for the boats still existed. These drawings were sold to foreign navies, including Japan; the firm of Kawasaki, in Osaka, began building submarines based on the plans of German U-boats in the early 1920s. Japanese builders were assisted by German designers, who were forbidden to design submarines in their own country. Designing submarines for the Japanese navy would provide invaluable experience for these engineers and draftsmen in the not-too-distant future, when U-boats would be built for a new and modernized German navy.

But unexpected problems began cropping up at the Kawasaki shipyard, many created by the interference of the Japanese government as well as bureaucrats within the Japanese navy. In the spring of 1924, the German Admiralty, the Marineleitung, ordered Lieutenant Commander Canaris to travel to Osaka to find out exactly was hampering submarine construction. If anyone could do the job, it was Canaris, who had a reputation as an expert negotiator and arbitrator. The fact that he did not speak a word of Japanese should not interfere with his ability to solve the problems, whatever they happened to be, at the Kawasaki works. The Admiralty had justifiable confidence in Canaris and his skills as a negotiator in any language.

As soon as he arrived in Osaka, Commander Canaris scheduled a conference with senior Japanese naval officers. If he had any misgivings concerning this meeting and a possible negative Japanese attitude toward foreign involvement in its submarine program, they were very quickly put to rest; Japanese officials could not have been more cooperative or accommodating. Commander Canaris was informed that the Japanese admiralty was hoping for extensive German cooperation with the building of its submarine service, since Germany was the acknowledged expert in that particular field. Japan had ambitions in the Pacific and, like Germany, was counting on a modern submarine force to help realize them. The commander assured everyone that Germany had every intention of helping the Japanese navy meet its goals.

On his voyage back to Germany, Commander Canaris had time to reflect on his visit. Although it had not been an unqualified success—even though Japanese officers and executives had been obliging, they struck the commander as too bureaucratic and inefficient—he was more than satisfied with the results of all the talks and meetings. Germany now had a new ally in the East, Commander Canaris could report, a country committed to developing its own fleet in the Pacific with the backing and assistance of Germany. The report he submitted to the Marineleitung convinced senior German officers to send yet another expert on submarines to Osaka. If the Japanese navy wanted help in designing and building their submarines, then the German Admiralty should do everything possible to cooperate.

But the admirals at the Marineleitung really had in mind the construction of submarines for Germany, not some foreign country. They had already taken a giant step in that direction by establishing a secret design bureau for submarine construction in The Hague, far away from the prying eyes of the Allied Disarmament Commission's inspectors. This bureau, called Ingenieurskantoor voor Scheersbouw (IvS) was managed by two former U-boat officers and employed about thirty designers and engineers. The IvS designed and managed the construction of submarines for several countries, including Argentina. The actual sea trials of these boats were supervised by the former naval officers. A new mine-laying submarine was developed and built for the Finnish navy in the mid-1920s. The IvS also had the drawings and the personnel to begin building U-boats for the Reichsmarine when the opportunity presented itself. The German Admiralty just needed a more sympathetic government to replace the Weimar Republic, a regime that would help to circumvent the Treaty of Versailles. When that happened, Germany would be able to build submarines for its own navy.

In the early part of 1925, Commander Canaris was given an opportunity of his own to promote submarine construction in a foreign country. A chief advisor at IvS, Lieutenant Commander Blum, had been ordered to travel to Madrid; he was directed to confer with Spanish officials about the possibility of building German submarines in Spanish shipyards. Commander Blum was not opposed to the idea, but he was not familiar with Spain and did not want to make the trip by himself. He asked that another officer, someone who knew the country, be assigned to go with him. Since Wilhelm Canaris was the Admiralty's "Spanish expert," someone who was not only fluent in the language but had actually spent time in the country as an intelligence agent during the war, he was assigned to accompany Commander Blum. The two officers left Germany for Spain at the end of January 1925.

Commander Blum's request to have a "Spanish expert" go along with him turned out to be an excellent, if not brilliant, idea. Warships of the Spanish navy, including submarines, had been designed by British shipbuilding firms for a good many years. Spain's submarines were entirely of British design and construction. But the success of German U-boats during the war against the British gave senior Spanish naval officers the idea of using German designs for their submarines, and they had begun to consider the possibility of doing business with the Germans instead of with British firms.

Commander Canaris learned about this change in outlook during conversations with Spanish officers and saw an opportunity. He sent a report to the Marineleitung, suggesting a partnership with a leading Spanish industrialist, Horacio Echevarrieta, and also advised cooperation between the Reichsmarine and the Spanish navy. The Admiralty agreed and formed an alliance with another foreign power—thanks mainly to Commander Canaris's intervention. The commander was also instrumental in arranging the financial backing of the Deutsche Bank for "Herr Echevarrieta"—with the condition that he would only work with IvS and use only German plans and drawings. Commander Canaris also managed to work out an agreement with Spanish security police. This security force would control Spain's political police after Francisco Franco became dictator in 1939. Commander Canaris had certainly lived up to his reputation as the Marineleitung's "Spanish expert." Senior German naval officers would always make it a point to consult with the commander whenever they had to make contact with Madrid.

But because of his enthusiasm for German rearmament, Commander Canaris also made his share of enemies. Left-wing and pacifist groups, along with the Social Democrat Party, denounced him as a warmongering right-wing extremist, as well as the "shrewdest member of the warrior caste."[1] Commander Canaris had certainly become one of the more offensive of Germany's military officers in the eyes of the Social Democrats. He had also become the favorite target of left-wing newspapers—editors went out of their way to vilify Canaris, describing him as a republic-hating, war-loving monster.

All of this negative criticism did not seem to bother Commander Canaris, but it certainly upset senior officers at the Marineleitung. Just about every day, newspapers that supported the Social Democrats had something uncomplimentary to say about the commander. With time, the anti-Canaris bias became an antinavy bias; the entire officer corps was being compared with the Huns and the Vandals. Bad publicity for the Reichsmarine was exactly what the Admiralty was trying to avoid. Lieutenant Commander Canaris had become a liability for the naval service, in spite of his impressive war record and everything he had accomplished since.

Commander Canaris was ordered to report for duty aboard the battleship *Schlesien* in June 1928 as the ship's executive officer. This assignment took Canaris safely out of Germany and, more specifically, out of Berlin. At the time, the battleship was taking part in exercises in the North Sea. The senior officers at the Marineleitung hoped that the left-wing newspapers would forget about Canaris now that he was no longer in the country. Canaris might be able to return to Berlin eventually, but not as long as he was a visible target for the Social Democrats.

If Commander Canaris was disappointed by the loss of his job in Berlin and the fact that he was no longer in a position to help rearm and modernize the navy, he did not let it show. According to the *Schlesien's* captain, his new executive officer threw himself into his duties. He was the strictest officer on board; he drove not only the officers and crew but also himself. Lieutenant Commander Canaris was promoted to the rank of full commander within a year, both as a reward for his devotion to duty aboard the *Schlesien* and also as a sort of consolation prize for having been sent off to the North Sea.

In September 1930, he was given another promotion of sorts: the post of chief of staff of the North Sea Naval Station, which had its headquarters at Wilhelmshaven. But Commander Canaris did not think very much of the promotion or the appointment. He also did not think very much of the other officers at the North Sea station, and the feeling was mutual: his colleagues thought the unhappy new chief of staff was aloof and uncongenial. Canaris had wanted to go back to work for the Marineleitung, where he could use his talents as a diplomat and an intriguer to help rebuild the Reichsmarine; instead, he had been sent off to Wilhelmshaven. An election had taken place in May 1928, and the Social Democrats had received the most votes. The leader of the party was now chancellor of Germany. With a left-wing government in power, there was no chance at all that Canaris would be allowed back in Berlin.

Commander Canaris would remain at the North Sea Naval Station, whether he liked it or not. Even though he was promoted to captain in October 1931, this was not much in the way of consolation. He would clearly not receive another assignment as long as the Social Democrats controlled the government. He would only escape his dead-end job by leaving the naval service. For the second time, his career seemed to have come to an end.

But the Weimar Republic looked as though it might be entering its last phase in the early 1930s. Not very many Germans had anything good to say about it. Monarchists hoped for a return of the kaiser. Conservatives wanted a right-wing regime to rearm the German armed forces. Socialists wanted a government similar to Joseph Stalin's regime in Soviet Russia; the Social Democrats were not far enough to the left to suit them. Nobody was satisfied with the current republic.

By September 1930, the government at Weimar had become so unpopular and unemployment so widespread that another general election was called. After all the votes had been counted, Adolf Hitler and the Nazi Party had the second-highest total. Hitler was so encouraged by the election results that he began making a series of speeches throughout Germany—emotional, sometimes fanatical speeches promising to restore Germany's economy as well as her military power. Through these speeches, the Nazi Party "was arousing the old feelings of German patriotism and nationalism which had become so muted during the first ten years of the Republic." When he was asked exactly what he meant by the German national revolution he intended to carry out with his Nazi Party, Hitler said, "This means exclusively the rescue of the enslaved German nation we have today. Germany is bound hand and foot by the peace treaties. . . . [T]he National Socialists do not regard these treaties as law, but as something imposed upon Germany by constraint."[2]

Hitler's speeches mesmerized crowds throughout Germany—he was saying exactly what everyone wanted to hear. Naval officers frequently sat in the audience when Hitler spoke and were in complete agreement with him. They often said the same things themselves aboard ship, in the officers' mess, or when off duty. The captain of the cruiser *Köln* heard one of Hitler's talks and invited him to visit his ship when it was docked at Wilhelmshaven. Hitler agreed and came aboard the *Köln* at the end of May 1932.

Hitler gave a nice little performance for the benefit of the *Köln's* officers—he made a few pertinent observations regarding the ship's guns and other aspects of its armament and general construction. The things he said certainly had their desired effect: the officers, especially the junior officers, were highly impressed with his aggressively pro-navy attitude. He told everyone, "I shall expand the fleet within the framework on the Versailles Treaty," and "If I say a ship is ten thousand tons it is ten thousand tons, no matter how big it really is." (The Treaty of Versailles limited German warships to a maximum displacement of ten thousand tons.) In other words, if he was not able to circumvent the treaty to get what he wanted, he would just ignore it completely. Hitler made a good many friends for himself that day.[3]

Hitler and the National Socialists were making friends and amassing votes throughout Germany. On July 31, 1932, the third national election in five months was held. As a result, the National Socialists became the dominant party—they received 13.745 million votes and came away with 230 seats in the Reichstag. The Social Democrats lost 10 seats, giving them a total of 133. Even though the Nazis did not yet have a clear majority, Hitler was determined that he would obtain it somehow. And once the Nazis had the power, they were just as determined to keep it. "Once we have the power we will never give it up," Propaganda Minister Josef Goebbels wrote in his diary in August 1932. "They will have to drag our dead bodies out of the ministries."[4]

Capt. Wilhelm Canaris was certainly not unhappy that the National Socialist Party was gathering momentum. He had no use for the Social

Democrats and absolutely no faith in the Weimar Republic. Hitler and his party were just what Germany needed, at least to his way of thinking; they represented nationalism, patriotism, and a strong military force. Friends and fellow naval officers could not help but note that Captain Canaris had become quite enthusiastic about the Nazis. With the left-wing Social Democrats losing ground in the Reichstag, Captain Canaris looked forward to the day when the National Socialists would become the dominant party in the German government.

The day Captain Canaris hoped for was not far off. He had been reassigned to the battleship *Schlesien* in September 1932, this time as the ship's captain. Canaris was much too busy with his new responsibilities as the battleship's commanding officer to pay much attention to politics. But at the end of January 1933, an event took place that captured his attention even though he was at sea. On January 30, 1933, President Paul von Hindenburg named Adolf Hitler to the post of German chancellor. The news was broadcast all over Germany. Everyone aboard the *Schlesien* also heard the broadcast. A historian would later write, "The Germans imposed the Nazi tyranny on themselves."[5]

Two weeks after the announcement, Captain Canaris brought the *Schlesien* back to Kiel for an overhaul. He was impressed by the changes that had taken place in the city. The most visible change was in the number of uniforms on the street. Naval uniforms had always been very much in evidence, Kiel being a port city, but now many others were just as conspicuous: the black uniforms of the Schutzstaffel (SS); the brown shirts of the Sturmabteilung. Everyone appeared to be more content and more confident; the general point of view seemed to be that Hitler and his new regime would create a revitalized Germany. Captain Canaris was absolutely convinced that Adolf Hitler was the best thing that could have happened to the country. An acquaintance of Canaris would write, "He then believed that the new regime was infinitely better than anything that had gone before, and that, for the time being, there was absolutely no alternative."[6]

Even though the Nazis were now in power and the Social Democrats were nothing more than an annoying memory, the change in political climate did not improve Captain Canaris's naval career. If anything, his prospects diminished until they almost faded from sight. Canaris's main difficulty was that he did not get along with his immediate superior, Rear Adm. Max Bastian. The two officers just did not like each other. For one thing, Admiral Bastian did not appreciate Captain Canaris's enthusiasm for Adolf Hitler and the National Socialists and thought that his subordinate spent entirely too much time giving lectures to the *Schlesien*'s crew on the benefits of the Nazi regime and its plans for a new and better Germany. Admiral Bastian and Captain Canaris also had completely different personalities: Bastian was blunt and outspoken, whereas Canaris tended to be reserved and withdrawn, especially in the admiral's presence. The two men rarely spoke to each other unless it was absolutely necessary. Canaris did his best to avoid the admiral altogether.

Admiral Bastian could not help but notice that Captain Canaris went out of his way to steer clear of him. Even though he returned the compliment and only spoke to Canaris in the line of duty—he did not like Canaris any more than Canaris liked him—the admiral was still offended by his subordinate's behavior. He decided to do something about his anger: Admiral Bastian wrote a letter of complaint to the Admiralty. Captain Canaris should make an effort to get along with him, he wrote, and should also become less introverted and withdrawn.

Captain Canaris was informed of Admiral Bastian's complaints and did his best to comply with the admiral's directive. He tried to be more sociable and less reserved. But the admiral was still not satisfied with Canaris or his performance and in September 1934 advised the Admiralty that he would be best suited for an organizational position instead of a command at sea. Admiral Bastian advised that Captain Canaris, with his diplomatic skills and talent for privacy and reticence, should be a perfect fit for an administrative post, possibly as head of an intelligence network—maybe the Abwehr, Germany's military intelligence organization.

The Marineleitung read Admiral Bastian's recommendation and approved it. But the Admiralty did not send Captain Canaris to the Abwehr. Instead, they sent him off to another organizational job—at Fort Swinemünde, where he would assume duties as the installation's commanding officer. Fort Swinemünde was the Reichsmarine's equivalent of Siberia—a seaport on Germany's Baltic Sea coast that, as far as

Canaris was concerned, might as well have been on the dark side of the moon. Both Captain Canaris and Admiral Bastian knew that this was a dead-end assignment, which might very well have meant the end of Canaris's naval career. But less than a month after reporting for duty at Swinemünde, something happened that would completely change Captain Canaris's career, as well as his life.

* * *

At the beginning of 1934, the head of the Abwehr, Capt. Conrad Patzig, was forced to submit his resignation. He was having a remarkably similar problem to Captain Canaris's difficulties with Admiral Bastian: Captain Patzig was finding it impossible to get along with the director of the newly created Sicherheitsdienst (SD), the security branch of Heinrich Himmler's SS. The director of the SD was none other than Canaris's protégé from his days aboard the training ship *Berlin*: Reinhard Heydrich.

Heydrich was no longer an awkward nineteen-year-old naval cadet. He was now an ambitious Nazi, determined to make a name for himself in Adolf Hitler's new Germany.

Captain Patzig strongly suspected that Reinhard Heydrich had ambitions to absorb the Abwehr into his SD and take over the military intelligence branch himself, which led to increasing friction and bad feelings between the two. Finally, after more than two years of disputes and partisan infighting, Heydrich brought some political influence to bear and pressured Captain Patzig into leaving the Abwehr.

Before leaving his position, Conrad Patzig recommended that Wilhelm Canaris replace him as Abwehr director. He had known Canaris for some time. As far as he was concerned, no one else had Canaris's talent for deception and subterfuge, at least no one else in the German navy. The fact that Canaris was also on friendly terms with Reinhard Heydrich was another contributing factor in Patzig's recommendation: it would be better to have Heydrich as an ally of the Abwehr than an antagonist. Captain Patzig's endorsement, along with Admiral Bastian's passing suggestion, resulted in Canaris's appointment as chief of the Abwehr.

When he received his new appointment, Wilhelm Canaris breathed a sigh of relief. Not only had he been rescued from the purgatory of Fort Swinemünde, but he had been given a real job, an appointment with a future. He was warned about the rift between the Abwehr and the SD, but he was not worried. Captain Canaris was convinced that he was the right man for the job—a loyal National Socialist who would do his best to succeed as director of intelligence for Adolf Hitler and his regime.

CHAPTER THREE

Turning against Hitler

ON MARCH 16, 1935, CAPT. WILHELM CANARIS RECEIVED A COMMUNI-
qué from Propaganda Minister Josef Goebbels that left him absolutely
astonished. Dr. Goebbels's announcement stated that a new law had
gone into effect. The Law for the Re-creation of the National Defense
Forces declared that Germany would now begin expanding its peacetime army of one hundred thousand men into a conscript army of three
times that size. The Reichswehr, which had been limited in size by the
Treaty of Versailles, would be renamed the Wehrmacht and would also
be increased to 350,000 men. Adolf Hitler had nullified the Versailles
Treaty, restored universal military service, and announced the formation
of an army of thirty-six divisions. It was an incredible piece of news.
Captain Canaris could hardly believe it.

On the following day, Gen. Werner von Blomberg, commander in
chief of all armed forces, made a formal announcement of Hitler's new
law at the Berlin Opera House. A ceremony honoring Germany's war
dead was the occasion for General von Blomberg's remarks; he spoke to a
gathering of senior German officers—"a sea of military uniforms."[1] Hitler was also present, sitting in the royal box just a few feet away.

General von Blomberg began by informing the assembly, "The
world has been made to realize that Germany did not die of its defeat
in the World War." He went on in the same tone, "Germany will again
take the place she deserves among the nations. We pledge ourselves to a
Germany which will never surrender and never again sign a treaty which
cannot be fulfilled. We do not need revenge because we have gathered

glory enough through the centuries." Hitler did not add anything to these remarks. He sat quietly at General von Blomberg's side and "looked on approvingly."[2]

It would not be an exaggeration to say that Captain Canaris was thrilled by the news—it was just the sort of thing he had come to expect from Adolf Hitler. Hitler had promised to do away with the Versailles Treaty—in *Mein Kampf* he had written, "No nation can remove this hand from its throat except by the sword."[3] Although Canaris enthusiastically supported what Hitler had done, he had the feeling that the French and the British were not just going to sit back and allow Germany to break the treaty. The Allied countries did not trust Germany any more than the Germans trusted them.

Everyone wondered what London and Paris would do. "They could fight a 'preventive' war and that would be the end of Hitler," in the opinion of an American reporter who viewed the defiance of the Versailles Treaty as "a terrible blow to the Allies."[4] Britain and France did extend protests through their respective embassies and were expected to take some sort of military action in response to Hitler's challenge. As head of the Abwehr, Captain Canaris was instructed to find out exactly what plans these countries might have in mind.

The new Abwehr director went right to work as soon as he received his orders. In a letter dated March 19, 1935, he instructed agents in every Abwehr station "to ascertain what military developments, if any, are occurring in neighbouring countries."[5] Captain Canaris also made a personal visit to each station during the next few weeks, asking the staff of each what data they might have been able to gather regarding enemy troop movements. He also spoke with members of the Hungarian intelligence service, along with the head of Italy's military intelligence, on the same subject. After several weeks of accumulating reports from a variety of sources, Captain Canaris came to an extraordinary conclusion: the British and the French had no intention of doing anything in response to Hitler's flagrant violation of the Treaty of Versailles. Apart from a few notes passed between embassies, no action was taken. Hitler had certainly won his gamble that nothing would happen. Captain Canaris, along with everyone in Germany, was overjoyed by the Allied failure to retaliate.

By the time it had become evident that the British and French would not challenge Hitler, Canaris had his own personal triumph: in May 1935, he was promoted to the rank of rear admiral. His promotion to flag rank coincided with the expansion of the Abwehr—beginning in 1935, German counterintelligence would come under the auspices of the Abwehr. The agency was already responsible for gathering military and political information that would be useful to the Hitler regime. The admiral would now be in charge of protecting German rearmament from the prying eyes of British and French agents. Admiral Canaris directed every Abwehr office and station to be especially alert for enemy spies. Now that Adolf Hitler had expanded the army and was rapidly rearming Germany, Canaris did not want any foreign interference with the new Reich that Hitler was creating from the wreckage of the Treaty of Versailles.

But besides doing away with the Versailles Treaty and rearming Germany, Hitler was also doing other things inside his new Germany, things that Wilhelm Canaris did not yet know about. In April 1935, American journalist William L. Shirer was visited by a "successful" Jewish lawyer who had just spent several months in a Gestapo prison. The visitor, identified as "Dr. S" by Shirer, said that no charges had been brought against him "other than he was a Jew or a half-Jew." He had also offended the Nazis by defending Ernst Thälmann, leader of the German Communist Party. "Many Jews come to us these days for advice or help in getting to England or America," Shirer wrote in his diary, "but unfortunately there is little we can do for them." Shirer went on to say that his hotel was "mainly filled with Jews and we are a little surprised to see so many of them still prospering and apparently unafraid." He ended the entry with this ominous note: "I think they are unduly optimistic."[6]

At that point, Admiral Canaris would have been far more interested in another incident. In June 1935, Britain agreed to give Germany parity in tonnage allowed for submarine construction—the German navy would be allowed to build as many submarines as the British navy. "Germany gets U-boat tonnage equal to Britain's," William Shirer wrote with some disbelief on June 18, 1935. "Why the British have agreed to this is beyond me. German submarines almost beat them in the last war, and may in the next."[7] This is just what Admiral Canaris had been hoping for: more submarines for the German navy. And with the permission of the British! If another war with Britain should break out, the navy would be ready. So would the Abwehr.

* * *

Admiral Canaris certainly was enthusiastic about his new position as head of the Abwehr—so enthusiastic, in fact, that he showed up for his first day of work on New Year's Day, January 1, 1935, which was a legal holiday. He was also grateful to have such an important job. Instead of being shunted off to a thankless, dead-end position at Swinemünde, he was now in charge of Germany's entire military intelligence organization. But even though he was more than qualified for the job—not only because of his talent for subterfuge but also because of his ear for languages and his diplomatic abilities—Admiral Canaris certainly did not look like anybody's idea of the director of an intelligence agency.

The Abwehr's new chief seemed to go out of his way to look as unmilitary as possible at all times. In January 1935, just a few weeks after the appointment, American writer Ladislas Farago met Admiral Canaris. He later admitted that he was not impressed. For one thing, Canaris was only five feet, three inches tall—he certainly did not look the part of a spy in a detective novel. Also, he gave the impression of being dull, uninteresting, and generally not very bright. "I could not believe that this rumpled, tongue-tied, absent-minded little man was the new chief of the Abwehr," the writer would recall.[8]

Canaris's disheveled appearance also earned him any number of uncomplimentary remarks from his fellow officers, who were just as unimpressed. Senior naval officers had any number of other unflattering things to say about him as well: he did not seem very interested in military topics and preferred studying foreign languages to reading about naval matters; he could be maddeningly vague; he never seemed to give a straightforward yes or no to a question and frequently answered with another question. When he was still a junior officer, quite a few of his superiors had disliked Canaris personally. One such officer was future grand admiral Erich Raeder, who could see no future for him in the naval service.

By 1935, when Admiral Canaris was forty-eight years old, his hair had turned completely white. This was probably a genetic trait, not a sign of premature aging. Among the staff at Abwehr headquarters in Berlin, the admiral was known by a number of nicknames: the Old Man, Old Whitehead, and Old Nosy. His office at 72–76 Tirpitz Ufer was sometimes referred to as the Fox's Lair and its inhabitant as the Old Fox—a devious, wily senior officer who kept to himself and did not say very much to anybody.

The Abwehr under Admiral Canaris concentrated most of its energy on detecting foreign espionage agents, as well as on rooting out any treasonable activities being carried out by communists or other anti-Nazi individuals. Army units were constantly being warned, "Feind Hört Mit"—"The enemy is listening." Anyone showing any hostility or disloyalty toward the new regime was to be reported. Beginning in 1935, the Abwehr screened government bureaus and military units for politically disagreeable persons, meaning anyone who might be communist leaning or have socialist sympathies. Admiral Canaris was never satisfied with the effectiveness of the Abwehr's counterespionage system, even though Abwehr agents seemed to be everywhere, including in munitions and armaments plants. New agents were constantly being recruited—after being thoroughly screened for their political reliability. By 1938, the Abwehr was an excellent intelligence agency, but Admiral Canaris was always trying to make it better.[9]

The admiral wanted to do everything possible to support Adolf Hitler and National Socialism. Hitler had rescued Germany from both the Treaty of Versailles and the Weimar Republic and had also succeeded in rearming the country's military forces: Germany's army, navy, and air force were now the most modern in the world. Admiral Canaris expected every member of the Abwehr to stand behind Hitler and the Nazi Party and told them as much. He said to a group of Abwehr officers, "Adolf Hitler's ideas are imbued with the following soldierly spirit: honour and a sense of duty, courage, military preparedness, a readiness for commitment and self-sacrifice, leadership, comradeship and a sense of responsibility."[10]

But by the early part of 1938, Admiral Canaris was already beginning to have second thoughts about Hitler. His turning away from Hitler began with an incident that had nothing to do with him and would take him some time to understand and accept. In January 1938, Gen. Werner von Blomberg married Erna Gruhn at the Reich War Ministry in Berlin. Because von Blomberg was minister of war as well as commander in chief of all German armed forces, the wedding was a leading social event. Among the guests were Adolf Hitler and Hermann Göring. Admiral Canaris was only slightly interested in the event; he had heard talk that the fifty-nine-year-old von Blomberg would be marrying a much younger woman but did not pay much attention to the gossip. He had been in Spain when the wedding took place and did not hear very much news from Germany.

Shortly after General von Blomberg was married, a police file was uncovered that produced a very embarrassing piece of evidence concerning his wife: the former Erna Gruhn was a convicted prostitute and had also been a model for pornographic photos. When this news became known, no one knew what to do. General von Blomberg was not only one of Germany's highest-ranking officers but also a close confident of Adolf Hitler. The commissioner of Berlin's police force notified Gen. Wilhelm Keitel, who knew General von Blomberg personally. General Keitel's reaction to the news was typical of him—he said he did not want to involve himself in the incident. The commissioner next went to Hermann Göring, who immediately informed Hitler that the head of the armed forces was married to a prostitute. Hitler was shocked and angered by the news, but he also saw that the incident created an opportunity for him. He would demand von Blomberg's resignation, on the grounds that Germany's highest-ranking general had committed an immoral act by marrying a prostitute; after the general stepped down, he would assume the title of supreme commander himself. Hitler had been looking for justification to solidify his control of the armed forces; the von Blomberg scandal gave him a tailor-made excuse. General von Blomberg resigned in January 1938, and Adolf Hitler immediately replaced him as supreme commander.

At the same time, a scandal was fabricated to remove another high-ranking general, Werner von Fritsch, from his post as Wehrmacht commander in chief. General von Fritsch did not agree with Hitler's aggressive attitude toward the Soviet Union. He was afraid that Hitler's belligerence would lead to a war with Stalin's Russia, a war he knew Germany could not win. Although the general was not outspoken or overly negative in his criticism of Hitler's policies, both Hitler and Göring decided that he had to be dismissed from his post. No disagreement would be tolerated from any senior officer, especially not one with as much rank and authority as von Fritsch.

The method used to dispose of General von Fritsch was both simple and brutal. He was charged with having homosexual relationships and engaging in homosexual activity, which was a criminal offense. A witness was produced to testify before Hitler and Göring that von Fritsch had a homosexual encounter with a young boy in Potsdam. The general was a bachelor; unmarried men were often accused of being "queer."

General von Fritsch vehemently denied the charge and demanded that he be tried by a court of honor. As a result of the trial, he was acquitted of all charges. But even though he had been found not guilty, the general's career was finished—his reputation had been damaged beyond any possible repair. Early in February 1938, General von Fritsch resigned from the army. Hitler had removed another general who had disagreed with him, which helped to solidify his control over the army.

News of the Blomberg-Fritsch crisis was the leading story throughout Germany as well as in the international press. American correspondent William Shirer was in Vienna at the time of the crisis and read all about the incident on the day after the two officers were banished from the army. "Doings in Berlin," he wrote in his diary. "Today's papers say that Blomberg and Fritsch, the two men who have built up the German army, are out. Hitler himself becomes a sort of 'Supreme War Lord,' assuming the powers of Minister of Defense."[11]

Shirer did not seem all that surprised by this turn of events—he had been in Europe for four years and had come to expect this sort of behavior from Hitler. But Admiral Canaris was taken completely by surprise. He did not realize the part Hitler had played in the scandal until the end of January 1938, when he was told exactly what had happened. The news that Hitler had ruined the lives and careers of two of his most senior officers, all for the purpose of making himself supreme overlord of all German forces, angered him. Until that time, he had thought of Hitler as an honorable head of state, a leader who represented everything that was good in Germany. But when he learned about the Blomberg-Fritsch matter, he gleaned that Hitler had only his own interests at heart. As far as Admiral Canaris was concerned, Hitler could no longer to be trusted—he said noble things about Germany but was only interested in his own power and influence.

The von Fritsch scandal was actually a complete frame-up, as Canaris would discover. It had not been Gen. Werner von Fritsch but a Captain von Frisch who had had a homosexual affair. The Gestapo knew this but proceeded with the case against General von Fritsch just the same. When this false accusation was revealed at the trial, the prosecution's entire case collapsed. Despite the general's acquittal, Hitler still accepted von Fritsch's resignation and would not allow the release of any information that might clear his name. The witness who had testified against the general at his trial, one Hans Schmidt, was shot to prevent him from disclosing the truth about the Fritsch incident. "This was the time," a close friend of Admiral Canaris remembered, "when Canaris began to turn from Hitler. . . . If you have to mark any one event as the crisis of loyalty between Canaris and Hitler, this is it."[12]

But besides the Blomberg-Fritsch incident, several individuals were also instrumental in changing Admiral Canaris's mind regarding Hitler and the Nazis. One of these was Col. Hans Oster, who would leave an indelible impression on Canaris's point of view. Oster and Canaris met for the first time in 1931. At the time, Canaris was chief of staff of the North Sea station, and Hans Oster was serving as staff officer with the Sixth Infantry Division. They almost immediately discovered that they had a great deal in common—for one thing, neither one of them supported the Weimar Republic—and quickly became very good friends.

Colonel Oster turned against Hitler in June 1934 when hundreds of opponents of the Nazi regime were murdered by Hitler's order. The incident became known as the "Night of the Long Knives." Most of those killed during Hitler's purge were the brownshirts of the Sturmabteilung, who were shot by members of Heinrich Himmler's Schutzstaffel. Oster was both outraged and sickened by the killings. The mass executions convinced him that the Hitler government was a criminal organization of gangsters and assassins. Canaris did not agree with his friend's opinions but decided not to take any actions against Oster; after the Blomberg-Fritsch episode, however, he shared Oster's sentiments.

Hans von Dohnanyi was another influence concerning Canaris's change of heart regarding Hitler. Von Dohnanyi was an attorney as well as a legal advisor to the Ministry of Justice. He was also the brother-in-law of theologian Dietrich Bonhoeffer, who became a leading opponent of Hitler. In his capacity as legal advisor, von Dohnanyi had access to all documents pertaining to the case against Werner von Fritsch and was just as disgusted by the incident as Admiral Canaris. Even before the Blomberg-Fritsch incident, von Dohnanyi had begun to keep a sort of logbook of all the Nazi atrocities and misdeeds that he could uncover, everything from bribery and corruption within the government to the deporting of "undesirables" or "disruptive individuals" to concentration camps. Admiral Canaris was moved by what von Dohnanyi had to say about the Nazi government in his calm yet passionate tone. The lawyer's detailed accounts reinforced Canaris's increasingly unsavory opinion of Hitler and the Nazis.

But the incident with the farthest-reaching effect upon Admiral Canaris and his estimation of Hitler was the Night of Broken Glass, or *Kristallnacht*, which took place on November 9, 1938. On this night, coordinated attacks were carried out against synagogues and Jewish-owned businesses throughout Germany. This was done in retaliation for the assassination of a staff member at the German embassy in Paris, Ernst von Rath, by a Polish Jew named Herschel Grynszpan. Reinhard Heydrich ordered the destruction of all Jewish temples in Germany and Austria, an order that was carried out with a vengeance. Otto John, an executive with Lufthansa Airlines who would become a member of the anti-Nazi resistance, recalled that during the destruction "everywhere the police, acting under orders, remained passive onlookers."[13]

Before the night was over, hundreds of synagogues had been vandalized, along with thousands of Jewish shops and businesses. Fragments of broken glass from smashed windows covered streets and pavements. The effect of light reflected by the shards reminded bystanders of crystal ornaments, which gave rise to the name "Crystal Night." The name has become synonymous with Nazi Germany and the barbarity of the Hitler regime throughout the world. In the days following *Kristallnacht*, Otto John recalled, "life in Germany seemed to me increasingly sinister."[14]

Admiral Canaris certainly agreed that Hitler's Germany had become sinister and threatening. As soon as he heard about the events of November 9, the admiral sent an angry letter of protest to Feldmarschall Wilhelm Keitel, who had become the head of all German armed forces. In his letter, Canaris did not skimp on the details; his account described the destruction and vandalism by the mobs accurately and at length. He also complained that the unchecked night of violence ruined the image of Germany throughout the world, which was absolutely correct. Every newspaper in Europe and the United States reported on the attacks. The front page of the *New York Times* ran the headline "Nazis Smash, Loot and Burn Jewish Shops and Temples."[15]

But Feldmarschall Keitel was not interested in the admiral's protests. He had no intention of criticizing any members of the Nazi hierarchy. He especially did not want to oppose Adolf Hitler, who had been ultimately responsible for *Kristallnacht*. Of all the high-ranking Nazis, only Hermann Göring objected to the night of violence and destruction, and his opposition was based on economics, not moral scruples—he had been informed that the damage done on November 9 would cost German insurance companies millions of dollars in claims, which would have a disastrous effect on the economy.[16]

The Nazi-sponsored chaos of November 9, combined with the Blomberg-Fritsch crisis, destroyed Admiral Canaris's faith and confidence in Adolf Hitler and his government. Although Hitler had certainly showed himself to be a German nationalist, he had also demonstrated that he could not be trusted. Canaris finally came to realize that Hitler was malicious, amoral, and unscrupulous. He had ruined the careers of General von Blomberg and General von Fritsch to foster his own ambition, and he had approved a night of vandalism that had not only shocked and offended Canaris personally but also turned world opinion against Germany. No one could say for certain exactly what he would do next. But whatever it was, it would probably be violent and self-centered, as well as dangerous for Germany. Canaris could no longer allow himself to support Adolf Hitler.

Admiral Canaris might have resigned in protest—given up his post as head of the Abwehr as well as his commission as a naval officer—but he was much too ambitions to consider this. He held the rank of rear admiral and had been appointed head of the Abwehr. He had not held on to his naval career through the years since the 1914–1918 war, including the dismal years of the Weimar Republic, just to give it up for a principle. Instead, he decided to use his rank and position to work against Hitler in secret, in his own way, taking clandestine action against the Nazi regime whenever the opportunity presented itself. Given the violent and aggressive manner in which Hitler had been governing the country, Admiral Canaris figured some sort of opportunity would present itself in the very near future.

* * *

Admiral Canaris was not the only German deeply offended by *Kristallnacht*. A pastor who lived in the same Berlin suburb as the admiral, a minister by the name of Dr. Heyden, heard about the "horrendous" episode on the radio. It had left him and his wife feeling "shocked and helpless." On the Sunday after *Kristallnacht*, Dr. Heyden decided to say something regarding the incident in the course of his sermon: "What a terrible harbinger of events to come for our Germany, the land of the Reformation, that the synagogues of our fellow human beings should be ignited and burned down with deliberate criminal intent."

Several people—"about five," according to one account—walked out of the church in protest. One of them reported Dr. Heyden to the police; as a result, he was ordered to report to the local police station the following day to answer questions. During the course of his "intense questioning," the pastor suggested that his interrogators contact Admiral Canaris regarding the subject of his sermon; the admiral was one of his

A Nazi boycott of Jewish shops. Such demonstrations were instrumental in changing Canaris's mind about Hitler and the Nazis. *Source:* National Archives.

parishioners, he explained. The police took Dr. Heyden up on his suggestion and paid Canaris a visit. His response to the police inquiry was short and to the point: "The Reverend Hayden would never say such a thing." Apparently satisfied with the admiral's defense of the pastor, the police dropped all charges against him. This would not be the last time that Admiral Canaris came to the rescue of someone in peril. During the next several years, he would save many others from the prisons and concentration camps of the Nazi government.[17]

CHAPTER FOUR

Cheating the Gestapo

ADM. WILHELM CANARIS'S FIRST REAL OPPORTUNITY TO ACT AGAINST Adolf Hitler and his regime came in the summer of 1939, when Germany was preparing to attack Poland. The actual day that he began his plan of subversion was August 22, 1939, during a meeting with Hitler at the Berghof, Hitler's retreat in Bavaria. The meeting had been called by Hitler himself. Most of the senior officers of all the German forces—Wehrmacht, Luftwaffe, and Kriegsmarine—were in attendance, including Hermann Göring. After a light breakfast on the terrace of his picturesque house, Hitler informed everyone why he had called them together: he intended to invade Poland in order to make the port city of Danzig German again and eliminate the hated Polish Corridor. Only war would accomplish these two items, Hitler said, and he intended to wage his war against Poland as soon as all of his forces were in place along the Polish frontier.

Hitler's words stunned everyone in the room, but he still had a lot more to say. The political situation was favorable for an attack, he went on. It would be to Germany's advantage to start a war as quickly as possible because the country's relationship with Poland had become untenable. He only hoped that no do-gooder from France or England would step forward with a plan for a negotiated peace at the last moment. He intended to overrun Poland and was not about to let Britain, France, or anybody else stand in his way.[1]

The meeting went on all throughout the morning, with Hitler doing most of the talking, and recessed for lunch early in the afternoon. After lunch Hitler continued with his discussion of the planned invasion of Poland. Among other things, he said that he would invent an excuse for starting the war; the excuse did not have to be plausible. "Our strength consists in our speed and in our brutality," he went on. "Genghis Khan led millions of women and children to slaughter—with premeditation and a happy heart. History sees in him solely the founder of a state. It's a matter of indifference to me what a weak western European civilization will say about me."

He was not concerned with what any of his officers thought of him, either, including those present. "I have issued the command—and I'll have anybody who utters but one word of criticism executed by a firing squad—that our war aim does not consist in reaching certain lines, but in the physical destruction of the enemy. Accordingly, I have placed my death-head formations in readiness—for the present only in the East—with orders to them to send to death mercilessly and without compassion, men, women, and children of Polish derivation and language. Only thus shall we gain the living space (*Lebensraum*) which we need. Who, after all, speaks today of the annihilation of the Armenians?" He was referring to the Armenian Genocide during World War I, when between one and one and a half million Armenians were slaughtered by the Turks. Finally, almost exhausted by his tirade, Hitler told everyone that he had done his duty; now it was up to them to do theirs.[2]

Admiral Canaris was shaken and upset by Hitler's proclamation. An attack on Poland would lead to a war with Britain and France, he could see that. He also knew that once the British entered the war on Poland's side, they would somehow manage to involve the United States in the fighting. With the Americans on their side, Britain would win the war. It was as simple as that. The admiral saw that he had to do something to stop Hitler from instigating a war.

As soon as the meeting ended—Commander in Chief Walter von Brauchitsch advised everyone to return to their posts immediately—Admiral Canaris traveled to the Hotel of the Four Seasons in Munich. He had jotted down a brief summary of Hitler's remarks in pencil while the conference was still in progress, even though everyone present at the meeting had been forbidden to take notes. At the hotel, the admiral wrote down everything he could remember about Hitler's speech, using his notes as a reference. He gave this summary to fellow anti-Nazi conspirator Col. Hans Oster. Oster rewrote the entire document, making Hitler's violent and aggressive remarks seem even cruder and more lurid.

According to Colonel Oster's version, Hitler had called the British and French heads of state cretins and imbeciles and also said that after the death of Joseph Stalin, who was gravely ill in Oster's account, he would attack Soviet Russia. One item that Colonel Oster did not have to invent was Hitler's urging his officers to act mercilessly and barbarously. He did add some of his own embellishments, writing that European citizens must be made to recoil from the barbarity of German troops. Europe, along with the rest of the world, certainly would react with horror to the atrocities committed by Hitler's troops in Poland.[3]

After Colonel Oster finished with his revision of Hitler's words, Admiral Canaris gave the edited speech to the Dutch military attaché in Berlin, Maj. G. J. Sas. Major Sas made certain that the representatives of both Britain and France received copies of the document, including Maj. Francis Foley, who had been the British military representative in Berlin for the past nineteen years, since 1920.

The falsified version of Hitler's address did exactly what Admiral Canaris intended. Both Britain and France went on full alert. In Britain, the army was mobilized with all leaves cancelled, the Admiralty brought the navy to full war footing, and all coastal defenses and antiaircraft units came to readiness. French premier Edouard Daladier brought the Maginot Line defenses to maximum alert, along with all troops stationed along the French-German frontier. Also, both countries promised to come to Poland's aid in the event of an attack by Germany. Another unexpected turn of events took the admiral completely by surprise: Italian dictator Benito Mussolini informed Hitler that he would not come to his assistance if Germany went to war with Poland.

Admiral Canaris hoped that all of these events would change Hitler's mind concerning his planned attack on Poland. With the British and the French on full alert and Mussolini's flat refusal to back Germany in the war that would certainly take place, Hitler could see that this was not going to be the quick and easy conquest he had in mind when he announced his plans at the Berghof meeting. The admiral was even optimistic enough to think that Hitler's generals might stage a revolt over having a probable two-front war on their hands—against Poland in the east and Britain and France in the west.

Others throughout Germany shared Admiral Canaris's optimism and hoped that Hitler would change his mind regarding the invasion. "Of course, no one can be sure with Hitler," noted Ulrich von Hassell, the former German ambassador to Italy, on August 31. "It is not entirely out of the question that he will recoil at the last moment."[4] But the admiral's ruse merely caused Hitler to postpone his attack, not to cancel it. The invasion of Poland, originally scheduled for 4:30 a.m. on August 29, was pushed back to September 1. The Luftwaffe began bombing targets inside Poland at dawn on that Friday; the Wehrmacht joined the attack a few hours later. Both Britain and France declared war on Germany two days after that, on Sunday, September 3, as they had promised.

When Admiral Canaris was given the official word that the attack would go ahead, his spirits collapsed; the optimism that had maintained his morale for the past week turned to outright pessimism. He told Dr. Hans Bernd Gisevius, who had been an official at the Gestapo National Headquarters before he turned against Hitler, "This means the end of Germany."[5] At the same time, he made a promise to himself: "Nothing should be omitted that would shorten the war."[6]

But during the first weeks of the Polish campaign in September, Admiral Canaris seemed to forget his doubts about the war, along with his opposition to Adolf Hitler. He had been an officer in the German navy for the past thirty-four years, ever since his cadet days at Kiel, and was proud of his service. His years dedicated to the navy and to his country, along with his ingrained habit of obeying all orders from his superiors, seem to have overridden his contempt for Adolf Hitler and the Nazi regime. To evaluate the "situation" personally, Admiral Canaris made several trips to the Polish front in the first days of the offensive— back in Berlin he had been reading eyewitness reports of the fighting, but this was no substitute for being in Poland and seeing it for himself. On September 3, when he visited Gen. Gerd von Rundstedt's headquarters, the admiral was informed that the German Fourteenth Army was approaching Krakow (which would be captured on September 6). Other German units were pushing eastward through enemy territory as well. All throughout his time in Poland, he heard nothing but good news. The admiral was greatly impressed with the Wehrmacht's progress, even proud of it—in his mind, the war had suddenly become Germany's campaign, not Hitler's. It was as though Canaris did not want Hitler to win the war, but he did not want Germany to lose it either.

This moral and ethical split personality did not last very long, however. On September 29, the signing of the German-Soviet Boundary and Friendship Treaty brought back all the hostility that Admiral Canaris felt toward Hitler. Under the terms of this treaty, after Russian troops had invaded Poland from the east on September 17—sixteen days after the German army attacked from the west—Germany and the Soviet Union agreed to divide control of occupied Poland between them. Twenty-two million Poles became unwilling subjects of Nazi Germany, while Russia gained the oil fields of eastern Poland as well as a barrier against the west. Admiral Canaris was horrified and sickened by this agreement. As far as the admiral was concerned, Hitler had betrayed Germany when he agreed to cooperate with Soviet premier Joseph Stalin, head of Bolshevik Russia, the sworn enemy of Germany. From Admiral Canaris's point of view, the so-called Boundary and Friendship Treaty would bring the country nothing but ruin and misfortune. A Wehrmacht officer called September 29 a day of shame for Germany. Admiral Canaris could not have agreed more and considered Hitler and his Nazis nothing but self-serving politicians at best and criminals at worst. The admiral had always been anti-communist and anti-Bolshevik, along with most German nationalists, and could see nothing but trouble for Germany as a result of the treaty with Stalin, trouble brought on by Hitler and his Nazi regime.

By the time the German-Soviet treaty had been signed, Admiral Canaris's opinion of the fighting inside Poland had also taken a dramatic turn. He made several other visits to the front after stopping at von Rundstedt's headquarters on September 3; each time he returned to Germany, he was increasingly despondent about the brutality and ruthlessness of the German troops. Everywhere he looked, he could see nothing but destruction and desolation: ruined houses, homeless civilians living in terror, the wreckage of completely burned-out buildings. He spent several hours being driven through the ruins of Warsaw, which left the admiral especially disheartened and depressed. Ulrich von Hassell, who knew Canaris and shared his feelings toward Hitler, wrote that Canaris "had come back from Poland completely broken" after he had seen "the results of our brutal conduct of the war, especially in devastated Warsaw." Von Hassell also mentioned that German troops were surrounding entire villages and setting them on fire "because of civilian snipers, while the population inside shrieked frantically."[7]

Toward the middle of September, Admiral Canaris began receiving information that would persuade him to take direct action against Hitler's policy of brutality. He was given firsthand reports of mass executions of Polish "undesirables": Jews from all social levels, university professors who lectured on subjects considered offensive to Hitler's New Order, members of the old Polish aristocracy who refused to acknowledge German authority, Catholic priests who would not preach sermons based on Nazi doctrine—anyone considered difficult or nonconforming or hostile to the Nazis. In his Berghof speech on August 22, Hitler had ordered his commanders to act without mercy or compassion toward all men, women, and children "of Polish derivation and language."[8] The officers and men of Heinrich Himmler's Schutzstaffel (SS) and Reinhard Heydrich's Sicherheitsdienst (SD) had taken Hitler's words to heart and were waging his battle against Polish civilians with a vengeance.

This was not the kind of war that Admiral Canaris expected or anticipated. Murder and mass executions carried out against an entire country's population, as well as its culture and way of life, was not war. To the admiral's way of thinking, it was atrocity. Abwehr officers had reported seeing murder squads, *Einsatzgruppen*, forcing Polish civilians to dig their own graves before shooting them, sometimes with machine guns. "Whatever we have now disavowed in the way of a Polish ruling class must now be liquidated," Hitler declared; "whatever grows again we must take into our safekeeping and eliminate in due course."[9] Reinhard Heydrich straightforwardly told the admiral that he intended to kill all the priests, Jews, and aristocrats in Warsaw as soon as his men moved into the city. Canaris was appalled. Through Heydrich, Hitler was planning to liquidate anyone in Warsaw and throughout Poland who might be considered inconvenient or threatening to the Nazis.

Wilhelm Canaris was a cautious soul by nature and did not like taking unnecessary chances, but in this case he decided to make an exception. On September 12, during a visit to Hitler's headquarters train, he lodged an official complaint with Gen. Wilhelm Keitel, the supreme commander of all German armed forces. The admiral found General Keitel in his office aboard one of the railway carriages and came right to the point. "I have information, Herr Colonel General, that mass executions are being planned in Poland, and that members of the Polish nobility and the Roman Catholic bishops and priests have been singled out for extermination. I feel obligated to give you a word of warning," he went on. "For such outrages, the world will eventually blame the Wehrmacht, if only because it acquiesced in these unheard-of atrocities."

General Keitel was not happy to hear what Admiral Canaris had to say. "If I were you, Herr Canaris," he said in an unfriendly tone, "I would not get mixed up in this business. This 'thing' has been decided upon by the Fuehrer himself. He has told General von Brauchitsch that since the Wehrmacht does not want anything to do with this 'thing,' it [the Wehrmacht] will have to let the SS and the Gestapo do it. As a matter of fact," the general continued, "every military command in Poland will from now on have a civilian chief besides its military head, the former

During the early 1930s, Canaris had no idea that Hitler's new Germany would include concentration camps such as Buchenwald. *Source:* National Archives.

to be in charge of the 'racial extermination' [*Volkstuemliche Ausrottung*] program."[10]

The Wehrmacht did not want to get involved with mass executions, but Wehrmacht officers were more than willing to look the other way while the Gestapo, SS, and SD performed the killings. One general, Johannes Blaskowitz, did speak out against the atrocities and was promptly relieved of his command. In demoting General Blaskowitz, Hitler made his point: if you value your Wehrmacht commission, follow orders and do not contradict *der Führer*. The injunction to exterminate all politically, socially, and racially unacceptable Poles was another *Führerbefehl*, an order issued directly by Adolf Hitler himself.

Shortly after General Keitel informed Admiral Canaris of the *Führerbefehl*, Hitler himself entered the general's carriage. General Keitel motioned for the admiral to keep quiet by putting his index finger to his lips. Canaris complied; he realized that he had no hope of stopping the extermination campaign that Reinhard Heydrich and his men were carrying out since they were doing so on Hitler's personal order. The admiral was also aware that some of his own Abwehr officers had been implicated in working with Heydrich's SD men in committing the killings.

After the usual greetings were exchanged, Hitler asked Admiral Canaris if he had any news from the western front, where French and British troops faced German units across their defenses. The admiral replied that French troops and artillery were being assembled in the Saarbrücken area, which indicated "a systematic and methodical offensive" in that vicinity. This took Hitler completely by surprise. "I can't imagine that the French will attack in the Saarbrücken area," he said, and went on to explain that German defenses were strongest in that region. "They may risk an adventure by crossing the Rhine," he went on, "although we are prepared there, too. I do not consider an attack through Holland and Belgium to be likely. It would be a breach of neutrality."

Hitler did not believe Admiral Canaris's prediction of a Saarbrücken offensive. Along with General Keitel, Hitler thought of the admiral as a "cautious pessimist" with a tendency to see the negative side of every situation and disregarded his report. This time the attempt by Canaris to plant misinformation with Hitler did not work, but he would continue doing his best to keep Hitler and his generals misinformed regarding Allied forces and their strategy whenever he had the opportunity.[11]

Another highly effective method Admiral Canaris would use to sabotage the authority of the Nazi regime was to assist victims of the Gestapo and the SD—specifically, to help these outcasts escape Hitler's *Einsatzgruppen* and racial extermination programs. An opportunity to rescue one such victim unexpectedly presented itself while the admiral was traveling by train through western Poland. When his train made a stop in the vicinity of Poznan, one of his officers, a Colonel Hartwig, introduced him to a vaguely familiar Polish woman. After a moment, he recognized the woman as Halina Szymańska, an acquaintance from Berlin in the days before the war.

Madame Szymańska was the wife of Antoni Szymanski, who had been the most recent Polish military attaché in Berlin. When war broke out, he left Germany and returned to Poland, where he joined the Polish army. Madame Szymańska and her husband were well known among members of the "Polish colony" and also socialized with many Germans during their nearly six years in Berlin. Among the people they met were generals and senior military officers, including Adm. Wilhelm Canaris. "I remembered this Admiral Canaris, because he was a singular man," she recalled, "not stiff and hard-voiced like some of the officers—the opposite, in fact, soft-voiced and friendly." Almost as an afterthought, she added, "Of course, I had no idea who he was, nor do I think did anyone else."[12]

When the war came, Madame Szymańska was living in eastern Poland, near Lublin, with her three daughters. Before long, the entire vicinity was overrun by Russian and Ukrainian troops. "The Ukrainians plundered us and stole my handbag," she said, "which contained my identity card and money." Shortly afterward, she was informed that Russian troops were in the area and moving toward Lublin. She decided that it would be best for her and her children to travel westward, toward the German lines, instead of waiting for the Russians to arrive. Russian troops were known for their brutality, especially toward women. She hoped that the Germans would be more civilized toward a woman in her position and that she might even meet someone she knew from her years in Berlin.

The first German officer she encountered wanted to know who she was. Madame Szymańska identified herself as the wife of the former military attaché and asked for diplomatic immunity. The officer seemed skeptical and asked if she knew any Germans who might give her a reference. She mentioned an army officer and a Luftwaffe general whom she had known in Berlin. "Then I remembered the friendly little naval officer and added: 'And Admiral Canaris.'"

Mentioning the admiral's name certainly had its desired effect. "I noticed that the German officer found it hard to conceal his astonishment when I uttered this name," Madame Szymańska remarked. "His whole tone and bearing altered. He told me that he could not give me a pass to go westwards, but he ordered a military vehicle to take me on its way to Posnan."[13]

Colonel Hartwig discovered Madame Szymańska and her daughters near Poznan, in a refugee camp with other political prisoners. Like most of the others in the camp, she was waiting for someone, preferably a German officer, to identify her. The colonel recognized her and asked her to come with him and talk to Admiral Canaris in his nearby railway carriage. "Can he not identify me here?" she asked, apprehensive about the prospect of boarding a German train.

"It will be difficult for him to talk to you among these people," Colonel Hartwig explained. Madame Szymańska complied with the colonel's request and went along with him to the admiral's carriage. She had managed to keep her composure up to this point, but when she entered the carriage and met Admiral Canaris for the first time in several years, her rigidly controlled poise disappeared. Just seeing "the friendly little naval officer" brought back memories of the days before the war, when she had lived a comfortable life with her husband and children, before she ever heard of refugee camps. Within moments of entering the admiral's compartment, Madame Szymańska burst into tears and began talking about her escape from the Russians. She was also very concerned about the Polish army and its fighting record against the Wehrmacht. "Our armies have been routed," she blurted out. "I fear they have not stood and fought."

The admiral did his best to calm her. The Polish armies have fought "well and bravely," he said. "They were simply out-mechanized by our armies and could do nothing against such a weight of material." He also asked Madame Szymańska if there was anything he could do to help her. When she replied that she wanted to reach her parents' house in Warsaw along with her children, Admiral Canaris frowned and shook his head. "I would not go to Warsaw," he said with some foreboding in his voice. He realized that no place in Warsaw, or in all of Poland, would be safe for her. She was not a Jew, but as the wife of the former Polish military attaché, Madame Szymańska would be in danger from Reinhard Heydrich and the SD as long as she remained in the country. He looked at a large wall map and ran his finger across it. "Switzerland," he said, "that is the best place."[14]

Admiral Canaris had the rank and the authority to arrange all the documents necessary to guarantee Madame Szymańska and her children safe passage to Switzerland. The signature on any paper of an admiral in the German navy, as well as the head of the Abwehr, would not be questioned. It took a few days, possibly a week, before all the documents were prepared and signed. As soon as everything was in order, Madame Szymańska boarded a train for Switzerland and managed to find an apartment for herself and her daughters in a comfortable section of Bern. She reported to the Polish Legation in Bern, where she was registered as a member of the Free Polish movement. At the legation, Madame Szymańska told the story of her rescue by Admiral Canaris, an old friend of hers from prewar days in Berlin. The Polish officials were extremely interested in her story about the German admiral who helped her to escape from the Nazis and wanted to know more about him. When British intelligence agents heard the story, they became interested in the admiral as well.

Admiral Canaris also took the trouble to find out exactly where Madame Szymańska's mother and father lived in Warsaw. When he was informed of the street address, he had his driver take him there. Madame Szymańska's parents were very glad to hear that their daughter and three granddaughters were safe and living in Switzerland, out of harm's way. The admiral also acted as a sort of post office between Madame Szymańska and her parents, forwarding all letters and correspondence addressed to him to either Switzerland or Warsaw.

This particular story has a happy ending: a Polish woman, a member of the upper stratum of Polish society, was successfully rescued from the SD and the Gestapo and resettled in Switzerland. (Madame Szymańska's husband, Col. Antoni Szymański, had been captured by the Red Army and was a Russian prisoner of war.) But this was not the end of the story.

In addition to cheating the SD of another victim, Admiral Canaris also accomplished something else: Madame Szymańska became one of his contacts with the Western Allies. The admiral met Madame Szymańska several times in her Bern apartment, at 10 Schonemweg, to discuss information regarding future German offensives, information that she passed on to British intelligence. Shortly after arriving in Switzerland, she started working as an agent for Britain's Secret Intelligence Service (SIS). "Halina was recruited by the Allied secret intelligence services through a network of Polish officers in Bern, Switzerland, who made contact with the British," according to one source. "Szymańska's mission was to provide a conduit of information between the Allies and Admiral Wilhelm Canaris, chief of the German Abwehr."[15] She reported directly to the head of the Bern SIS station, a Maj. Vanden Heuvel.[16]

In addition to meeting with Admiral Canaris, Madame Szymańska also met with his "courier," Hans Bernd Gisevius. "Szymańska played an important role, as an intermediary, in secret contacts between the Allies and German anti-Nazi conspirators," as it was reliably reported.[17] Some of the information she passed along to the Allies came from Admiral Canaris himself. "He told me that winter of 1940 that Germany would certainly make war on her treaty partner Russia sooner or later," she said. "Next spring he was in Berne again, and when I asked him whether the troop movements in the Balkans were aimed against Turkey, he simply replied, 'No, Russia perhaps.'"[18]

In the spring of 1941, Madame Szymańska received advance warning concerning Operation Barbarossa, the coming German attack on the Soviet Union. About four months after the offensive began, in October

1941, Admiral Canaris came to see her again and said that "the German front had run fast and bogged down in Russia and that it would never reach its objectives."[19] She related each of these conversations directly to British intelligence. "During World II," one commentator said, "she became one of the most effective MI6 [British SIS] agents."[20] One of the main reasons behind this effectiveness was the information that Admiral Canaris divulged to Madame Szymańska during his visits to her apartment. When Admiral Canaris helped her to escape the SD in Poland, he also helped to further the cause of the German resistance against Hitler.

Admiral Canaris's primary concern would continue to be the overthrow of Hitler and his regime. A major part of this concern consisted of helping anyone being persecuted by the Gestapo, the SD, or any other Nazi organization. From his point of view, aiding and abetting "undesirables" and political dissenters in their attempt to escape Nazi persecution was as vital to the anti-Nazi resistance as passing information to the Allies. Albert von Kessel, an employee at the Foreign Office who knew the admiral and has been described as "on the fringes of the conspiracy," said that Canaris was "the kind of man who took every opportunity to pry a victim from the Gestapo."[21] Admiral Canaris was well aware that a good many of the potential victims hiding from the Gestapo in Poland were Jews.

In the autumn of 1939, not long after Admiral Canaris helped Madame Szymańska and her children escape to Switzerland, another chance to rescue a potential Gestapo victim was passed along to him indirectly, via Washington, DC. The American consul general in Berlin, Dr. Raymond Geist, had been contacted by high-ranking US government officials regarding a "very delicate" matter. Dr. Geist, in turn, contacted German state councilor Helmuth Wohlthat.[22] Dr. Geist and Councilor Wohlthat had known each other for some time (Dr. Geist had been the consul general since 1929) and were on friendly terms. The delicate matter they discussed had come to the attention of Supreme Court Justice Louis Brandeis and Secretary of State Cordell Hull, who had passed it along to the consul general. Dr. Geist wanted to know if his friend Councilor Wohlthat might be able to help him resolve the matter.

The problem that Dr. Geist had been handed by Washington consisted of a prominent rabbi from Warsaw, Yitzhak Yosef Schneerson, and more specifically how to rescue him before the Gestapo discovered his whereabouts and deported him to a concentration camp. The US Department of State, through Cordell Hull, made the rescue of Rabbi Schneerson a matter of some importance and instructed Dr. Geist to begin proceedings that would lead to the rabbi's removal to a neutral country. Rabbi Schneerson was a spiritual leader of the Chabad movement, as well as of European Jewry overall. He had resided within the Warsaw Ghetto all throughout the fighting of September 1939. Senior members of the Chabad movement wanted to remove him from Warsaw, and from Poland, before it was too late; they knew it was only a matter of time before the Gestapo or the SD caught up with him.

If Rabbi Schneerson had been an American citizen, Dr. Geist simply would have gone to the German Foreign Office and made arrangements to transport the rabbi away from the war zone—in September 1939, the United States was still firmly neutral. But Rabbi Schneerson was a Latvian citizen,[23] as well as a Jew; getting him out of Poland was not going to be a simple matter, which is why Dr. Geist asked his friend Wohlthat for help. Councilor Wohlthat realized that removing the rabbi from Poland would present its share of difficulties. It would also be a dangerous, possibly deadly, undertaking. Any German caught trying to smuggle a rabbi out of any German-occupied country would find his life in peril.

Councilor Wohlthat knew that he could not possibly go to Foreign Minister Joachim von Ribbentrop for help, and he knew better than to ask anyone like Reichsmarschall Hermann Göring, head of the Luftwaffe, or General Keitel. Having heard something about Adm. Wilhelm Canaris and his sympathies, he decided to take a chance and visit the admiral at his office in the Tirpitz Ufer to talk over the problem. The admiral turned out to be reassuring and encouraging, even though he also realized that getting a rabbi out of Warsaw was not going to be easy, and the visit was exactly what Wohlthat was hoping for. After the councilor explained the situation, Admiral Canaris agreed to assign officers to locate Rabbi Schneerson and escort him out of Poland. He may or may not have been motivated by the fact that the US State Department also had an interest in saving the rabbi. The admiral's main interest was depriving the SS and the Gestapo of another murder victim.

The job turned out to be as difficult as Admiral Canaris and Councilor Wohlthat thought it would be, but for different reasons. As he had promised, the admiral assigned three officers to carry out the task. One of the officers he chose was Maj. Ernst Bloch, a badly scarred veteran of World War I who had fought at Verdun, the Somme, and Flanders. His face had been severely disfigured by a bayonet wound during the fighting, which gave him a slightly sinister appearance. His father was Dr. Oscar Bloch, a Jew. Admiral Canaris was well aware of Major Bloch's parentage.

The admiral sent Major Bloch and his fellow officers to Warsaw with instructions to work with the Abwehr office in that city. Their assignment seemed simple enough: find Rabbi Schneerson and his family and get them safely out of Warsaw. But just finding him turned out to be a complicated affair: the rabbi's followers were not inclined to give any useful information to German officers regarding his whereabouts. For nearly two months, throughout October until the end of November, Major Bloch and his two men searched Warsaw for anyplace that might be a likely hideout for the rabbi, asking questions and sometimes going from door to door in a particular area. Finally, at the end of November, Rabbi Schneerson was found in a Warsaw apartment house. Major Bloch took him into protective custody and informed Abwehr headquarters that the rabbi had been found alive.

Now that Rabbi Schneerson had finally been located, getting him out of the country presented another set of problems. Major Bloch was informed that he was also expected to arrange the escape of about a dozen additional Orthodox Jews, along with the rabbi and his family. This meant that additional visas would have to be arranged, both in Europe and the United States, including with the government of Latvia; Latvia was not inclined to cooperate with Nazi Germany. Finally, after all arrangements had been made, Rabbi Schneerson, his family, and his followers finally left Warsaw under the protection of Major Bloch, as well as Admiral Canaris, on December 22, 1939. They traveled by train from Warsaw, out of Poland to Berlin, where they stayed in the Jewish Federation offices, before traveling on to Latvia and finally to neutral Sweden.

One of Rabbi Schneerson's followers gave some idea of what the party went through on their journey: "German soldiers were bloodthirsty like wild animals to hurt our group of Jewish men with beards and side-locks as soon as they saw us."[24]

The American visas for the rabbi and his party, which authorized the group to enter the United States, were finally granted in early January 1940. "Ironically, it took longer to get the visas from the American government than to rescue the Rebbe from the Nazis,"[25] a news report grumbled, but on March 19, 1940, Rabbi Schneerson, along with his wife, several family members, and the other members of his group, finally landed in New York. The rabbi's library of 135 crates of books—another complication as he had refused to leave Warsaw without them—arrived from Warsaw a few months later.

Dr. Geist promised that he would do his best to keep the names of the "German personalities" who had taken part in the Schneerson rescue, including Helmuth Wohlthat and Admiral Canaris, from leaking beyond his office.[26] But Councilor Wohlthat had heard about the admiral's friendly inclinations toward "undesirables," anyone being persecuted by the party or the Gestapo, long before the rescue had taken place. There had been rumors that Admiral Canaris was assisting Jews and other refugees to get out of Germany even before Poland was invaded. Sometimes Abwehr officers were approached by perfect strangers and asked for help—they had friends or relatives who had to leave the country. It is not surprising that the SD got wind of what was going on over at the Tirpitz Ufer. If Helmuth Wohlthat had heard the rumors, so had Reinhard Heydrich.

Heydrich may have been Canaris's neighbor, as well as a frequent visitor at his house to attend musical evenings, but he was not above collecting information that he could use against the admiral when the opportunity presented itself. Among other things Heydrich did to accumulate evidence was have his SD agents follow Abwehr officers and eavesdrop on their conversations. He also had Admiral Canaris's office wiretapped. As head of the SD, Heydrich was one of the most powerful and influential men in the Nazi Party. But he was also one of the most ambitious, and he was always looking for an excuse to absorb the Abwehr into the SD and assume control of both agencies.

But Heydrich never used the information he had collected for a very practical reason: Admiral Canaris had compiled a dossier filled with incriminating information on Reinhard Heydrich. While Heydrich was eavesdropping on Abwehr agents and bugging the admiral's office, Admiral Canaris was doing some dirty work of his own. He acquired a copy of Heydrich's *Ahnenliste*, literally a listing of ancestors, which all Nazi Party members had on file. He claimed to have evidence that some of Heydrich's ancestors were Jewish, which would have made his position as head of the SD untenable. At least one of Heydrich's biographers, French writer André Brissaud, believed that he had Jewish ancestors. It has been suggested that one of the primary motives behind Heydrich's obsessive persecution of Jews was to prove that he was not Jewish himself. One of the Nazi Party's "racial experts" declared that Heydrich was not of German blood and had no German forbears.[27]

Whatever it was, be it proof that Heydrich was part Jewish or some other bit of incriminating evidence, something in Admiral Canaris's dossier frightened Reinhard Heydrich enough to keep him quiet regarding any suspicions he might have about the admiral and his rescue activities. Heydrich knew all about Canaris's dossier and its contents—the admiral told him all about the file himself. Admiral Canaris also let it be known to Heydrich that he had sent the report to a friend in Switzerland, along with instructions to forward it to the *New York Times* in the event that anything "suspicious" happened either to him or to his family. Heydrich knew the admiral well enough to realize that he meant what he said.

Although the mysterious dossier gave him some protection from Heydrich and the SD, Admiral Canaris knew that this protection could only be temporary. There was no guarantee that one of Heydrich's men would not come across some proof of Canaris's actions to help Jews elude the SD and, in a fit of patriotism or political fanaticism, go to a Gestapo official with his evidence. In spite of his precautions, Admiral Canaris knew that he could never be entirely safe from Reinhard Heydrich and his intrigues.

CHAPTER FIVE

Opening a Spanish Door

ADOLF HITLER'S ARMIES OVERRAN POLAND WITH AN AGGRESSIVENESS and single-mindedness that surprised even him. The last active Polish fighting unit surrendered on October 5, just over a month after the German invasion began; Hitler issued a peace offer to the ravaged country the following day. "The campaign was fierce and brilliant," journalist John Gunther wrote. "Nothing quite like it has been seen in military history."[1] Adm. Wilhelm Canaris continued to work against the Nazi regime even after Poland surrendered and in spite of the fact that Hitler seemed unstoppable at that point. He knew that the war was far from over and that Poland was only the beginning. He did his best to keep informed of any Jews or any other probable Sicherheitsdienst (SD) victims who might be in need of assistance, but he also took other steps to undermine Hitler's war effort. One such step consisted of sending information to the Allies, especially information regarding German troop movements and future strategy. But the admiral also managed to send other forms of data whenever an opportunity came his way. In fact, Admiral Canaris sometimes received credit for sending data that somebody else forwarded along to Allied intelligence.

One evening in November 1939, Dr. Reginald V. Jones had a small package deposited on his desk while he worked at his office at 54 Broadway in London. Dr. Jones was a principal scientific advisor for the Secret Intelligence Service (SIS) as well as a scientific officer at the Air Ministry. The colleague who dropped the parcel said, "Here's a present for you!" and explained that it had come from "our Naval Attaché in Oslo."

It contained "some seven pages" of typewritten documents, as well as a small, sealed box. Dr. Jones was afraid that the box might be some sort of bomb and opened it with no small amount of anxiety. Instead he found an electronic vacuum tube, which turned out to be a sensor for an anti-aircraft shell proximity fuse.[2]

The typewritten papers that Dr. Jones found in the naval attaché's "present," which would become known as the "Oslo Report," provided SIS with technical and highly classified information regarding some of Germany's most secret weapons programs. "It was probably the best single report received from any source during the war," Dr. Jones would write. During the course of the war, SIS would receive many pieces of valuable information from any number of sources, including reports from resistance and underground groups as well as aerial photographs. Most data from resistance organizations came as the result of dozens, sometimes hundreds, of people working in close connection with each other. But the Oslo Report was an altogether different article, with an altogether different history. "The Oslo Report, we believed, had been written by a single individual who in one great flash had given us a synoptic glimpse of much of what was foreshadowed in German military electronics," according to Dr. Jones.[3]

The report proved to be invaluable, not only to the SIS but also to Allied strategy in general. Among other things, it revealed that the Germans had two different types of radar equipment; many scientists and technicians did not believe that the Germany had any radar at all. Documents in the report also showed that a German rocket testing site existed at Peenemünde, on an island in the Baltic Sea. The report also revealed that long-range rockets, later known as the V-2 rocket, as well as jet-powered drones, the V-1 flying bomb, were being developed there. There were also drawings for a navigational aid that guided German bombers at night, as well as for torpedoes that homed in on the sound of a ship's propellers. A number of Dr. Jones's colleagues, including members of the Admiralty Research Laboratory, were convinced that the Oslo Report was nothing more than an elaborate hoax. But Dr. Jones himself did not share their skepticism and believed that its contents were genuine. "The value of the Oslo Report was to become evident as the war progressed," he later said.[4]

But the biggest mystery concerning the reports and its contents was its creator: Who could have been responsible for collecting so much material and delivering it without anyone knowing about it? Along with all of its papers and drawings, the package also contained a note mysteriously signed "a well-wishing German scientist,"[5] which was the only clue. But the method by which the parcel had been delivered, dropped anonymously and without explanation at the British embassy, indicated that it was the handiwork of only one man: Wilhelm Canaris. No one but the admiral would have had the rank and the authority to collect an entire package full of secret documents and drawings, then smuggle them out of Germany, right past the Gestapo and SD, and have them delivered safely to Norway. "It seemed quite possible that the Report was Canaris's doing," said Dr. Robert Cockburn of Britain's Telecommunications Research Establishment. "But we never found out. And we never discovered who else but Canaris or his agent could have done it."[6]

Many years after the war, Dr. Jones discovered that Admiral Canaris had not been responsible for the Oslo Report after all, in spite of all the indicators and hunches, and was able to identify the "well-wishing German scientist" as engineer and physicist Hans Ferdinand Mayer. Dr. Mayer was certainly a German scientist; he was director of communications research at Siemens and had access to a wide range of information regarding military and electronic technology being developed in Germany at the time. He never met Admiral Canaris and did not belong to Canaris's group of anti-Nazi conspirators, but he had a great deal in common with the admiral—especially concerning his views on Hitler and the Nazis. Appalled, like Canaris, by the atrocities being carried out in Poland by the Gestapo and the SD, he decided to act against Hitler and his party in his own way. He took a trip to Scandinavia in the autumn of 1939, allegedly on business, and delivered his report to the British embassy in Oslo in November. Dr. Mayer's sole motivation for taking such a risk was his determined opposition to Hitler and the Nazi government, a motivation he shared with Admiral Canaris.

For reasons that had nothing to do with the Oslo Report, the Nazis arrested Dr. Mayer in 1943—the Gestapo detained him for listening to British radio broadcasts as well as for criticizing the Nazi regime. Following his conviction, he was sent to the Dachau concentration camp. "The Nazis never learned of the Oslo Report," one writer commented, "a fact that probably saved his life."[7] Dr. Mayer managed to survive his term in concentration camps—he was transferred to four other prisons before the war ended—and became a professor of electrical engineering at Cornell University in 1947. The principal beneficiary of the Oslo Report, Dr. Reginald V. Jones, discovered the identity of the "well-meaning German scientist" through a group of mutual friends in the scientific community. The two met in 1955; Dr. Mayer requested that his role in the Oslo Report incident be kept a secret from the public until after his death. "Mayer died in 1980, and his identity was not revealed until nine years later."[8]

Even though Hans Ferdinand Mayer had no connection with Admiral Canaris or his anti-Nazi conspiracy, his sympathies certainly coincided with Canaris's way of thinking, and like the admiral, he had the courage of his convictions.

* * *

Admiral Canaris was given another opportunity to act against Hitler, along with another chance to free a number of Jews from concentration camps, in the autumn of 1940. In September, after the Luftwaffe lost the Battle of Britain, Hitler "indefinitely" postponed his plan to invade southern England and looked for another way of attacking Britain. His advisors suggested that one possible means would be to invade and capture Gibraltar. With Gibraltar in German hands, the argument went, Britain would be cut off from her forces in North Africa as well as—and this was a major point—from access to the Suez Canal. The idea was "that Hitler's armies might march through Spain and seize Gibraltar, suffocating the Empire by cutting its Mediterranean lifeline."[9] The invasion was given the code name Operation Felix, and the officer assigned to command the operation was Wilhelm Canaris.

Adolf Hitler in Paris in June 1940, after France surrendered to German forces. By this time, Canaris had turned completely against Hitler. *Source:* National Archives.

The choice of Admiral Canaris to head the attack on Gibraltar seemed logical. He spoke fairly fluent Spanish and had visited Spain many times over the years. He admitted that he felt at home among the out-of-the-way towns of Castile. It gave him great pleasure to travel along the country's back roads, visiting local restaurants and spending the night in small guesthouses. But even more important than his love Spain and his knowledge of the country and the language, Admiral Canaris had one other attribute that gave him an advantage over every other German officer: he was on very friendly terms with Spain's fascist dictator, Generalissimo Francisco Franco, whom he had known for years. The two had met possibly as far back as 1916 and 1917, when the young German naval officer had come to Madrid during World War I, and they always had a high opinion of each other. Franco not only liked Canaris personally but also remembered that he had been instrumental in arranging German military assistance for the fascists during the three-year civil war, which had ended in victory for Franco in April 1939. No one else in the Abwehr, or probably in any of the German forces, seemed to have qualifications for heading Operation Felix comparable to those of Admiral Canaris.

Canaris was so much at ease when he visited Spain that he sometimes allowed himself to discuss politics and air his political viewpoints. During one of his trips through the Spanish countryside, the admiral and some accompanying junior officers happened to come across a flock of sheep. He recommended that the officers always give the "Heil Hitler" salute whenever they encountered any sheep. "You never know," he would advise, "there might be some high-ranking official personality among them."[10] Admiral Canaris was usually extremely careful when it came to expressing his opinion, especially when it came to politics, but sometimes he let his true feelings show in spite of himself.

In July 1940, the admiral and a few staff officers left Berlin for Madrid. Everyone used different methods of transportation, traveled by different routes, and wore civilian clothes. Their assignment was to meet with Abwehr agents in Spain and to discuss the feasibility of Operation Felix. After the Abwehr officers and the admiral had their discussion and made their evaluation, Admiral Canaris sat down to write a report on the probability of the operation's success. He could see that the capture of Gibraltar by the Germans would be disastrous for Britain and an unqualified triumph for Hitler. In his report, Canaris did not even try to make an impartial evaluation regarding the feasibility of Operation Felix. Instead, he gave a completely negative account of what he had learned in Spain regarding Gibraltar.

Operation Felix could only be a very slow and hazardous operation, the admiral predicted. Just moving troops through Spain would be sluggish and frustrating; the few good, paved roads were too narrow to accommodate German mechanized transport. Traveling by train did not look to be much of an improvement, since the gauge of Spanish rail lines differed from that of French tracks, which meant that all German units would have to change trains at the border.

Any attempt at a surprise attack on Gibraltar was out of the question, the admiral's report continued. The British had mined the narrow strip of land that connected Gibraltar with the mainland and had also reinforced the defense force with fresh troops while the admiral was in Madrid. Machine guns and artillery emplacements had been dug into solid rock along the approaches to Gibraltar; neutralizing these positions would be difficult, at best, even with aerial bombing. In his report, Admiral Canaris did not offer much hope of success for Operation Felix. In fact, the way the admiral slanted his information made any attempt at an invasion sound like a full-scale disaster for Germany.

Admiral Canaris handed his report to recently promoted Feldmarschall Wilhelm Keitel, who passed it along to Hitler. The admiral's conclusions regarding Operation Felix only served to reinforce Feldmarschall Keitel's and Hitler's opinion of Canaris as a pessimist who only saw the negative side of every situation, and they decided to ignore his conclusions, just as they had ignored his prediction about a Saarbrücken offensive in 1939. Hitler was not about to be discouraged by some absentminded little admiral, especially since he had been wrong before in his predictions, and decided to go ahead with his planned invasion of Gibraltar. But before he could do anything, he would have to approach Generalissimo Franco for his permission to attack Gibraltar from Spain.

He did not foresee any problem with this since he had always been on friendly terms with the Spanish dictator.

But Admiral Canaris had known the generalissimo a lot longer than Hitler and was on much friendlier terms with him. He arranged for Dr. Josef Müller, a friend and confident who was also the Abwehr representative in Rome, to meet with Serrano Suñer, the Spanish foreign minister and Franco's brother-in-law. The message Dr. Müller delivered to Foreign Minister Suñer came as complete and total shock. "The Admiral asks you to tell Franco to hold Spain out of this game any all costs," he said, then warned that Germany's military position was not as strong and powerful as Generalissimo Franco might have been led to believe. "It is in reality desperate, and we have little hope of winning this war. Franco may be assured that Hitler will not use force of arms to enter Spain."[11]

Admiral Canaris himself went to Madrid to discuss Operation Felix with Generalissimo Franco as well as to talk about Hitler's impending visit to Spain. The admiral briefed Franco on what to say to Hitler when he arrived. Among other things, he advised the generalissimo to demand 15-inch guns—knowing full well that Hitler did not have anything resembling artillery of that caliber—as well as other items that Hitler either did not have or could not afford to provide. Franco listened to his old friend with some surprise, but he did not require much persuasion to stay out of the war. The Spanish Civil War had ended just a year and a half earlier; it would take some time before the country and its economy recovered from its effects. Franco was well aware that he needed to concentrate on problems at home, especially the problem of staying in power. He knew that he could not afford to be distracted by Hitler and his war with the British, and he had no desire to help the German dictator establish a worldwide Nazi empire.

On October 23, the two dictators met at the French border town of Hendaye to talk about Operation Felix and Spain's role in the operation. Hitler had traveled all the way from Berlin by train to speak with Franco. The generalissimo deliberately kept Hitler waiting, intentionally arriving at Hendaye two hours late for the meeting. Ulrich von Hassell summed up what happened next in his diary. "Hitler did not get on well with Franco, who was very reticent; he said Franco was probably a pretty good soldier but had become the head of his state by accident," von Hassell recounted. Hitler called Suñer "the worst kind of 'business politician.'"[12]

According to British writer Ian Colvin, Hitler "sought to overbear Franco" with a nine-hour tirade, "a suffocating flow of language with which he habitually stupefied his victims."[13] Among other things, he gave a monologue on German military successes in Poland, the Low Countries, and France, as well as on the U-boat successes against Allied shipping and the bombing of London, and promised similar successes in the near future. It was an impressive performance, or would have been if Dr. Müller had not already informed Franco of what Hitler was going to say. But because he had been forewarned, the generalissimo knew exactly what to expect from Hitler and had all of his answers prepared.

Franco refused to make any concessions regarding Operation Felix. Instead he kept asking for concessions from Hitler: for Spain to join the Axis, he insisted upon large shipments of grain and fuel oil from Hitler—the United States would almost certainly stop selling both items to Spain if he signed any sort of alliance with Germany. Hitler kept talking, asking Franco to join the war on the side of Nazi Germany on January 10, 1941; this agreement would correspond with the planned invasion of Gibraltar at the end of the month. He used every trick of persuasion and intimidation he knew to convince Franco to enter the war on the side of Germany, but Franco was determined to remain neutral and stubbornly refused to cooperate. He even told Hitler that if German troops did manage to occupy the British Isles, Britain would continue to fight from Canada with American help. Admiral Canaris's report, which had been delivered by Dr. Müller, was certainly having its desired effect. Franco gave vague reassurances of cooperation with Hitler but would make no definite promises. "Franco, to be sure, pledged absolute loyalty to the Axis," von Hassell noted in his diary, "but reserved to himself the timing of his participation."[14]

After hours of bluster and bombast, Hitler finally concluded that he would not to get anywhere with Francisco Franco and gave up. When the two dictators left Hendaye following their meeting—which Ulrich von Hassell cynically described as "squabbling with the Spaniards about an undertaking against Gibraltar"[15]—Hitler was thoroughly angry and frustrated. "I would rather have four teeth taken out than go through that again," he told Italian dictator Benito Mussolini afterward.[16]

Ian Colvin, who as a British news correspondent had seen Admiral Canaris in Berlin before the war, wrote that the admiral "had achieved something lasting" in Spain. "He had saved this mysterious land from prolonged torture."[17] He also compared Hitler's setback at Hendaye to the German defeats at Stalingrad and El Alamein and in the Battle of Britain. Admiral Canaris can be given full credit for this reversal of Hitler's plans. If Franco had been persuaded or pressured into allowing German troops to invade Gibraltar through Spain and the invasion had succeeded, the war would almost certainly have taken a different turn. With Gibraltar in German hands and its strait closed to British shipping, as well as British warships, this advantage might very well have allowed Feldmarschall Erwin Rommel and his Afrika Korps to capture the Suez Canal. By warning Franco about Hitler's intentions regarding Operation Felix, Admiral Canaris changed the course of the war.

By helping to keep the Germans out of Spain, Admiral Canaris also kept a door open for Jews escaping from Nazi-occupied territory. In the Berlin suburb of Zehlendorf, thirteen Jewish men were deported to different concentration camps. These men were married to non-Jewish women who were not sent off to camps but knew exactly where their husbands had been sent. The wives informed the local pastor, Reverend Heyden, of their husbands' whereabouts. This was the same Dr. Heyden who had been saved by Canaris in November 1938. Reverend Heyden compiled a list of names and camps and handed it to Admiral Canaris. "All of them were released, thanks to the combined efforts of Canaris and his staff," the reverend's son commented. The admiral also organized the transport of all thirteen men to Madrid in a closed railway compartment; once there, they came under the protection of Generalissimo Franco. "Canaris used his connections to put up the thirteen in private homes in Madrid before some of them were flown to England," Reverend Heyden's son continued. "Most of these men joined the British military."[18]

Thousands of Jews managed to escape Nazi concentration camps by way of Spain with the assistance of both Admiral Canaris and Francisco Franco. The fact that Spain bordered on German-occupied France shortened the travel route for refugees. The main barrier for anyone hoping to escape to Spain was physical—the Pyrenees—instead of political. "The Pyrenees separated 'free' Spain from Vichy France, making the passage over this mountain range the virtual equivalent to the freedom passage through the Swiss Alps."[19] A newspaper report estimates that "after the fall of France in 1940, an estimated 20,000–35,000 Jews did manage to cross the Pyrenees" and make their way across Spain "to Portugal and freedom"—passage across the Atlantic Ocean either to South America or the United States.[20]

Admiral Canaris helped a great many of these escapees to leave both Germany and German-occupied France and make their way to Franco's Spain. Once they had arrived in Spain, these Jews, along with other outcasts, were no longer in danger of arrest by the Gestapo. "Spain's collaborative relations with Germany placed Spanish diplomats in the best position to help the Jews"[21] and also helped Admiral Canaris's Abwehr agents in Spain make life easier for the refugees while they were in the country. These "unpatriated citizens" were only allowed to remain in the country for thirty days before moving on to their final destination, usually by way of a Portuguese or Spanish port. The visas issued to these refugees required them to be "in transit"; they were not allowed to settle in Spain. As Foreign Minister Francisco Gomez-Jordana phrased it, they had to pass through the country "like a light goes through glass, without a trace."[22] The Spanish government did not want these stateless refugees to have any impact or influence in Spain—at least that was the implication. Admiral Canaris used his connections, as well as his agents, to take over where the Spanish government left off. Franco allowed the Jews to enter the country; the admiral did his best to see that they were able to get along while in Spain, until they moved on.

Generalissimo Franco certainly was directly responsible for helping to rescue thousands of Jews from the Nazis, but his reasons for coming to the aid of so many exiles has been the subject of controversy since the early 1940s. Some take a romantic view of the generalissimo's motives. "Franco not only stood up to Hitler and adamantly refused to hand over the approximately 40,000 European Jews who had sought refuge in Spain," one writer declared, "he also provided protection for Jews in

Nazi-occupied Eastern Europe with Spanish passports."[23] But many others have been much more cynical in their outlook. "By helping the Jews, Franco's regime was able to gain some good publicity without actually having to do all that much or even allowing the Jews to stay," another source claims. "In this way, Franco could get good press and enrich Spain's economy via Jews in transit without even allowing them to settle permanently in Spain."[24] The same writer goes on to say, "Jews were mere chess pieces to be used and manipulated in Franco's larger game."[25]

There are also those who point out that Franco actually helped the Nazis in their persecution of the Jews. "The Spanish dictator, General Francisco Franco, whose apologists usually claim that he protected Jews, ordered his officials to draw up a list of some 6,000 Jews living in Spain and include them in a secret Jewish archive," a London newspaper reported. This report also claims, "That list was handed over to the Nazi architect of the so-called 'final solution,' the German [Schutzstaffel (SS)] chief Heinrich Himmler."[26] Admiral Canaris may have rescued Jews out of moral convictions, critics argue, but Franco only wanted to enhance his own image in the world, especially in the United States.

Regardless of his motives, others argue that Franco did come to the rescue of thousands of Jews who needed his help. Among those who held this point of view was Israeli prime minister Golda Meier, who was anything but an apologist for any fascist dictator. Prime Minister Meier told a Spanish news magazine that her country remained grateful for "the humanitarian attitude taken by Spain during the Hitler era, when it gave aid and protection to many victims of Nazism."[27]

* * *

Members of the anti-Hitler conspiracy had firmly made up their minds to end the rule of Adolf Hitler and his government, but not all of its members could agree upon exactly how this coup should be carried out. Admiral Canaris, the chief of intelligence, responded with a spy's mentality. His idea was to oust Hitler by doing everything possible to cost him the war: supply the German High Command with a steady stream of misinformation and bogus intelligence reports regarding Allied intentions and, at the same time, send the Allied powers genuine information concerning German plans and intentions. Another member of the conspiracy, a thirty-three-year-old colonel named Count Klaus von Stauffenberg, read the reports of the mass executions in Poland and reacted from a soldier's point of view, which was to take direct action. He decided that the only certain way to eliminate Hitler was to have him killed. Ulrich von Hassell, the former German representative to Italy, had his own idea, which stemmed from his background as a diplomat: the conspirators should not attempt to remove Hitler by themselves but should ask Britain to help them with their coup.

This seemed a logical course of action to von Hassell. The British government would certainly be willing to help a clique of anti-Nazi conspirators who were at work inside Germany, he thought. Backing a movement to oust Hitler and his party could have nothing but positive results for the Allied cause and would almost certainly help to shorten the war. Even though he had been removed from his post as Italian ambassador several years earlier—he was dismissed from his post by Foreign Minister Joachim von Ribbentrop when he opposed the alliance between Hitler and Mussolini in 1937—von Hassell still had the connections to arrange a meeting between top-level British officials and himself. During the early part of 1940, he began making preparations to meet with a representative of Prime Minister Neville Chamberlain's government.

Along with Admiral Canaris and the other members of the anti-Hitler movement, Ulrich von Hassell had also heard the stories of the atrocities carried out by the SD. An acquaintance gave him a lurid image of Poland under the Nazi occupation. "The hungry workers are gradually getting weaker. The Jews are systematically being exterminated, and a devilish campaign is being launched against the Polish intelligentsia with the express purpose of annihilating it." To illustrate his point, the man gave von Hassell a specific example of this "devilish campaign." "For the death of one SS man, who allegedly had been murdered while looking for a cache of arms, five hundred intellectuals were taken at random from the lists of lawyers, doctors, et cetera, and murdered."[28]

In October 1940, von Hassell received word of an edict that Hitler had issued to Feldmarschall Wilhelm Keitel concerning the occupation of Poland, along with instructions on how to deal with any rebels who defied the Nazis. Of the decree and its contents, Von Hassell noted in his diary, "After the war we shall have many rebellious peoples to rule; in order to manage them, he [Hitler] wishes to put in control not the Army but the combat units of the SS." The diary entry continued, "He therefore wants the SS transformed into a special service branch, equipped with all arms, including air weapons, and under his reprisal command."[29] Hitler was sending the armed elements of the SS, the Waffen-SS, to enforce Nazi rule in Poland, which would mean still more killing. Von Hassell also noted, "It is being said openly that there are no decent Poles, just as there are no respectable Jews."[30] He decided to do whatever he could to put an end to the Nazis and their murders. During the winter of 1940, von Hassell began his campaign to involve Britain in the plot to overthrow Hitler.

In February 1940, von Hassell met with an associate of British foreign minister Lord Halifax in Arosa, Switzerland. The meeting had been secretly arranged through the intercession of von Hassell's son-in-law, Detalmo Pirzio Biroli. Von Hassell did not mention the name of this "associate" of Lord Halifax and only identified him as "Mr. X." "Mr. X" was in fact James Lonsdale-Bryans, an amateur diplomat whom Lord Halifax had allowed to meet "unofficially" with von Hassell and who thus did not have as much authority as von Hassell imagined. A handwritten note from an official in MI5, Britain's counterintelligence and security agency, stated, "He went to Italy with the knowledge of the FO in order to develop his contacts. He greatly exceeded his instructions."[31] The two met three times in von Hassell's hotel. "I spoke at length with X, and finally gave him the attached (but unsigned) statement on a durable peace," von Hassell wrote in his diary.[32]

Lonsdale-Bryans had said something to the effect that "conservative Englishmen hoped for a monarchy" to replace Hitler. A leading candidate for this new kaiser was Prince Louis Ferdinand of Prussia, the grandson of Kaiser Wilhelm II. "A monarchy is very much to be desired," von Hassell wrote, "but that would be a problem of the second stage." In other words, the first priority was the removal of Hitler by German efforts. After he had been ousted, the problem of a successor could be dealt with.[33]

Lonsdale-Bryans was not very reassuring regarding von Hassell's proposal for obtaining a "durable peace" or overthrowing Hitler. "Mr. X considers a negotiated peace with the present German regime an absolute impossibility," von Hassell said matter-of-factly. In response to an inquiry by Lonsdale-Bryans regarding the identity of the men in the anti-Hitler movement, von Hassell flatly refused to answer the question. "I am not in a position to name the men who are backing me," he said. "I can only assure you that a statement from Halifax would get to the right people."[34]

The articles of the unsigned statement that von Hassell gave to Lonsdale-Bryans, which (in Sections VI and VII) listed "certain principles" regarding the "treaty of peace and the reconstruction of Europe," seem idealistic, especially in view of what was to come during the next five years. But von Hassell wanted to try his own approach to overthrow Hitler, just as Admiral Canaris and Count von Stauffenberg would attempt theirs. Below is von Hassell's own English version of the document:

Confidential

i. All serious-minded people in Germany consider it as of utmost importance to stop this mad war as soon as possible.

ii. We consider this because the danger of a complete destruction and particularly a bolshevization of Europe is rapidly growing.

iii. Europe does not mean for us a chess-board of political or military action or a base of power but it has "la valeur d'une patrie" in the frame of which a healthy Germany in sound conditions of life is an indispensable factor.

iv. The purpose of a peace treaty ought to be a permanent pacification and restablishment of Europe on a solid base and a security against a renewal of warlike tendencies.

v. Condition, necessary for this result, is to leave the union of Austria and the Sudeten with the Reich out of any discussion. In the same way there would be excluded a renewed discussion of occidental frontier-questions of the Reich. On the other hand, the German-Polish frontier will have to be more or less identical with the German frontier of 1914.

    vi. The treaty of peace and the reconstruction of Europe ought to be based on certain principles which will have to be universally accepted.

   vii. Such principles are the following:

       1. The principle of nationality with certain modifications deriving from history. Therefore

       2. Reestablishment of an independent Poland and of a Czech Republic.

       3. General reductions of armament.

       4. Restablishment of free international economical cooperation.

       5. Recognition of certain leading ideas by all European states, such as:

           a. The principles of Christian ethics.

           b. Justice and law as fundamental elements of public life.

           c. Social welfare as leitmotiv.

           d. Effective control of the executive power of state by the people, adapted to the special character of every nation.

           e. Liberty of thought, conscience, and intellectual activity.[35]

In London, von Hassell's statement was not read with very much enthusiasm, although his principles of "Christian ethics" and "liberty of thought, conscience, and intellectual activity" probably raised a few eyebrows.[36] But the British government was not interested in an opportunity to end the war by using the subterfuge of underground movements and had no confidence in any anti-Hitler conspiracy operating inside Germany. The von Hassell document made no mention of the fate of Jews or any other outcasts being victimized by the Nazis, but mentioning Nazi persecution would not have fazed anyone in London either and would not have made the British government change its mind. If the anti-Nazi conspiracy could be used to cause Hitler to lose faith in his military and naval leaders, as well as in his chief of intelligence, that was all Britain wanted or expected from them. And if the conspirators somehow managed to overthrow Hitler, so much the better. But no one wanted to give them any assistance or even any hope. A British historian wrote of the

anti-Hitler conspirators, "Brave though they were, they should have realized that the British were now fighting a total war, and that the Schwarze
Kapelle," a name given to the anti-Hitler movement by the Gestapo,
"would be considered merely as another weapon in that war."[37]

Committed to a land war against the German army in France and
the Low Countries as well as to a war at sea against the Kriegsmarine,
Britain did not feel inclined to get involved with a group of well-meaning
amateurs who would probably not be able to overthrow Hitler anyway.
The war would be fought "to the bitter end," to use Winston Churchill's
phrase.[38] Force would have to be met with force, not with trickery or the
activities of underground conspirators.

Von Hassell did not get the reaction he had been hoping for from his
meeting with James Lonsdale-Bryans or from his statement. But as the
war went on, the anti-Hitler conspirators would contact the Allies again
and keep trying to convince British and American leaders that they were
worth taking seriously.

CHAPTER SIX

Suspicions and Brutalities

THE ATTACK ON RUSSIA THAT ADM. WILHELM CANARIS HAD PRE-
dicted and mentioned to Madame Halina Szymańska in the spring of
1941 took place on June 22, 1941. From the very beginning, he was
convinced that the invasion was a serious mistake. The Abwehr was duty
bound to distribute false reports of the transfer of German troops to
northern France. These reports were meant to mislead British and French
intelligence into believing that the next German offensive would take
place in southern England instead of the Soviet Union. But the admiral
was adamantly against the Russian campaign. One of Admiral Canaris's biographers stated that he considered a war with the Soviet Union
nothing less than "a national calamity" and feared that in sending bogus
information to mislead France and Britain, "he was abetting a crime
which might claim millions of lives." He was convinced that the planned
invasion, code-named Operation Barbarossa, would be disastrous for
Germany, Nazi and non-Nazi alike.[1]

In spite of the admiral's misgivings, the early stages of the invasion
were a brilliant success. In fact, the offensive reminded Canaris of the
Polish campaign. During the first weeks of Barbarossa, as stated by a
British historian, "the Wehrmacht achieved some of the greatest victories
in the annals of war." The Wehrmacht's chief of staff declared that the
campaign had been won within fourteen days of the start of the offensive.
By the second week of July, the Red Army had lost three thousand prisoners to the advancing Germans, along with twenty-five hundred tanks.

Adolf Hitler began planning a victory parade to be held in Moscow by the German army by the end of August.[2]

Admiral Canaris read the reports of the Wehrmacht's almost irresistible advance toward Moscow and of the overwhelming of the Russian armies. But he also began receiving information about the Sicherheitsdienst (SD) and the activities of their *Einsatzgruppen*. Just as they had done in Poland, these groups entered Russian towns after the Wehrmacht had passed through and began conducting their reign of terror against Jews and others they considered to be inconvenient. The primary victims of these death squads were, once again, intellectuals, Jews, and communist officials. The *Einsatzgruppen* were divided into four units and totaled about three thousand men. They tracked down these unfortunates and shot them by the thousand.

"The whole war in the east is terrible—a return to savagery," Ulrich von Hassell wrote in his diary. He mentioned a young officer who had been ordered to shoot 350 civilians, "allegedly partisans, among them women and children," who had been herded together in a barn. The officer, reluctant to carry out his orders, was warned that the penalty for disobedience was death. After hesitating for a short while, he ordered his machine gunners to carry out the assignment. The incident upset him so much that "he was determined not to go back to the front." Such stories from the Russian front were fairly common.[3]

Abwehr units in Russia began sending reports of mass executions within a few weeks of the invasion. On August 10, Feldmarschall Gerd von Rundstedt issued a statement expressing his displeasure with these executions and sent a copy of the document to the Abwehr. Just as upset by the reports, Admiral Canaris issued a statement of his own regarding the activities of the SD and their *Einsatzgruppen*. He sent a communiqué to Gen. Erwin von Lahousen, the head of Abwehr II, forbidding members of the Abwehr to take part in politics—Abwehr activities were to be strictly confined to military matters. Abwehr agents were instructed to avoid taking part in any and all political activities, including working with the SD, in spite of any previous orders they might have received. Admiral Canaris wanted to make absolutely clear that none of his agents were to cooperate with the SD in their campaign against the Jews or anyone else the Nazis considered to be politically objectionable.

Admiral Canaris might have done his best to prevent his agents in Russia from taking any part in the SD's mass murders, but there was nothing he could do to prevent the SD from carrying out their executions. The reports from the East kept coming in, cold-blooded, matter-of-fact inventories listing the number of people shot, along with a brief description of the victims. One such report, labeled "Incident Report No. 153" and submitted by the officer in charge of Einsatzgruppe D, stated, "Subunit's field of operations cleared of Jews, particularly in smaller localities. Those shot during period under review comprise 3,176 Jews, 85 partisans, 12 looters, and 122 Communist officials. Running total: 79,276." A similar report, from Einsatzkommando 6, gave these figures: "Of the remaining 30,000, approximately 10,000 were shot." And Einsatzgruppe C submitted these figures: "As of 6.9.1941, Special Detachment 4a had disposed of a total of 11,328 Jews."[4] The SD's murder campaign in Russia seemed even more aggressive than it had been in Poland. The killings were certainly more organized and orderly, an indication that Reinhard Heydrich's men were becoming more efficient with practice.

The SD had also made a pact with the Wehrmacht, an agreement that allowed members of both the SD and the Gestapo to inspect prisoner of war camps in search of Jews, Communist Party leaders, and other political "undesirables." These individuals would be singled out from the other prisoners and removed from the compound, usually never to be seen again. Sometimes they were executed in front of Wehrmacht troops. When informed that Reinhard Heydrich's men were murdering Russian prisoners, Admiral Canaris was outraged. No decent or respectable military should even consider executing prisoners; this ran contrary to all the rules of warfare. The admiral sent Erwin von Lahousen to confront representatives of the Wehrmacht with a strongly worded communiqué; he wanted to register his objections to the Wehrmacht's agreement regarding enemy prisoners. The admiral himself preferred to stay in the background during such disputes, not wanting to call attention to himself or to his antipathy for the Nazis. He was afraid that Heydrich and the

Gestapo would become suspicious of his political sympathies and might uncover his activities with the anti-Hitler opposition.

General von Lahousen had a very uncomfortable meeting with a general named Reinecke, who was head of the department within the German Armed Forces High Command that had made the pact with the SD and the Gestapo. Heinrich Müller, a leading Gestapo chief nicknamed "Gestapo" Müller, was also present. General von Lahousen let the two of them know, in no uncertain terms, that the massacre of prisoners of war (POWs) went against all the rules and statutes of international law and also adversely affected the morale of German troops forced to witness these executions—if the Germans did this to Russian POWs, the Russians would do the same thing to them if they were captured. The general was a lawyer by profession and made his point with eloquence and no small amount of anger, but his argument impressed neither Reinecke nor Müller. Gestapo Müller rejected the protest out of hand.

The Abwehr legal department also drafted a written protest to Feldmarschall Wilhelm Keitel. It was actually written by Count Helmuth James von Moltke, who was attached to the legal branch of the Abwehr's foreign intelligence section. He was also a member of the anti-Nazi opposition. Von Moltke wrote that the German High Command's agreement with the SD and the Gestapo regarding the killing of prisoners of war could only serve to "negate the validity of standards prescribed by the rules of war in the fight against Bolshevism." He went on to present the Abwehr's "strong objections" to the agreement "not only from the standpoint of principle but because of the adverse consequences that would certainly ensue from the political and military aspect."[5]

Von Moltke's letter was typed, dated September 15, 1941, signed by Adm. Wilhelm Canaris, and dispatched to Feldmarschall Keitel. Feldmarschall Keitel was no more interested in the letter or in the protest than he had been in Canaris's protest of mass executions during the Polish campaign. "These objections accord with soldierly conceptions of a chivalrous war," he responded, implying that the war against Russia would be carried out in a manner that was anything but chivalrous. "What matters here is the destruction of an ideology"—the annihilation of all communists and communist sympathizers, including Jews and

Jewish Bolshevists. "I therefore approve and endorse these measures," he concluded, meaning the measures that the SD had been carrying out against POWs. The admiral had raised his voice in protest to the head of the German Armed Forces High Command and formally objected to the routine killings being carried out with official approval. Once again, the admiral's complaints had come to nothing.[6]

Any number of Admiral Canaris's contemporaries, including Ulrich von Hassell, criticized the admiral for not being more forceful and active in the anti-Hitler resistance's campaign against Hitler and his regime and for having Erwin von Lahousen meet with General Reinecke and Gestapo Müller instead of confronting them himself. But there are several good reasons for this. For one thing, von Lahousen was a lawyer. A protest based on international law sounded more convincing coming from an attorney than from an admiral. Also, not all Abwehr officers sympathized with Admiral Canaris and his anti-Hitler views. A good many of the admiral's subordinates had no use at all for either Jews or communists and would willingly have seen every member of both groups exterminated.

The head of the Abwehr's Russian command, Maj. Hermann Baun, did not seem to be disturbed by the treatment of Jews in Russia at all. In fact, he seemed to agree with the prevailing anti-Semitism in both the German and the Russian forces—Russian soldiers had been reported as saying that the Germans certainly knew how to deal with Jews. And Col. Franz-Eccard von Bentivegni, head of the Abwehr section that dealt with finding and eliminating enemy spies, was glad that the Jewish residents living in Berlin were restricted to the eastern end of the city. In Colonel von Bentivegni's opinion, all Jews were either communist sympizers or Russian spies. Keeping them all in one section of Berlin and requiring them to wear a distinguishing yellow Star of David, made them easier to track and identify.[7]

Admiral Canaris had to be very careful that his rescue activities did not come to the attention of officers like Major Baun or Colonel von Bentivegni, both for his own sake as well as for the protection of his fellow conspirators in the anti-Hitler conspiracy. Fortunately for the admiral, there were also a good many Abwehr officers who agreed with him and supported his rescue efforts. One such officer was Maj. Walter Schultze-Bernett, commander of Abwehr headquarters in The Hague.

Major Schultze-Bernett had been assigned to the Abwehr's Hague office in 1940, shortly after the Netherlands had been overrun by German troops. He had been a member of the Abwehr since 1935 and had played an active role in intelligence gathering prior to the German invasion—he was a captain at the time. Because of his activities in preparation for the Wehrmacht's campaign in Holland, which were instrumental in the success of the operation, Schultze-Bernett was promoted to the rank of major. But after German forces occupied Holland, the major was horrified by the SD's treatment of Jews and other Nazi outcasts. He could not bring himself to accept what the SD and their *Einsatzgruppen* were carrying out in the name of Hitler and his regime. "Schultze-Bernett was probably a cosmopolitan man to whom the Master Race was suspicious," a German historian wrote. "In addition, he came from a middle-class background, and the brutality of the Nazis was contrary."[8] The cruelty and violence of the Gestapo and the SD turned him away from Hitler and toward Admiral Canaris and his way of thinking.

As the director of the Abwehr's Hague headquarters, two of Major Schultze-Bernett's main functions were to establish and develop military intelligence services in Belgium, France, and the Netherlands and to strengthen the Abwehr's overseas intelligence services. When he investigated the state of the intelligence networks on the other side of the Atlantic, the major was not encouraged by what he found. "Our connections to overseas, particularly to the USA and South America, were rather thin and almost shattered," he wrote.[9] After making his evaluation, he wrote an official report in which he expressed his opinion of the sorry state of the Abwehr's foreign intelligence networks and submitted his findings to the Abwehr's main headquarters in Berlin. He probably expected his assessment to be filed away in a desk drawer and forgotten.

But in March 1941, the Berlin office reacted to Major Schultze-Bernett's report by ordering that intelligence services be established in Central and South America. Headquarters also directed that these outposts should be staffed by trained Abwehr agents. The major read the directive, which had obviously been prompted by his report on the "thin and almost shattered" state of the Abwehr's overseas services, with no small amount of surprise. Berlin had not only listened to what he had to say about the Abwehr's intelligence services abroad but also given him the authority to send Abwehr personnel to foreign countries. He saw the order as an opportunity to send Jews out of the country and away from "the now ongoing activities in the Netherlands against the Jews by the Sicherheitsdienst (SD), to have the possibility of their emigration, which should then officially take place."[10]

In March 1941, the major had "the ingenious idea" of using diplomatic connections in several Latin American countries to help mount a large-scale Jewish rescue operation—sending Jews overseas disguised as Abwehr agents. Admiral Canaris gave his full approval for this operation and agreed that Jews should be employed as "agents" in the Abwehr's overseas departments. Major Schultze-Bernett called this plan Operation Aguilar—Operation Eagle in Spanish. Admiral Canaris described it as the "infiltration of agents in North, Central, and South America." He also insisted on one stipulation: "The Abwehrstelle Netherlands had to keep completely in the background, so as not to appear as the initiator of this action in appearance and thus to reveal the intentions of the action."[11] The admiral wanted to make absolutely certain that Reinhard Heydrich never discovered anything regarding Operation Aguilar. For the sake of everyone in the anti-Hitler movement, as well as everyone involved in Aguilar, it was absolutely imperative that the operation be kept a complete and total secret.

Sending some five hundred Jews out of Nazi-occupied Holland past the watchful eyes of German officials, not to mention the SD and the Gestapo, required no small amount of planning. Each of the "agents" had to be supplied with identification cards and other forms of documentation, essential to offer proof that these individuals were genuine Foreign Service Office employees. None of these documents were fakes or forgeries. All passports and other credentials were signed by Admiral Canaris himself or by another senior Abwehr officer—every officer had to be sympathetic to the anti-Hitler movement. Some of the newly recruited agents were taught simple codes to make their cover stories more convincing. "You had better teach them a code or two," the admiral advised his chief of staff, Hans Oster, "for I have claimed them as my agents."[12] Consulates in the destination countries had to be contacted to inquire if they would be willing to grant entry visas to Jewish refugees.

After all the negotiations and necessary preparations had been completed, arrangements had to be made to get the emigrants out of Holland. Six trains were acquired to take the five hundred refugees to Spain and Portugal. The trip had an auspicious beginning when a Dutch security official, a member of the Schutzstaffel, decided to cooperate with Major Schultze-Bernett and allowed the departure of the refugee train without any problems or complications. "Much to our surprise, we found the head of the security department in The Hague, Mr. Pilling . . . without regard to the possible consequences, gave his consent and support in promised implementing," the major remembered. Albin Pilling, the security man, "provided the necessary certificates." Each train was met at the French-Spanish frontier by a "defense officer," presumably a colleague of Pilling, "so there were no incidents at the border."[13]

The journey was coordinated by a non-Nazi named Harry W. Hamacher, a Roman Catholic who was also the head of the travel agency Brach and Rothstein. "Mr. Hamacher probably also spoke with human motivation to help Jews to escape their probable fate," Major Schultze-Bernett went on to say. But Mr. Hamacher also "earned a lot of money with the emigration of Jews," so his motives were not entirely noble and humane. As their predecessors had done, the refugees traveled through Spain to the coast of Portugal and then on to the New World to begin new lives beyond the reach of the SD and the Gestapo. After departing from harbors in Spain and Portugal, Operation Aguilar's five hundred exiles were scattered all over Latin America: Cuba, Argentina, Brazil, Mexico, Haiti, the Dominican Republic, Venezuela, Columbia, Panama, Ecuador, and, according to some accounts, the United States. Each person was allowed to take only two suitcases. Major Schultze-Bernett traveled with the first train, which departed on May 11, 1941, and well as with the second, bound for Hendaye, "to make sure of a smooth process." To avoid attracting attention, he wore civilian clothes instead of his uniform.[14]

The five hundred Jewish refugees who escaped the Nazis through Operation Aguilar may have been out of danger from Reinhard Heydrich and his SD, but Admiral Canaris was not. Heydrich had been intent for quite some time on absorbing the Abwehr into his Sicherheitsdienst, which would allow him to take control of both intelligence agencies, and was always on the lookout for the chance to write a bad report concerning Admiral Canaris, the Abwehr, or both. Although he was cruel and ruthless by nature—German historian Hans Bernd Gisevius, who was well acquainted with Heydrich, said that his "dominant trait" was brutality—the head of the SD could also be subtle and devious when it suited his purposes.[15]

Heydrich had his spies quietly investigate Admiral Canaris and his activities and managed to get wind of the fact that five hundred Abwehr agents had been sent to Latin America. He almost certainly had not heard the name Operation Aguilar, or he would have taken immediate action against Canaris, but he realized that something was wrong. Why had so many agents been sent overseas, all of them to Central and South America, and in such a short period? And why did so many of them have Jewish names? There was something very peculiar about these "agents." Heydrich had nothing concrete against the admiral, just vague doubts and suspicions. But he intended to keep his eyes and ears open and was prepared to wait patiently for the Abwehr chief to make a slip. When he had assembled enough evidence to prove that Wilhelm Canaris was conspiring against the government by recruiting Jews as agents, he would take his proof directly to Adolf Hitler himself. Admiral Canaris would then be eliminated, removed as head of the Abwehr, and Heydrich would become director of the combined Abwehr-SD agencies. It was only a matter of time—or so it seemed to Reinhard Heydrich.

Admiral Canaris realized that Heydrich and the Gestapo had their suspicions about his activities and feared that one of them would eventually discover something incriminating about him. The stress and strain of being an active member of the anti-Hitler movement was visibly taking its toll on the admiral. Those who saw him every day could not help but notice how tired and worn he looked and how edgy and depressed he seemed. Never known for a crisp and military appearance, he had seemed sometimes to go out of his way to be as disheveled and unkempt as possible, but now his personal appearance bordered on the alarming—his uniform was frequently unbuttoned or misbuttoned, with bits of food and cigar ash clinging to its front. Even more alarming was his frequently apathetic and dispirited manner. He seemed even more preoccupied and absentminded than usual, as though he did not really care about his job. The details of running his office seemed to interest him less and less; he began thinking about retiring to civilian life so that he could forget about the Abwehr and everything that went with it. He worried that some sort of evidence connecting him with Madame Szymańska or Operation Aguilar would fall into the hands of the SD or the Gestapo, who would not hesitate to use it against him and the other members of the anti-Nazi resistance. Like Heydrich, he seemed to think it only a matter of time before such an event took place.

* * *

Members of the anti-Hitler movement still nurtured the idea of keeping in touch with the Allied powers concerning their goals and intentions. Their idea was to develop contacts with the Western Allies who would assist them in their plot against Hitler—even a word of encouragement would give the movement a boost in morale, if nothing else—and in their efforts to rescue Jews and other Nazi victims simply by spreading the word of the Hitler regime's atrocities. With the reelection of Franklin D. Roosevelt as president of the United States in November 1940, the anti-Nazi resistance had the idea of making contact with Roosevelt to ask for his support, as well as to keep him advised of exactly what was going on inside Nazi Germany. Even though the United States still professed to be officially neutral, President Roosevelt and Prime Minister Winston Churchill had signed the Atlantic Charter in August 1941. (Although the charter made the United States an overt ally of Britain, the German press largely ignored the signing—the fighting in Russia just about monopolized news headlines.) President Roosevelt was obviously thinking ahead; he could see that the United States would almost certainly be going to war against Germany in the near future and wanted Prime Minister Churchill to know that he would be with Britain when that time came. The anti-Hitler resistance intended to keep the president informed of its plans and intentions.

Before anything else could be accomplished, the anti-Nazi resistance had to decide exactly what kind of government Germany would have after Hitler had been ousted. The person selected to lead the provisional post-Hitler government was Prince Louis Ferdinand, the grandson of Kaiser Wilhelm II and head of the House of Hohenzollern. Ulrich von Hassell had mentioned Prince Louis as a possible head of government early in 1940, when he spoke with British diplomat James Lonsdale-Bryans. The fact that President Roosevelt and Louis Ferdinand had known each other before the war provided an enormous advantage for the opposition—during their honeymoon in 1938, the prince and his wife had visited the president and Mrs. Roosevelt. If all went according to plan and the Hitler government was overthrown, Germany would be transformed from a fascist dictatorship into a constitutional monarchy. And this transformation would be accomplished with the approval of Franklin Roosevelt. At least that was the anti-Hitler movement's idea.

Pulitzer Prize–winning American journalist Louis Lochner, head of the Associated Press office in Berlin as well as a friend of Prince Louis, was chosen to act as liaison between the prince and President Roosevelt on behalf of the anti-Nazi opposition. Louis Lochner knew absolutely nothing about the opposition, its objectives, or any of its followers. He was given a carefully worded briefing on the anti-Hitler opposition at the home of another member of the opposition, Otto John, an attorney and a civilian executive at Lufthansa Airlines. During the course of the meeting, Lochner was informed of the anti-Nazi movement's "moral disgust" toward Hitler and the Nazis but was also advised of its members' relative powerlessness, which had forced them "to look for allies among people in foreign countries who thought as [they] did." Lochner listened to the briefing and was impressed by the dedication of Otto John and the other opposition members. "Germany must become a state based on law once more," he was told; "everything else is secondary."[16] The anti-Nazi resistance was committed to the overthrow of Hitler and everything he stood for; establishing a new government would come afterward.

Both Louis Lochner and Otto John were friends with the American naval attaché at the American embassy in Berlin, Cdr. Albert Schrader, as well as with the assistant military attaché, Maj. William Hohenthal. They were planning to use these two contacts for the purpose of reaching out to President Roosevelt to act as preliminary liaisons—the opposition members wanted to advise the president of their goals and objectives. The members also wanted their two Berlin embassy liaisons to pass on a letter from Louis Ferdinand to President Roosevelt. If the anti-Hitler resistance managed to oust the Nazi government, they wanted to know if the Roosevelt administration would be willing to assist them in negotiating with the British government, which had been so reluctant to deal with them. It was hoped that a favorable reply from President Roosevelt might also persuade "one of the field marshals" of the German army to lead a coup d'état against Hitler, which would give the opposition and its efforts some additional weight and authority.[17]

Otto John did not like the idea of telling the two American attachés anything about the anti-Nazi movement or its activities. Americans were being carefully watched by Reinhard Heydrich's SD agents these days; everything the US embassy staff said or did was being more strictly scrutinized than ever before. He discussed this with Hans Oster as well as with Hans von Dohnanyi, another leading member of the opposition, and also consulted Admiral Canaris. The admiral sent an urgent communiqué urging the opposition not to give the Americans anything in writing. Ever since September 1941, when President Roosevelt ordered American warships to shoot at any German ships found in US waters, all Americans in Germany were regarded as belligerent. Also, any Germans who made contact with American nationals were seen as potential traitors. Otto John was warned "to be more watchful than ever for S.D. drawing-room spies and for Gestapo agents."[18] Any incriminating note or document found in the possession of a member of the opposition would almost certainly prove fatal.

Before making contact with President Roosevelt, Louis Lochner had to be supplied with quite a lot of "detailed information" regarding "our plans and the members of our circle" at an arranged briefing. With the details given to him at this briefing, Otto John thought that Lochner "should be in a position to give Roosevelt a first-hand picture of the men, the forces, and the political tendencies in Germany to overthrow the regime."[19] But Lochner was well aware of the danger he would be placing himself in by taking notes. Instead of writing everything down, he used a sort of shorthand—jotting down a few key words and phrases that he could memorize. After he had memorized the gist of the information that he had been given, Lochner would destroy his shorthand notes. Since he was scheduled to leave Berlin for Switzerland in December, Otto John, Admiral Canaris, and all the other opposition members thought it would be a good idea if Lochner waited until he reached Switzerland before getting in touch with President Roosevelt—"we wondered whether he should not contact Roosevelt from there," as John phrased it.[20]

The opposition's "requests" and points of view would be transmitted to President Roosevelt by Louis Lochner instead of by Commander Schrader and Major Hohenthal—he would have transferred his mental notes to paper by that time—along with "a friendly covering note" from Louis Ferdinand. Otto John and the other members of the opposition listened to Admiral Canaris's warning about giving the Americans anything in writing. Presumably, everything would have been sent from Switzerland by diplomatic pouch. The main points of the prince's letter were that the opposition planned to overthrow the Hitler regime "with the help of disaffected generals," to end the war "as rapidly as possible," and to restore the rights of "oppressed peoples and persecuted persons."[21] The full text of the letter was short and to the point:

1. We were endeavouring to overthrow the regime with the help of disaffected generals, to end the war as rapidly as possible and to re-establish the rule of law in the State.
2. In the event of a rising we requested the enemy powers not to attempt to exploit internal unrest for strategic purposes.
3. The rights of the oppressed peoples and persecuted persons would be restored.
4. Our efforts could be assisted from outside by announcements or confidential communications to the effect that the Western Powers would be prepared to conclude peace with the German people once they were purged of Nazism.

5. We requested the President to support us in the interests of a rapid termination of hostilities.[22]

Louis Lochner never had the chance to contact the president regarding the anti-Nazi resistance and its plans or to transmit Prince Louis Ferdinand's letter. Before he was able to leave Berlin, Japanese carrier-based aircraft attacked the American naval base at Pearl Harbor on December 7, 1941. Three days later, on December 11, Adolf Hitler declared war on the United States; President Roosevelt reciprocated later the same day. With the United States and Germany at war, every American reporter in Germany was arrested and interned, including Louis Lochner—"the Gestapo dragged him from his bed."[23] He was not allowed to return home until June 1942, after six months of internment at Bad Nauheim, near Frankfurt. By that time, any interest Franklin Roosevelt might have had in the anti-Hitler movement had disappeared.

President Roosevelt intended to concentrate on winning the war; as far as he was concerned, the only certain way of reaching "a rapid termination of hostilities" was by achieving a military victory over German forces, not by "endeavouring to overthrow the regime with the help of disaffected generals."[24] Eleanor Roosevelt was not very sympathetic toward the anti-Nazi resistance either and did not even try to change her husband's opinion of the movement. When Otto John spoke with her about the possibility of Prince Louis Ferdinand replacing Hitler, she was "distant and condescending." She reacted to the idea of a constitutional monarchy by telling John, "Do these dear little children"—meaning the Hohenzollerns—"really think that there would ever be a chance for them to get back on the throne?" Otto John tried to explain that the idea of a Hohenzollern restoration did not come from Prince Louis but was the product of the "pure moral indignation" of the anti-Hitler resistance—Admiral Canaris, Hans Oster, and the other members of the movement. But Mrs. Roosevelt was not interested and had no inclination to listen to what he had to say.[25]

Dealing with members of the anti-Nazi conspiracy and listening to plans for overthrowing Adolf Hitler and installing Louis Ferdinand as the head of a constitutional monarchy struck President Roosevelt as a complete waste of time. From his point of view, the only sure way of ousting Hitler and rescuing Jews and any other victims of Nazi oppression was to win the war by armed force. Everything else was beside the point.

* * *

Reports of mass executions and other Nazi atrocities had been reaching the United States well before Pearl Harbor, and President Roosevelt was aware of the stories. But there was a tendency not to believe them on the part of not just the president but a good many people throughout the country. Americans had heard stories like this before, twenty-five years earlier. During World War I, the Germans had also been accused of murders, massacres, and an array of violent crimes. Stories of atrocities committed by soldiers in the kaiser's army frequently appeared in the American press—the murder of Belgian and French civilians, the torture of prisoners of war, and the slaughter of babies by running them through with bayonets. These stories were widely circulated by newspapers throughout the United States. After the war, the American public was outraged to learn that most of these lurid tales were completely fictitious, mostly concocted by propagandists in London to turn American opinion against Germany.[26] The stories coming out of Europe since the invasion of Poland had the same ring to them. President Roosevelt remembered the anti-German propaganda from World War I very well and was more than just skeptical about what he had been hearing lately. The stories struck him as more fabrications.

President Roosevelt was not alone in his skepticism of the atrocity stories that were coming out of German-occupied Europe. Polish diplomat Jan Karski risked his life to escape occupied Europe and come to the United States and had seen for himself exactly what the SD and the Gestapo had done in Poland. In Washington, DC, he told his eyewitness accounts of the horrors to, among others, US Supreme Court Associate Justice Felix Frankfurter. Justice Frankfurter, whose family had included many rabbis over the generations, was absolutely incredulous—everything Jan Karski said seemed too shocking to be true. He did arrange for President Roosevelt to hear Karski's stories but remained highly skeptical

President Franklin D. Roosevelt signing the declaration of war against Japan in December 1941. President Roosevelt had no interest in the anti-Nazi movement. His only priority was to win the war by military force. *Source:* National Archives.

of what he had been told. "I did not say that he was lying," he explained. "I said that I cannot believe him. There is a difference."[27]

President Roosevelt's reaction to Jan Karski's accounts probably coincided with Justice Frankfurter's—he could not bring himself to accept that these things were actually taking place. After hearing the first reports of *Kristallnacht* in November 1938, he told members of the White House press corps, "I myself could scarcely believe that such things could occur in twentieth century civilization."[28]

CHAPTER SEVEN

A Diplomat, an Assassination, and a Pestilent Priest

"THERE IS AN ANTI-NAZI POTENTIAL IN GERMANY, WHICH UP TO NOW has not been utilized," wrote Austrian socialist Karl B. Frank, using the pseudonym Paul Hagen, to Allen W. Dulles in April 1942. "It has hardly been recognized in its importance for political warfare," the memorandum went on. Actually, the "anti-Nazi potential" had been completely ignored up to that point, not just unutilized—Franklin D. Roosevelt had known about it for months. But the point of the memo was to suggest a "practical way" of using "this hitherto neglected front." Frank reminded Allen Dulles, who was attached to the Coordinator of Information (COI) office in New York at the time, "It may be remembered that American armies have worked with underground movements previously, in Asia as well as in South America."[1]

The memo pointed out that the anti-Nazi movement had already done a fair amount of damage to the German war effort. Slowdowns in factories staged by members of anti-Hitler groups had cost German industry an estimated $300 million between September 1941 and March 1942. The best way of employing these groups more effectively, Karl Frank suggested, would be through the "careful study" of their members and their contacts, as well as by making every effort to contact the group leaders. In order to accomplish these objectives, "a small staff of a few dozen experienced people should be prepared, supported with technical facilities (papers, etc.) to look up as soon as possible all contacts in

Sweden, Switzerland, etc., where contacts to inside groups might possibly be organized." Such an agency would be particularly useful "at a time when mere Intelligence work is less successful considering the totalitarian blockade of information behind the Nazi lines." In other words, the underground would be able to supply Allied intelligence with information when more conventional methods, including aerial reconnaissance and spies, were not able to provide Allied intelligence services or the COI with some piece of critical data. Frank did not mention anything about Nazi atrocities or the rescue of Jews and other victims of the Nazi government, although he did make a passing reference to "Jewish refugee knowledge."[2]

Karl Frank's suggestions regarding a link between Allied intelligence and the German anti-Nazi resistance was given serious official consideration in Washington. Two weeks after Frank sent his memo to Allen W. Dulles, US Assistant Secretary of State Adolf A. Berle responded to it with a memorandum of his own. "I believe that the time is due (if not overdue) for an all-out political campaign to upset the Nazi government in Germany," he began. "It is fairly well established that one group of German generals has been actively canvassing the possibility of a change in government, so as to place Germany in a better position to make peace." The British government had known that an anti-Nazi group was operating in Germany for quite some time; James Lonsdale-Bryans met with Ulrich von Hassell in February 1940. Now, the US State Department was becoming aware of the same thing—some sort of underground movement to overthrow Adolf Hitler actually existed within the upper ranks of the German armed forces.[3]

Dulles read Berle's "interesting memorandum" on the anti-Nazi resistance and sent a few suggestions of his own to COI head William J. Donovan. (The COI became the Office of Strategic Services in June 1942.) Dulles had in mind the instigation of a "subtle propaganda" campaign directed against Germany. Specifically, he favored an operation that would "fan the flames," deepening the split between the Wehrmacht on one side and the Gestapo and Sicherheitsdienst (SD) on the other—the Nazi atrocities in Poland and Russia angered a good many German soldiers and turned them against the Nazis and their *Einsatzgruppen*. He wanted to start "an open struggle for power, possibly an open revolution between the Nazi authorities and the Military authorities."[4]

Dulles was convinced that Adolf Berle's plan should be taken seriously. Berle was a high-ranking member of the State Department with access "to material not available to me," Dulles commented. If Berle favored a plan of action against the Nazi government, his proposal deserved every consideration. Dulles also thought that President Roosevelt should play an important role in any propaganda program directed at Nazi Germany. "Certainly the time will come when a propaganda drive based on a comprehensive statement to be made by the President should be undertaken," he wrote, and went on to say that it would be a good idea to start "our propaganda campaign" sometime during the autumn of 1942. "When Hitler falls it should not come through a quiet coup d'état," Dulles concluded, "but as the result of an open conflict between the Nazi and military elements."[5]

But President Roosevelt did not agree with Frank, Berle, or Dulles. He did not want any part of a coup d'état, an open revolution, or any sort of negotiated peace settlement with Germany. The only acceptable ending to the war in Europe, according to President Roosevelt, was the military defeat of Germany, followed by the total surrender of the German government and all German armed forces. Any change in government would come only when Hitler was removed by an Allied military victory. Nothing less would even be considered.

President Roosevelt remembered very clearly what had happened inside Germany after World War I ended in November 1918—he was assistant secretary of the navy at the time. Although Allied forces had defeated the German army in the field in 1918, no Allied armies ever marched into Germany and occupied the country. Kaiser Wilhelm abdicated, an armistice was signed, the German army disbanded and went home, and the Weimar Republic was established. But many Germans never accepted the idea of a military defeat; they believed that the German army had not lost the war on the battlefield but had been stabbed in the back by Bolsheviks, Jews, and Social Democrats at home. Hitler frequently referred to the "stab in the back" principle, which he called the *Dolchstoss*, in his speeches during the 1920s. The *Dolchstoss* became a very popular topic with the crowds: it gave them an excuse to blame the loss of the war on something other than the German army.

The word appeared in print as early as December 1918, only a month after the war ended, in the German-language Swiss newspaper *Neue Zürcher Zeitung:* "As far as the German Army is concerned, the general view is summarized in these words: It was stabbed in the back by the civil population."[6] Hitler added his own bias to the *Dolchstoss* by putting the entire blame for the German surrender on the Jews. He called the Jews *die Novemberverbrecher*, the November criminals, traitors who betrayed the Fatherland. The stab-in-the-back theory grew in popularity through-out the 1920s, during the Weimar Republic, and became one of the Nazi Party's main campaign issues—Hitler promised that if the Nazis came to power, Germany would become a major power again and would undo the effects of the November criminals and their stab in the back.

President Roosevelt was well acquainted with the stab-in-the-back principle and did not want to give Germany a similar excuse to start another war in another twenty or twenty-five years. Roosevelt also remembered Marshal Ferdinand Foch's prediction that the 1919 Treaty of Versailles, which formally ended World War I, was not really a peace treaty at all but nothing more than a twenty-year armistice. Marshal Foch's prediction turned out to be all too accurate. The president did not want another twenty-year armistice after the current war ended and would accept nothing less than the total defeat of Nazi Germany. He intended to force the Germans out of France and all the other countries in western Europe that their forces occupied and to keep pushing them until they were overwhelmed and had no option but to surrender. There must not be a third world war in another twenty years, and no fascist dictator must be given the chance to create a Fourth Reich in the 1960s. After the surrender, all war criminals would be put on trial, the Nurem-berg Laws would be repealed, and the "Jewish question" would be settled. But first the Nazis must be forced to surrender. There could be no nego-tiations and no dealings with any anti-Hitler underground.

In February 1942, Heinrich Himmler received yet another report involving a Jewish agent at work for Adm. Wilhelm Canaris and the Abwehr. This particular agent, said to be of 100 percent Jewish blood, was attached to the Abwehr office in Tangier. No one knows for certain where the report came from. It might have originated with Gen. Walter Schellenberg, the SD's chief of foreign intelligence. General Schellenberg was in the awkward position of working for Reinhard Heydrich and being on friendly terms with Admiral Canaris at the same time. "Seeing you two together, one would take you for bosom friends," Heydrich complained to Schellenberg about his relationship with the admiral. "You won't get anywhere by handling him with kid gloves."[7]

Although he was friendly with Admiral Canaris, General Schellenberg never forgot that he was also the subordinate of both Reinhard Heydrich and Heinrich Himmler. In his memoirs, Schellenberg mentions presenting "my reports about [Canaris's] various betrayals" to Himmler.[8] The general had been suspicious of Admiral Canaris and his motives for employing Jewish agents for some time and kept a wary eye on Abwehr personnel in Spain and North Africa, always on the lookout for incriminating evidence. Himmler was more annoyed than surprised by the report; by this time, it was just the sort of news he had come to expect in connection with the admiral, and he did not seem very interested. The Reichsführer's response to General Schellenberg's report was vague. He said that he would let Hitler know about Admiral Canaris's peculiar habit of enlisting Jewish "agents" the next time the two had a conference.

Hitler did receive the report on Admiral Canaris and his Jewish agents, although the information probably did not come from Reichsführer Himmler. After reading the report, Hitler sent for Feldmarschall Wilhelm Keitel to discuss the situation, as well as to decide exactly what should be done about the admiral. Hitler became so incensed during the meeting that the discussion quickly deteriorated into a tirade against Canaris. After working himself into a frenzy, Hitler ended the meeting by suspending Admiral Canaris from his duties as head of the Abwehr. Feldmarschall Keitel did not say anything at all during Hitler's rant, either in favor of Admiral Canaris or against him.

For the time being at least, Admiral Canaris was effectively out of a job. His replacement as head of the Abwehr was Vice Adm. Leopold Bürkner, the current director of the Abwehr's foreign section. Admiral

Bürkner was not a member of the anti-Nazi underground; he did not even know it existed. In fact, he was an admirer and supporter of Adolf Hitler and would never have considered taking any action against him or the Nazi Party—a British writer said that he "unfortunately conformed to Fuehrer Headquarters standards." A story used to circulate about Admiral Bürkner watching flags being placed on an intelligence map in Hitler's headquarters. German forces were represented by blue flags, Russian units by red flags. Concerned that too many Russian flags would alarm Hitler, he shouted, "Ach, don't put so much red on the map!"[9]

The appointment of Admiral Bürkner as interim head of the Abwehr put Admiral Canaris in serious danger. He realized that if Bürkner happened to come across any evidence that connected him with Operation Aguilar or the anti-Hitler conspiracy, he would not hesitate to report his findings to Heydrich or even to Hitler himself. The admiral asked Feldmarschall Keitel to talk to Hitler and intercede on his behalf; Keitel had enough influence to persuade Hitler to reverse his decision. But the *feldmarschall* refused to help or to intervene. Admiral Canaris realized that his only hope to regain his position as Abwehr chief, as well as to remove the threat of danger posed by the appointment of Admiral Bürkner, would be to see Hitler in person. Since Feldmarschall Keitel would not help, he decided to arrange a face-to-face meeting with Hitler himself.

No one knows exactly what took place during the conference or what Admiral Canaris said to Hitler. But whatever argument the admiral used to convince Hitler that he should be reinstated as head of the Abwehr must have been very persuasive—by the time the meeting ended, Hitler was convinced that Admiral Canaris should be restored to his post and agreed to recall him immediately. Not only did the admiral talk his way back into his old job, he also managed to avoid any possible trouble at the hands of Admiral Bürkner and the SD. Directly after the meeting, Canaris returned to Berlin by air, probably hoping to get away from Hitler as quickly as possible, before he had the chance to change his mind. Shortly after returning to his office in Tirpitz Ufer, he received a telephone call from Keitel. The *feldmarschall* wanted to congratulate Admiral Canaris on his reinstatement and also claimed that he had played a major role in changing Hitler's mind and effecting the restoration. The admiral, unmoved by Keitel's congratulations, did not believe a word of what the *feldmarschall* had to say about any conversation with Hitler.

Admiral Canaris had escaped the latest effort to remove him as head of the Abwehr, but he was well aware that there would be others. And the next attempt was not long in coming. At the beginning of 1942, Reinhard Heydrich requested a meeting with the admiral to discuss the relative powers of the SD and the Abwehr and also to suggest ways of redefining the roles of the two agencies. He really had in mind the SD's absorption of as much of the Abwehr's authority as possible. He brought "Gestapo" Müller with him to the meeting, along with some high-ranking SD officers. Col. Franz-Eccard von Bentivegni, a senior Abwehr officer, accompanied Admiral Canaris and paid very close attention to Heydrich.

And Heydrich had a great deal to say. He explained that he wanted full control of all counterespionage activities to be shifted from the Abwehr to the SD, along with the complete authority over the Geheime Feldpolizei, or Secret Field Police, the department of the Abwehr that monitored all security concerns within the German armed forces. This proposal would not have eliminated the Abwehr entirely but would have greatly curtailed the agency's power and influence and reduced the authority of Admiral Canaris. The admiral listened to Heydrich's proposals and offered no objections to any of them. According to Walter Schellenberg, who was both a high-ranking officer in the SD and a friend of the admiral, "Canaris gave in all along the line."[10]

Colonel von Bentivegni was totally surprised and dismayed when the admiral acceded to Heydrich's demands without any opposition. Von Bentivegni was the head of Abwehr III, the department in charge of counterespionage and counterintelligence. Heydrich's proposal shifted all of Abwehr III's activities to the SD's jurisdiction. The colonel realized that if Heydrich's ideas for reorganizing the Abwehr and the SD were put into effect, he would lose his post and the Abwehr would lose a great deal of its power. After the conference broke up, Colonel von Bentivegni had his own meeting with Admiral Canaris and explained exactly what Heydrich had done. The admiral was so exhausted by this point that he had not completely focused on Heydrich's demands; he had agreed to all the changes and proposals just to end the meeting, along with the tensions it caused, as quickly as possible. The colonel managed to persuade Admiral Canaris to rewrite the proposal. The new draft removed almost all of the concessions that the admiral had made. When informed of this turn of events, Heydrich was angered by what he considered Admiral Canaris's betrayal and breach of good faith.

A new agreement was drawn up a few months later, in May 1942, in the city of Prague. This arrangement, which would become known as the "Ten Commandments," gave Heydrich most of what he wanted, although it was not as comprehensive as the first had been. Admiral Canaris was not visibly upset by the Abwehr's loss of authority, even though he was more disappointed than he let on, and said good-bye to Heydrich with no anger or recrimination when he left Prague. Colonel von Bentivegni was happier than the admiral; at least he was able to retain his position as head of Abwehr III.

Admiral Canaris was visibly worn down and depressed by the constant fighting with Reinhard Heydrich and the SD. Walter Schellenberg went horseback riding with the admiral on an almost daily basis; he could not help but notice the changes that had taken place in Canaris since the fighting with Heydrich had intensified. "Heydrich's ice cold tactics of the last months were beginning to show their effect," he noted. Canaris "felt insecure and restless and, so I thought, had something like a physical fear of Heydrich."[11] This was a pertinent observation—Heydrich, standing six feet, three inches, was a full foot taller than the admiral.

The admiral's fears were not helped by the fact that both the Gestapo and the SD were keeping a very sharp eye on anyone suspected of anti-Nazi activities. Ulrich von Hassell was given a direct warning that he was being monitored by the Gestapo. "I was being watched because I had criticized the regime, said Hitler must be removed, and such things," he wrote in his diary on May 1, 1942. In late April, he had been informed that "every step [he] took was observed." He was also advised to burn any notes or documents related to conversations he might have had with any opposition members.[12] Admiral Canaris was well aware that the SD and the Gestapo were keeping him under observation as well.

Canaris told Walter Schellenberg that Heydrich's intrigues had greatly upset him. Even though a sort of armistice had been worked

Capt. Wilhelm Canaris (*left*), head of the Abwehr, and SS Lt. Gen. Reinhard Heydrich, chief of the SD, in 1936. Heydrich suspected Canaris of plotting against the Nazis. Canaris became head of the Abwehr Section of the Reichswehr Ministry on January 2, 1935. *Source:* US Army.

out with Heydrich and the SD, the admiral knew that this agreement was only temporary at best. He said "in a resigned voice" that Heydrich "would attack again"; the agreement had given him nothing more than a little breathing space.[13] The relationship between the two had become "poisonous" by the spring of 1942, according to one of Heydrich's biographers.[14] As soon as Heydrich had more evidence against Canaris, proof that the admiral had been involved in rescuing Jews from German-occupied countries, he would present his evidence to Hitler. Both Canaris and Heydrich knew what would happen when that time came.

Reinhard Heydrich had a plan that, if it worked, would put European Jews beyond the reach of Admiral Canaris. His idea was to send them out of Europe to an overseas location. After France surrendered in June

1940, roughly five hundred thousand Jews came under the control of the Nazi government. Heydrich had no idea of what should be done with all of these people. He would like to have sent his *Einsatzgruppen* into France and the Low Countries so that they could repeat what they had done in Poland and Russia, but senior Wehrmacht officers objected to the SD's activities. Killing Jews, along with anyone the SD considered politically objectionable, did not play any useful role in winning the war and was actually proving counterproductive—the killings tended to lower the morale of German troops and stiffened opposition among resistance fighters. The Wehrmacht's objections limited what the SD was able to carry out in western Europe. Heydrich would have to come up with another idea.

Deportation seemed like a possible solution. Heinrich Himmler fully agreed with the concept—Himmler did not necessarily want to have all Jews and "undesirables" killed, just driven out of Europe. In May 1940, he sent a memo to Hitler stating that the term "Jew" should be completely eliminated from Europe "through the massive immigration of all Jews to Africa or some other colony."[15] After France surrendered in June 1940, the island of Madagascar was suggested as a possible destination for departing Jews. Madagascar had been a French colony, but after France surrendered the island became a German possession. Heydrich instructed his "Jewish expert," Adolf Eichmann, to draw up a plan for exporting European Jews to their new island home off the southeastern coast of Africa. By early July, Eichmann and a member of the German Foreign Office, Franz Rademacher, had written a memorandum on the subject of Jewish resettlement on Madagascar. In the 1930s, Rademacher had explored the feasibility of establishing a Jewish settlement in the Amazon rain forests of Brazil. The plan he created with Adolf Eichmann outlined the basic provisions of what became known as the Madaskar Projekt, or Madagascar Plan. The plan had five major points:

1. Negotiation of a peace treaty with Vichy France by which Germany would take over Madagascar under a mandate

2. Deportation of one million European Jews annually to the island

3. Establishment of a Jewish-sponsored bank to finance the establishment of the Gestapo state and the deportation of the four million Jews

4. Creation of a shipping pool large enough to transport them to Madagascar within the necessary period of years

5. Establishment of ports and supply bases for the German navy in the principal anchorages plus military bases in the interior[16]

The SD would be in complete control of the colony, since it "alone ha[d] the necessary experience in the field." The plan also mentioned that the Jews would be in charge of the local government, along with "police posts" and the railways, but overall political administration would remain in the hands of the Germans. "Thus the Jews will remain as hostages guaranteeing a suitable attitude on the part of the American co-religionists." In other words, having several million Jews in Madagascar would pressure the Jewish population in the United States, which would in turn pressure the US government, to maintain a more friendly attitude toward Nazi Germany.[17]

The plan was very carefully thought out. To ensure that the new colony would get off to a good start, or at least have the maximum number of advantages during its early stages, the first group of colonists would be made up of farmers, plumbers and other skilled tradesmen, and construction workers, along with their families. All the farmers and artisans would be required to bring the tools of their trade along with them. Each person was allowed to take a little over 440 pounds—200 kilograms—of luggage and personal belongings.

The colonists would travel to their new homes in Madagascar via captured British merchant vessels and transports. The German High Command expected to invade England sometime during the summer of 1940 and was confident that British forces would surrender to the Wehrmacht following a short and stunning blitzkrieg campaign, just as French forces had done a few weeks earlier. After the anticipated surrender, the British fleet and all other British ships, naval and commercial, would be taken over by the Germans. It would just be a matter of assigning the Jewish colonists to their transports and shipping them off to Madagascar.

Reinhard Heydrich put a great deal of his personal time and effort into creating the Madagascar Plan for the simple reason that he had a great deal to gain from it personally. If the plan succeeded, he would not just look good in the eyes of Adolf Hitler, although that was part of its attraction, but, even more importantly, removing four million Jews from the continent of Europe would certainly enhance his reputation among high-ranking Nazis. Establishing a Jewish colony on Madagascar would also strengthen his political influence within the Nazi regime. The success of the Madagascar Plan would give the SD more power, which would make the agency more influential than the Abwehr and might also give Heydrich an edge in eliminating the Abwehr altogether and taking over its authority. The Madagascar colony could be instrumental in eliminating Admiral Canaris as a rival and, with the Jews safely removed to an island several thousand miles away, would also put an end to the rescue operations that Heydrich had been powerless even to prove, much less prevent.

But the war did not turn out the way Heydrich or Hitler expected. The Luftwaffe lost the Battle of Britain, the invasion of England was postponed indefinitely, and the Madagascar Plan was cancelled. Because no British ships were captured, Heydrich had no way to transport his four million Jews to Madagascar. It was a setback for Heydrich, but only a temporary one. Hitler had decided that all the Jews in Europe should be eliminated, and Heydrich would play a major role in this operation. But instead of deporting the Jews to Madagascar, the SD would send them to eastern Europe, to extermination camps—Auschwitz, Belzec, and Treblinka. Admiral Canaris would do his best to keep frustrating Heydrich and his plans.

* * *

The conflict between Admiral Canaris and Reinhard Heydrich ended unexpectedly as well, and not at all the way that the admiral thought it would, although it did end dramatically. A few days after the Ten Commandments agreement was signed in Prague, Admiral Canaris was informed that Heydrich had been badly wounded in an assassination attempt by Czech partisans. Radio Prague confirmed the report on May 29, 1942, two days after the attack took place. Canaris immediately flew back to Prague to witness the situation for himself.

The report that the admiral received was accurate. Two Czech soldiers, who had been specially trained in England for the assignment, had attacked Heydrich while he was being driven to his office on May 27. They waited for him as his open Mercedes approached a sharp turn on the road to Prague. One of the Czechs aimed his machine gun at Heydrich and pulled the trigger at point-blank range, but the gun jammed. Heydrich shouted for his driver to stop, stood up, and drew his automatic pistol, which gave the second partisan a chance to throw a grenade. The grenade fell short, exploding next to the car instead of inside it. Heydrich was injured by the explosion but was still alive.

He was taken to hospital, where it appeared that his wounds were not serious. But X-rays showed that the explosion had broken one of Heydrich's ribs and also forced fragments of the car's upholstery into his spleen. The leading German surgeon in Prague removed the fragments, but Heydrich developed a severe infection that resulted in a high fever and coma. He died on June 4, eight days after the attack on the Prague road.

Both Hitler and Himmler wanted vengeance for Heydrich's death. On the same day as the attack, May 27, Himmler ordered the arrest of ten thousand hostages from the "Czech intelligentsia"—he wanted to have his full measure of revenge. "Out of the main body of this intelligentsia," Himmler ordered, "shoot this night one hundred of the most important." Dr. Josef Goebbels, head of the Nazi Propaganda Ministry, agreed that the "most brutal methods" should be employed against all Czechs who lived in the vicinity of the attack and against the Jews as well. He threatened to arrest five hundred Jewish residents of Berlin, and "I will warn the leaders of the Jewish community that for every Jewish plot and every Jewish attempt at rebellion, 100 to 150 Jews who are in our hands will be shot." Within a few days of the assassination, "several hundred" Jews were executed at Sachsenhausen concentration camp. The killings met with the full approval of Dr. Goebbels.[18]

The Gestapo was convinced that the two assassins, Josef Gabcik and Jan Kubis, were hiding in Lidice. The village was searched twice, but no trace of them was found. (Both were killed within the month by the SS.) In retaliation for Heydrich's death, Hitler ordered Lidice obliterated. On the evening of June 9, the village was surrounded by German troops and summarily destroyed. All houses and buildings were burned; anything left standing was bulldozed by the German Labour Service, which then planted grass on the remains to cover any traces of the village. The SS executed 199 men of the village; 195 women and 85 children were sent to Ravensbrück concentration camp. Eight of the village's children were "Germanized," that is, sent to Nazi foster homes. Of those who were sent to Ravensbrück, most were either gassed, died of malnutrition, or simply disappeared.[19]

Reinhard Heydrich's funeral took place in Berlin on June 9, 1942. His coffin lay in state for two days inside Mosaic Hall, part of the

Prisoners at Sachsenhausen concentration camp in 1938. Canaris arranged to disguise many Jews and other "undesirables" as Abwehr agents and send them away from Nazi-occupied territory, rescuing them from the fate of these inmates. *Source:* National Archives.

new Reich Chancellery. One of his biographers described the proceedings as a barbaric display, complete with massive banks of flowers and a steel-helmeted honor guard, in the same style as the ostentatious gangster funerals of 1930s Chicago. Most of the hierarchy of the Nazi regime was in attendance. Adolf Hitler gave a brief tribute, but the eulogy was delivered by Heinrich Himmler, who praised Heydrich for his courage, loyalty, and dedication to the Nazi regime and described him as irreplaceable. In his address, he very tactfully omitted the less attractive features of Heydrich's life: his sadism, his brutality, and the fact that he was known as the Butcher of Prague.[20]

Admiral Canaris also attended the funeral, standing in the front rank of the mourners and saying very little but with tears in his eyes. He said that he had lost a true friend in Reinhard Heydrich. He had certainly lost a dangerous opponent—his tears might very well have been tears of relief. Of all the tactful things said about Heydrich that day, the admiral recognized one of them as true: if nothing else, Heydrich was irreplaceable. Nobody else had his ruthlessness or ambition. Nobody else would have the motivation to keep on confronting and attacking Canaris with Heydrich's persistence. The admiral realized that the SD would be a different organization now that Heydrich was no longer in charge of it.

Heydrich's replacement as head of the SD, after an interim period under Heinrich Himmler, was Ernst Kaltenbrunner. Kaltenbrunner had been with Reich Security since the beginning of the war, but he was not nearly as driven or as ruthless as his predecessor. He was certainly no Butcher of Prague. Like Heydrich, he would have his suspicions of Admiral Canaris and would keep a wary eye on him. But the admiral would no longer be under be under the same kind of threat as when Heydrich was the SD's senior officer. In short, Heydrich's assassination let Admiral Canaris off the hook. He would now have more latitude in his activities against Hitler, including in his rescue campaign to save Jews and other politically incorrect victims of the Nazis.

* * *

The anti-Nazi resistance was still making every effort to convince the Western Allies that it was credible and should be taken seriously. In May

1942, Pastor Dietrich Bonhoeffer, an active member of the resistance, was informed that the bishop of Chichester, George Bell, would be in Sweden for three weeks. Bonhoeffer and Bishop Bell had been friends for many years, although they had not seen each other since before the war. The pastor was in Switzerland at the time. Before Bell went back to England, Bonhoeffer decided to call on his old friend to talk about the anti-Nazi movement. He was well aware that the bishop had direct connections to Winston Churchill's government—besides being bishop of Chichester, George Bell was also a member of the House of Lords—and hoped to persuade Bell to inform members of the government of the resistance and its accomplishments. He reasoned that a member of the government or possibly a member of Churchill's cabinet would be more willing to listen to a lord bishop than to a German pastor.

Pastor Bonhoeffer's dedication to the overthrow of Adolf Hitler and his government had been directly influenced by the plight of the Jews and other unfortunates in Germany. As early as April 1933, Bonhoeffer spoke out for resistance to Hitler's persecution of Jews, and he was informed about the increasing numbers of Jews being deported to extermination camps in Poland. He declared that the church must not allow these things to happen and determined to do something about the Nazi atrocities himself. He also declared that he would shoot Hitler himself if it became necessary—an astonishing statement coming from a Christian clergyman. As a young man, Bonhoeffer had many close friends of the Jewish faith, and he also fondly remembered many Jewish students from his days at the University of Berlin. As a Christian, and especially as a minister of God, Bonhoeffer was convinced that he could not just stand idly by and allow these atrocities to take place. To stop these crimes, which he considered offenses committed in the name of Germany by the Nazis, he would do everything possible to bring about the downfall of Adolf Hitler.

Admiral Canaris obtained a special courier permit that allowed Pastor Bonhoeffer to travel to Sweden. He left for Stockholm on May 30. The pastor met with Bishop Bell in the Swedish town of Sigtuna, accompanied by another pastor named Hans Schönfeld. Pastor Bonhoeffer knew the risk to his life—meeting with a British subject to discuss subversive activities against the German government could only have one ending if discovered by either the SD or the Gestapo—but he considered it worth taking. Among the things Bishop Bell and Pastor Bonhoeffer talked about was the installation of Prince Louis Ferdinand as the head of the new German government after Hitler had been removed from power. Bonhoeffer also gave the bishop the names of several of the anti-Hitler opposition members.

Bishop Bell seemed favorably impressed by what his friend had to say but warned that he should not get his hopes up as far as Winston Churchill's reaction to their conversation or his attitude on the subject of the anti-Hitler resistance. The bishop was well aware that the Churchill government had refused to make any sort of contact with the German opposition. Pastor Bonhoeffer thanked Bishop Bell for taking the time to confer with him. He ended his note of thanks, dated June 1, 1942, "Please pray for us. We need it."[21]

When he returned from Sweden, Bishop Bell wrote a letter to Foreign Minister Anthony Eden requesting a face-to-face meeting, reasoning that this would be the most effective way to state his case for the anti-Nazi resistance. His letter began, "I have just come back from Sweden with what seems to me very important confidential information about proposals from a big opposition movement in Germany."[22]

The conference took place on June 30. The bishop told Foreign Minister Eden about his talk with Bonhoeffer and Hans Schönfeld in great detail and also gave him a written memorandum on the discussion. Eden was noncommittal concerning what Bishop Bell had to say about the German underground, as well as about his memorandum. He did not respond to Bell's comments for two weeks, and then only after prodding by Sir Stafford Cripps, a member of Churchill's cabinet. His response to Cripps's message was not very encouraging. Foreign Minster Eden said that "it would not be in the national interest" to send Dietrich Bonhoeffer or any member of the anti-Nazi movement any reply at all.[23]

But the bishop was not easily discouraged. He wrote to Anthony Eden again regarding the anti-Hitler opposition on July 25. This time he quoted Winston Churchill to make his point. "Mr. Churchill said in his first speech as Prime Minister in the House of Commons on May

13th 1940 that our policy was 'to wage war against a monstrous tyranny never surpassed in the dark and lamentable catalogue of human crimes,' and that our aim was 'victory at all costs.'" He then went on to address the heart of his subject. "If there are men in Germany also ready to wage war against the monstrous tyranny from within, is it right to discourage or ignore them? Can we afford to reject their aid in achieving their end?" In the last line, he summed up his argument: "If we by our silence allow them to believe that there is no hope for any Germany, whether Hitlerite or anti-Hitlerite, that is in effect what we are doing."[24]

But Anthony Eden was not interested in anything that Bishop Bell had to say. In a letter dated August 4, the foreign minister advised Bishop Bell that he did not intend to encourage the anti-Nazi movement or to communicate with them. He reminded the bishop that he had already made a speech covering that very topic in Edinburgh on May 8. In the course of his speech, Eden said that no one would believe that the German people "really wished to see a return to a German state based on respect for law and the rights of the individual" until "they had taken active steps to rid themselves of their present regime." As far as Eden was concerned, he had already made his point. He informed Bishop Bell, "For the present, I do not think that it would be advisable for me to go any further in a public statement." This was Eden's official reply to Bishop Bell. But in the margin of a copy of his letter, the foreign minister wrote a note that revealed his true feelings toward the bishop along with his annoyance regarding both Bell and the anti-Nazi movement: "I see no reason whatsoever to encourage this pestilent priest!"[25]

Bishop Bell was also advised to take a copy of his Eden memorandum to the US ambassador in London, John G. Winant. Ambassador Winant seemed more than just slightly interested in what the bishop had to say about the anti-Hitler movement and promised to contact President Roosevelt regarding the memo. But Bishop Bell never received any response at all from Winant. The US government had no more interest in the German underground movement than Winston Churchill.

The Western Allies had no interest in rescuing Jews or anyone else; the sole objective of both Churchill and Roosevelt was to win the war. If the anti-Nazi movement could undermine the German war effort by creating suspicion and animosity between Hitler and his generals, this would be all well and good. But neither the British nor the Americans would make contact with anyone inside Nazi Germany, regardless of what Bishop Bell, Dietrich Bonhoeffer, or any other well-meaning clergyman had to say.

Dietrich Bonhoeffer was disappointed by the lack of concern shown by the British and American governments. Admiral Canaris was probably disappointed as well, but he would not have been surprised. By this time, he fully understood the situation: Allied leaders had no interest whatever in the anti-Hitler resistance, its accomplishments, or its objectives, including the rescue of Jews and "undesirables" from the Nazis. But this would not deter the admiral from carrying on with his activities to undermine the Nazi government, which included securing exit visas for as many Jews and other outcasts as possible.

CHAPTER EIGHT

A Hazardous Operation

ADM. WILHELM CANARIS WAS WELL AWARE THAT THE PLIGHT OF JEWS, along with other non-Aryans and political "unacceptables," in Germany and throughout German-occupied Europe was steadily getting worse. Although Reinhard Heydrich had been assassinated, his replacement as head of the Sicherheitsdienst (SD), Ernst Kaltenbrunner, carried on with his murderous program. This campaign was now being referred to as the *Endlösung der Europaischen Judenfrage*, the final solution of the European Jewish question. Heinrich Himmler wrote to Kaltenbrunner on the subject, "The essential thing, in my opinion, remains that as many Jews as humanly possible shall be shipped to the east."[1] Kaltenbrunner was in full agreement with Himmler and his opinion. Admiral Canaris emphatically did not agree and was determined to hamper the SD's shipments to the east with as much resolve as Kaltenbrunner had to increase them.

"There is a strong increase in the brutal treatment of the Jews," Ulrich von Hassell noted in August 1942. "The mixtures [half and quarter Jews] are also coming in for worse treatment." Von Hassell also commented, "More and more people are being deported. In Poland, as already stated here, they are simply murdered." He mentioned that an acquaintance of his had recently been sent to the East: "Old Weinberg, at eighty-one, is now in a concentration camp."[2]

The propaganda campaign against the Jews was so strident that it was beginning to backfire: it had become subject to ridicule and was making ordinary German citizens sympathetic toward the Jews and their predicament. Anti-Nazi jokes were beginning to circulate: "At a crossroads three cars, each with the right of way, collide—Hitler, the SS, and the fire department. Who is to blame? Answer: the Jews."[3] And a Swiss attorney, who had managed to save several Dutch Jews through the strategic use of bribery, asked an acquaintance, "You Germans are such great organizers; why, in the face of your transportation difficulties, do you first ship so many thousands to the east instead of simply murdering them at home?"[4]

Admiral Canaris was still doing his best to stop these "shipments" to extermination camps in eastern Europe. In the autumn of 1942, a train en route from Berlin to Basel, Switzerland, had fourteen people among its passengers who were "under great threat." One was a woman awaiting deportation to a concentration camp. Two others were half-Jewish girls who happened to be friends of Admiral Canaris's younger daughter Brigitte. (Canaris also had an older daughter, Eva.) Admiral Canaris was informed of the situation and was able to persuade the Gestapo that these people were actually agents working for Germany—"part of an important group of informers for Nazi Germany." Because of the admiral's intervention, these "agents" were given asylum in Switzerland instead of being sent to camps in the East. Admiral Canaris had saved another group from certain imprisonment and probable death at the hands of the SD.[5]

Several months earlier, in the spring of 1942, the admiral had become involved with another group of Jewish citizens in trouble with the Nazi regime. He received a report regarding seven Jews who were scheduled for deportation to extermination camps. Two of these were friends of Admiral Canaris; two were friends of Hans von Dohnanyi, who was Dietrich Bonhoeffer's brother-in-law. This was not an unfamiliar situation for the admiral. He plotted to have these seven individuals, along with their families, smuggled out of Germany and into Switzerland disguised as Abwehr agents. His plan would follow the same basic outline as Operation Aguilar: from Switzerland, the seven would eventually be sent across the Atlantic Ocean to the United States and South America. Because the rescue operation involved seven people, it was called Unternehmen 7, or Operation 7. Though the number of individuals would eventually increase to fourteen, the name remained the same.

Operation 7 turned out to be a lot more complicated than anyone expected; it was certainly more difficult and complex than Operation Aguilar. Admiral Canaris and Hans von Dohnanyi were able to remove the Jews from the deportation lists and also managed to obtain the necessary exit visas and other documentation. But this was only the beginning of the proceedings—and of Operation 7. In carrying out this rescue operation, Admiral Canaris would not be dealing with his old friend Francisco Franco, as during Operation Aguilar. Instead, he would be communicating with bureaucrats in Switzerland, who were not nearly as cooperative. For one thing, the Swiss officials insisted that their celebrated neutrality prevented them from giving asylum to anyone attempting to escape from Germany. Dietrich Bonhoeffer and one of his colleagues, Wilhelm Rott, did their best to persuade the Swiss that the refugees had to be allowed to enter Switzerland as quickly as possible, before their visas expired and they were sent to extermination camps. But the officials continued to insist that their neutrality prohibited them from offering any assistance and refused to help. Next, Rott wrote a letter to the Federation of Swiss Churches asking for help: "What we now ask you is whether, by urgent representations and official action by the Swiss churches, the door might be opened for just a few, or at least for one solitary case for which we specifically plead." But this request received no encouragement either.[6]

Pastor Bonhoeffer decided to write a letter to an old acquaintance, the well-known Swiss theologian Karl Barth, asking for his intervention. The two had known each other in the 1920s, when Bonhoeffer was still a student in Berlin. Barth, an outspoken critic of the Nazis, had been expelled from Germany in 1934 for refusing to declare his allegiance to Adolf Hitler. Bonhoeffer hoped that he might be able to persuade Barth to contact members of the Swiss government on behalf of the refugees and that Barth's name and influence might encourage Swiss officials to allow the fourteen exiles to enter Switzerland.

All the letters and communiqués finally had their desired effect: the Swiss government changed its mind and decided to let the refugees of Operation 7 into the country. But the government insisted on one condition: the new immigrants would have to bring enough currency to support themselves, since they would not be allowed to hold jobs in Switzerland. "The Swiss authorities, who were controlling their borders against a dreaded flood of Jewish refugees from Nazi-occupied Europe, had to be satisfied in their turn that the asylum seekers would not constitute any sort of financial burden on the country."[7] The anti-Nazi movement provided them with the money—$100,000 from funds that had been set aside for the resistance and its activities.[8] The job of supplying the refugees with the currency was given to Wilhelm Schmidhuber, a former Abwehr reserve officer attached to the Abwehr's headquarters in Munich.

Schmidhuber is usually described as fat and well-to-do—a "prosperous businessman from Munich," according to one acquaintance. As the honorary Portuguese consul in Munich, he liked to be addressed as "Mr. Consul." Otto John happened to meet Dr. Schmidhuber one occasion and hadn't thought much of him—"he gave me the impression as a self-important busybody," John noted after the war. Dr. Schmidhuber was also a member of the anti-Hitler movement and knew a great deal about Admiral Canaris as well as other members of the conspiracy.[9]

When all the visas were obtained and all the currency was distributed, the Jewish refugees left Germany for Switzerland. Some took the train from Berlin; others departed for Switzerland by other routes. At the Sudeten town of Cheb, which had been Czech until it was annexed by Germany in 1938, border guards inspected the luggage of one Jewish family. It was a routine search, the sort of inspection that the guards made every time a train passed through, but what they found in the suitcases was anything but routine: along with all the clothes and personal possessions were thousands of US dollars. The travelers were questioned about how they had managed to acquire the money—foreign exchange laws in Nazi Germany were very strict, and possession of American currency was almost unheard of, especially in such large amounts. The refugees explained that it had been given to them by Dr. Wilhelm Schmidhuber. The border guards immediately contacted the Gestapo about the fact that Jewish refugees were attempting to smuggle such a large amount of American currency out of Germany and also mentioned Dr. Schmidhuber as the person responsible for supplying the emigrants with it. The

Gestapo reacted at once. Dr. Schmidhuber was placed under arrest and detained at Gestapo headquarters in Berlin. The Jewish refugees were also arrested and their cache of US dollars confiscated.

From Berlin, Schmidhuber managed to contact Hans von Dohnanyi and asked him to arrange for his release. But according to Otto Hahn, von Dohnanyi was not inclined to help. Although the Gestapo did not have the authority to arrest any member of the Abwehr, Schmidhuber was no longer connected to the intelligence service, having been dismissed on ethical grounds. He had become involved in some unspecified illegal activities, possibly involving smuggling, which got him into trouble with customs officials in Prague. As a result, he lost his Abwehr commission, was discharged from the service altogether, and was ordered not to travel outside Germany again. In spite of this restriction, Dr. Schmidhuber went to Italy. He apparently was not very careful about his travel plans; an Abwehr officer found him and brought him back to Germany in handcuffs.

Because Dr. Schmidhuber was no longer connected with the Abwehr, and also because his dismissal had come as the result of his own dishonest business dealings and had nothing to do with any Abwehr activities, von Dohnanyi would not help him. Extremely upset when arrested by an Abwehr officer in Italy, Dr. Schmidhuber was outraged when von Dohnanyi refused to rescue him from a Gestapo jail. In retaliation for what he considered his mistreatment at the hands of von Dohnanyi and by the Abwehr in general, he decided to tell the Gestapo everything he knew about the Abwehr and its involvement in the anti-Hitler conspiracy.

During the course of the investigation, Dr. Schmidhuber did mention Admiral Canaris in connection with the conspiracy, but only briefly and imprecisely; he did not know enough about the admiral's part in the movement to give any definite information. But he was well aware of Gen. Hans Oster's hostility toward Adolf Hitler and the Nazis and also knew that Hans von Dohnanyi shared General Oster's anti-Nazi opinions. Among other things, Schmidhuber told his interrogators that von Dohnanyi had arranged the passage of several Jews to Switzerland and had made a profit of thousands of US dollars as the result of that venture. He also said that von Dohnanyi had used his influence to secure

a commission in the Abwehr for Dietrich Bonhoeffer, which kept Bonhoeffer from serving in the army, and also that Pastor Bonhoeffer had
secret connections with the bishop of Chichester. He was doing his best
to make his commentary as damaging as possible, both as revenge for von
Dohnanyi's refusal to come to his rescue and also to make himself look
good in the eyes of the Gestapo.

Dr. Schmidhuber did not give his information all at once. He presented his picture of von Dohnanyi's activities a piece at a time, over
a period of weeks and months—he described his method as "like a
mosaic."[10] Some of the things he had to say were not new to either the
Gestapo or the SD. Reichsführer Heinrich Himmler's remarks about
von Dohnanyi were surprisingly low-key: "I know that Dohnanyi is no
National Socialist, but at least he says what he thinks and one always
knows where he is with him."[11] Members of the anti-Hitler resistance
were very upset by Schmidhuber's arrest—everyone knew that he pos-
sessed a great deal of information about the conspiracy and would gladly
give either the SD or the Gestapo anything they asked for to save his own
life. Hans Oster wanted to have Schmidhuber assassinated, but this was
impossible as long as he was inside a Gestapo prison.

The matter of Hans von Dohnanyi was placed in the hands of
Dr. Manfred Roeder, a senior officer in the Luftwaffe's Judge Advocate General's office and a friend of one of the Gestapo's most feared
officials, "Gestapo" Müller. Dr. Roeder had recently made a name for
himself by obtaining death sentences for members of the Rote Kapelle.
The Rote Kapelle was essentially the eastern equivalent of the anti-Nazi
movement—a group of pro-Russian German officers who passed military information to Moscow. Now Dr. Roeder had an opportunity to
enhance his already formidable reputation by prosecuting the anti-Hitler
resistance and its members and was looking forward to his assignment.
He boasted that he would hang von Dohnanyi and "bring Canaris to
book" as well.[12] The anti-Hitler conspiracy, along with the possibility of
mounting any future rescue operations along the lines of Operation 7 and
Operation Aguilar, was suddenly in great peril.

Dr. Roeder took his time collecting his evidence against the resistance
and preparing his case, with Dr. Schmidhuber as his willing collaborator.

Not until April 1943, a year after the border guards confiscated the US dollars from the Jewish refugees at Cheb, did Dr. Roeder feel confident enough to make an arrest. On April 5, he appeared at the Abwehr offices in Berlin, accompanied by a Gestapo official named Franz Xaver Sonderegger, to take Hans von Dohnanyi into custody. "On the pretext of the foreign exchange control laws, Dohnanyi, his wife and brother-in-law have been arrested," Ulrich von Hassell noted.[13]

Because Hans von Dohnanyi held a commission in the Abwehr—he was a major in the Abwehr's foreign section—his arrest by Dr. Roeder was actually against the law. Under the prevailing statutes, von Dohnanyi could only be arrested by a member of the Reich Court Martial, not by either a Luftwaffe investigator or a Gestapo official. But Dr. Roeder was not interested in legal technicalities. He stated that both Hans von Dohnanyi and Dietrich Bonhoeffer were guilty of plotting to overthrow the Nazi government and that von Dohnanyi was guilty of "getting large-scale bribes for smuggling Jews into Switzerland."[14] Producing a search warrant, he proceeded to go through everything that might be of interest in von Dohnanyi's office and also emptied the contents of his safe. While all this was going on, von Dohnanyi, Oster, and Canaris could do nothing but stand by and watch.

The arrest took everyone by surprise. Not knowing that it was coming, no one had the chance to clean out von Dohnanyi's safe before Dr. Roeder and Franz Xaver Sonderegger arrived. Roeder discovered several slips of paper among the items inside the safe, each briefly outlining instructions for secret anti-Nazi intelligence operations. One of the papers concerned an assignment to the Vatican for Dietrich Bonhoeffer. Hans Oster spotted the document and, recognizing the possible danger if it fell into the wrong hands, picked it up and put it in his pocket. But Sonderegger saw General Oster pocket the slip and immediately told Dr. Roeder. Dr. Roeder took the paper from Oster, looked at it, and placed him under arrest. Hans von Dohnanyi was also arrested and taken from his office to a Wehrmacht detention prison. Dietrich Bonhoeffer was apprehended and taken to Tegel Prison, a short distance away from the Abwehr offices, where he was kept in solitary confinement. When Ulrich von Hassell heard about what had happened, he called the incident "a first-class mess." Admiral Canaris would probably have called von Hassell's appraisal a gross understatement.[15]

But the admiral could at least be relieved that von Dohnanyi and Pastor Bonhoeffer had not been sent to a Gestapo prison, where they would be subject to torture. Von Dohnanyi himself admitted, "No one can say how long he can hold out once the Gestapo has him in its power." Dr. Roeder did not have any real evidence that linked von Dohnanyi to Operation 7, at least nothing that would stand up under close examination, and had no means of extracting anything incriminating from him without the Gestapo and its methods. So he decided to use his own methods of torment to persuade von Dohnanyi to talk.

While in prison, von Dohnanyi was not allowed to read anything or to write any letters. Also, the notes he had taken during his interrogation, which he planned to use as part of his legal defense, were confiscated. These restrictions were designed to "soften up" the prisoner, as Dr. Roeder explained to the prison commandant, a Major Maass. The punishment that Von Dohnanyi endured was severe enough to make him seriously ill and to give him a dangerous case of phlebitis in both legs.[16]

But fortunately for von Dohnanyi, Major Maass was sympathetic toward his new prisoner and his political views. He allowed von Dohnanyi as many privileges as he could get away with, including allowing Frau von Dohnanyi to visit her husband twice a week and bring him food from home. Von Dohnanyi was also allowed to pass letters out of prison under the lids of his wife's food containers. These visits certainly helped to ease the tensions and pressures of von Dohnanyi's imprisonment, but they were carried out at considerable risk to Frau von Dohnanyi—as both she and Major Maass were well aware. Major Maass even gave Frau von Dohnanyi a straightforward warning: she should not be surprised if Gestapo agents met her at the prison gate during one of her visits and took her into custody along with her food parcels. But she was not put off by the major's advice and kept making her visits despite the danger and the warnings.[17]

At Tegel Prison, Dietrich Bonhoeffer also had the good luck of receiving privileged treatment from the guards. But for his first twelve days there, he was treated like a convicted felon. "The blankets on the camp bed had such a foul smell that in spite of the cold it was impossible to use them," he wrote shortly after being admitted. "Next morning a piece of bread was thrown into my cell; I had to pick it up from the floor." The jailers called him "scoundrel," among other things, when they spoke to him at all. He had not been told the reason for his arrest. The guards sneered and told him, "You'll find out soon enough." He was sometimes awakened out of a sound sleep by the "vile abuse" of other prisoners, inmates who were being held in nearby cells and physically tormented during interrogation in the middle of the night.[18] It was an uncomfortable and sometimes harrowing time for the pastor.

When the guards found out that the new prisoner was a pastor, their attitude changed. First they returned his Bible to him. After about a week and a half, the staff began to take a personal liking toward the quiet and sociable pastor. They not only became very friendly to him but also conspired to smuggle the pastor's letters out of prison. The attitude of the prison officials was very possibly influenced by the fact that the commandant of the Berlin district, their overall superior, just happened to be Dietrich Bonhoeffer's uncle. For his own part, Pastor Bonhoeffer did not let prison life upset him. Unlike the ailing and highly strung Hans von Dohnanyi, he was in good health, which helped him to maintain an optimistic attitude and state of mind. He tended to treat his time in Tegel as a sort of religious retreat; he spent much of it reading, writing, and thinking.

Dr. Roeder continued with his interrogation of both Pastor Bonhoeffer and Hans von Dohnanyi, but his methods were not having their desired effect. The fact that he did not have the necessary evidence to convict or hang either one of his prisoners did not stop him from using threats against them: "I shall not stop attacking you personally until I have destroyed you," he told von Dohnanyi.[19] These outbursts did not seem to have any effect on either von Dohnanyi or Pastor Bonhoeffer, although they were beginning to frighten other members of the anti-Hitler opposition.

Every one of the conspiracy members, including Admiral Canaris, knew very well that Dr. Roeder and Gestapo Müller were doing their very best to collect enough evidence to hang them all. "Roeder was frantically persistent with his inquiries into the 'Black Orchestra'"—the English translation of Schwarze Kapelle, the anti-Hitler movement. The anti-Nazi resistance had an abiding fear of Dr. Roeder; "he had the nose of a bloodhound and realized that he was on the right track." The evidence collected involving Operation 7 had strengthened his case as well as his resolve. He had ordered the Gestapo "into action" against the anti-Nazi resistance. The conspirators "had to assume that one day everyone would be caught and forced to talk under pressure." And when that day came, everyone in the conspiracy movement knew that they would be on their way to the gallows.[20]

Dr. Roeder kept on with his interrogation of, and threats against, Hans von Dohnanyi. He was certain that he was on his way to uncovering a massive political conspiracy, combined with a subversion plot. He was just as convinced that when he finished his investigation, he would find none other than Adm. Wilhelm Canaris, head of the Abwehr, at the center of the conspiracy. Dr. Roeder even kept Adolf Hitler informed of the investigation's progress; Hitler had taken a personal interest in the matter. But in spite of his determination and enthusiasm, Dr. Roeder very quickly discovered that he had an equally determined opponent in von Dohnanyi. As an attorney, von Dohnanyi was every bit as clever as Roeder, possibly even a bit more so.

Each time Roeder made an accusation, von Dohnanyi either side-stepped or refuted the charge. When Dr. Roeder claimed that von Dohnanyi had committed treason and conspired to overthrow the Nazi government, von Dohnanyi countered with a convincing argument that everything he had done in connection with the Abwehr was strictly in the line of duty. Roeder also accused him of accepting large sums of money in exchange for smuggling Jews out of the country. This was fairly easy to refute—as von Dohnanyi had never accepted any money, there was no evidence to support this accusation. And von Dohnanyi was able to explain that Dietrich Bonhoeffer's trip to England was actually a counterintelligence mission for Admiral Canaris carried out to give the enemy false information regarding German military intentions. Dr. Roeder was not able to substantiate any of his accusations and could not intimidate von Dohnanyi into making any sort of incriminating statement against himself. He had been totally frustrated in his attempt to collect evidence of high treason against von Dohnanyi, Canaris, and the other members of the anti-Nazi conspiracy.

Dr. Roeder's cold-blooded methods of interrogation very quickly came to the attention of the head of the Wehrmacht's legal department, Dr. Karl Sack. Dr. Sack had been on friendly terms with both General Oster and Hans von Dohnanyi since before the war and also shared their thoughts regarding Hitler and the Nazis. (A surprising number of senior officers disagreed with Hitler and his government, a number that had increased since the war both in Russia and North Africa began turning against the Germans.) Dr. Sack was irritated by Dr. Roeder's threats to "bring Canaris to book" but also saw this statement as a possible way of derailing the investigation.

Dr. Sack went directly to Feldmarschall Wilhelm Keitel to complain about Dr. Roeder and the intimidating method he was using to question Hans von Dohnanyi; he also made a special point of criticizing Roeder's threat to discredit Admiral Canaris. Dr. Roeder's true intent was not just to discredit the admiral, Dr. Sack explained, but also to make the entire German High Command, including the *feldmarschall* himself, appear inept in the eyes of Adolf Hitler. Manfred Roeder was a member of the Luftwaffe, Dr. Sack pointed out. By demeaning the High Command, he was really endorsing his superior officer, Luftwaffe chief Hermann Göring, for promotion as head of the High Command. In other words, Roeder's denunciation of Admiral Canaris and Hans von Dohnanyi was nothing but a political stab in the back—his real motive behind all the threats and bullying was to replace Feldmarschall Keitel with Reichsmarschall Göring.

According to British writer Anthony Cave Brown, Admiral Canaris also paid a visit to Feldmarschall Keitel to complain about Dr. Roeder and his methods. The admiral said that "Roeder was activated by a desire to besmirch the good name of the army by proving treason against the Abwehr."[21] Because Admiral Canaris outranked Dr. Sack, the *feldmarschall* was probably more inclined to listen to Canaris's complaint. But Keitel was impressed by the fact that the two officers presented the same argument: Dr. Roeder of the Luftwaffe was out to discredit both the

Wehrmacht and Feldmarschall Keitel for political reasons. His investigation had nothing to do with treason.

This argument certainly captured Feldmarschall Keitel's full attention. He was well aware that Hermann Göring had designs on replacing him as the head of the German High Command, so what Dr. Sack and Admiral Canaris had to say came as no great surprise. But the report prompted the *feldmarschall* to take action against Dr. Roeder and his investigation. He ordered the head of his own legal department, a Dr. Rudolf Lehmann, to begin his own investigation concerning Hans von Dohnanyi and any connection he might have with both the Schwarze Kapelle and Operation 7. Dr. Lehmann read all the files and documents related to the anti-Hitler movement. At the end of three days, he reported his findings to Feldmarschall Keitel: he concluded that Manfred Roeder's attacks on von Dohnanyi were based on nothing but "blind ambition" and that Dr. Roeder had "overreached himself" by carrying out such a heavy-handed investigation. His only motive for indicting von Dohnanyi for treason was to make Adm. Wilhelm Canaris look like a traitor, which would make the entire High Command, including Feldmarschall Keitel, appear incompetent in the eyes of Adolf Hitler. In short, according to Dr. Lehmann's findings, Manfred Roeder had no case against Hans von Dohnanyi.[22]

Ulrich von Hassell gave the prevailing opinion of "the Dohnanyi affair" in a diary entry dated July 18, 1943. "The Dohnanyi affair is a public scandal," he wrote. "Months spent in an endless investigation undertaken without legal warrant against a high military official."[23] This was exactly what Feldmarschall Keitel wanted to hear. On July 23, the *feldmarschall* ordered that the investigation be discontinued. From that point, any inquiry concerning von Dohnanyi would be confined to the possible abuse of his office. Feldmarschall Keitel also removed Manfred Roeder from the inquiry, just in case he decided to disobey orders and continue with his time-wasting witch hunt, and replaced him with an official named Kutzner, who had neither the zeal nor the ambition of Dr. Roeder. "We hailed this decision of Keitel's with relief," Otto John recalled. "The only case now remaining to Roeder could easily be refuted," the "case" being the acceptance of bribes for smuggling Jewish refugees out of Germany, which was a nonissue.[24] It looked as though the anti-Nazi movement had been reprieved; Operation 7 had been swept under the rug, and Admiral Canaris, Dietrich Bonhoeffer, and Hans von Dohnanyi had been given a very timely pardon.

But von Dohnanyi did not agree with this point of view. From his hospital bed, where he was being treated for phlebitis as well as a brain embolism that interfered with his speech and vision, he sent word to his fellow conspirators not to get their hopes up too high. Manfred Roeder was not about to give up with his persecution of Admiral Canaris and the resistance just because Feldmarschall Keitel issued an order. Dr. Roeder might have been replaced regarding the investigation of Operation 7, von Dohnanyi warned, but he was still living and still determined to do everything possible to hang Admiral Canaris, himself, and everyone else connected with Operation 7 and the anti-Hitler movement. Even though von Dohnanyi was undergoing treatment for his ailments and was confined to a hospital bed, he was still in custody, and Dietrich Bonhoeffer was still in Tegel Prison. Both were liable to be interrogated at any time, using any method that Dr. Roeder or any other investigator saw fit to employ. Von Dohnanyi could appreciate this ominous situation, even if Ulrich von Hassell and Otto John did not. "Unfortunately, it proved that Dohnanyi's appreciation of the situation was more accurate than ours," Otto John later admitted.[25]

Even though Operation 7 created a potentially lethal situation for the anti-Hitler conspirators involved in the incident, the story had a happy ending for the fourteen Jewish refugees—mainly because of Adm. Wilhelm Canaris. Shortly after the American currency incident at Cheb, Gen. Hans Oster informed Admiral Canaris about the situation—"laid the facts before him," according to Fabian von Schlabrendorff, who had been a member of the opposition since 1939—and asked the admiral to do what he could to help. Admiral Canaris came up with his own idea for releasing the Jews and sending them across the border to Switzerland. He immediately telephoned Heinrich Himmler and asked the Schutzstaffel (SS) leader to come and see him, explaining that the matter he wanted to talk about was much too sensitive to be discussed over the telephone. Himmler went to see the admiral "at once" and was taken completely by surprise when Canaris began to scold him for interfering with Abwehr activities.[26]

"How do you expect me to carry on with the Abwehr, Reichsfuehrer, if your people arrest my agents?" the admiral said. "I know that it is not your fault, but it is causing me a lot of trouble." Reichsführer Himmler, clearly not expecting a reprimand from the head of Hitler's Military Intelligence Service, was nonplussed by Admiral Canaris's outburst. He telephoned the officials who had arrested the Jewish refugees and ordered them to release the detainees to the Abwehr. A few hours after General Oster contacted Admiral Canaris about the problem, the admiral telephoned Oster to report that "his" Jews were being sent to Abwehr headquarters. From there, they were sent to Switzerland; Admiral Canaris used funds that had been set aside for counterintelligence operations to reimburse them for at least part of their confiscated funds. The admiral complained that General Oster always expected him to accomplish the impossible. He may not have done the impossible, but he did manage to save several more Jews from the Nazis. No one but Admiral Canaris could have talked Heinrich Himmler into releasing the fourteen Jews who were being held in custody—the *Reichsführer* seemed to be in complete agreement with the admiral. All of the refugees survived the war. Ironically, most of them outlived the anti-Hitler conspirators who had come to their rescue.[27]

* * *

By 1942, the members of the anti-Nazi movement, along with a good many senior officers in the Wehrmacht, were becoming increasingly motivated in their resistance to Hitler by the Nazi government's persecution of Jews and other outcasts. The atrocities were turning other members of the armed forces, not just generals but junior officers as well, against the Nazis. In October 1942, a twenty-four-year-old Wehrmacht captain named Axel von dem Bussche was present during the systematic execution of Jews near the Ukrainian village of Dubno. After witnessing the executions, he said that he regretted not having taken off his uniform and joined the victims and also said that there were only three honorable ways for an officer to react: "To die in battle, to desert, or to rebel."

Captain von dem Bussche decided to rebel against the Nazis. His first step would be a dramatic one: he volunteered to take part in an assassination attempt against Adolf Hitler.[28]

The assassination plot revolved around the presentation to Adolf Hitler of a new style of uniform overcoat during the autumn of 1942. Hitler was greatly interested in seeing these new coats, which had only recently been created for the Wehrmacht, and insisted upon inspecting them before giving his official approval. During the inspection, Captain von dem Bussche was to explain the advantages of the uniform's new features to a rapt and attentive Hitler. But Hitler would have no idea that Captain von dem Bussche was concealing two grenades in his own greatcoat. When he felt that the time was right, the captain would detonate the grenades. The explosions would kill both Hitler and himself.

Captain von dem Bussche traveled to Hitler's headquarters in East Prussia in November 1942, where the inspection was to take place, and waited for the date to be announced. But no announcement was ever made—the event was postponed several times; the captain was never given any sort of explanation for the delays. Toward the end of the year, he was informed that the inspection had been postponed indefinitely— the overcoats had been destroyed. They had been stored in Berlin in a freight car that had been blown up, with all of its contents, in an air raid. Another assassination attempt would be impossible, at least for the time being; it would take months for the coats to be replaced. There would be other attempts to kill Hitler, but Captain von dem Bussche would not take part in them. He returned to Russia early in 1943, where he was seriously wounded in combat and had a leg amputated as a result.[29]

* * *

In her secret annex in Amsterdam, Anne Frank wrote in her diary, "Our Jewish friends and acquaintances are being taken away in droves." She went on to report, "The Gestapo is treating them very roughly and transporting them in cattle cars to Westerbork, the big camp in Drenthe to which they're sending Jews. . . . We assume that most of them are being murdered." But she also mentioned that Jews were not the only people being persecuted. "Have you ever heard the term 'hostages'? That's the latest punishment for saboteurs."The hostages were ordinary German citizens arrested by the Gestapo in place of the saboteurs. "If the Gestapo can't find the saboteurs, they simply grab five hostages and line them up against the wall. You read the announcements of their death in the paper, where they are referred to as 'fatal accidents.'"[30]

In addition to Jews, the Gestapo and SD targeted anyone who did not fit their idea of racial and religious purity. Poles and Czechs were considered *untermenschen*, or subhumans. The disabled were also considered unfit to live, a drain on German resources. Hospitals were pressured into giving up their handicapped patients for "mercy killings." Legalized murders of the sick and the handicapped had become an official policy of the Nazi government. Besides people with mental or physical disabilities, the Nazis also persecuted homosexuals, gypsies, Poles and other Slavic peoples, and anyone else the Hitler regime thought of as inconvenient. The Nazis considered Gypsies racially inferior; about 1.5 million died in concentration camps during the mass killings, which they called the *Porajmos* in their language. The Nazis regarded anyone with any sort of mental or chronic illness as "unworthy of life." Institutions and asylums were sometimes converted into euthanasia centers; SS officers wore lab coats to look like doctors and to give the impression that they were running a medical facility. "Families were told their relatives had died from illness and given faked death certificates, when in reality up to 300,000 people in Germany and Austria were systematically murdered, usually in gas chambers disguised as showers. Their organs were used for experiments."[31]

Writer Elie Wiesel, who survived confinement in both Auschwitz and Buchenwald concentration camps, famously said, "While not all victims were Jews, all Jews were victims."[32] This came as cold comfort to hostages who were shot by the Gestapo as substitutes for fugitive saboteurs or to Poles and Czechs executed in concentration camps because they had been deemed subhuman. And none of these unfortunates could ever hope to be rescued through the efforts of Admiral Canaris, General Oster, or any other member of the anti-Hitler conspiracy.

* * *

Adolf Hitler had become angry with Admiral Canaris long before Operation 7 and Dr. Manfred Roeder's investigation. Dr. Roeder's findings did not prove anything one way or another—according to his data, the Abwehr may have been involved in smuggling Jews out of Germany but probably was not—although the incident did serve to increase suspicion regarding both the Abwehr and Admiral Canaris. But Hitler's confidence in the admiral's ability to act as head of his military intelligence service had been deteriorating for quite some time. As far as he could see, the admiral did not seem to know what he was doing. An event that took place in November 1942 caused Hitler to question Canaris's abilities even further.

That autumn, the German High Command began receiving intelligence communiqués regarding an Allied amphibious landing operation. An agent in England reported that a significant invasion would be taking place in the near future, although he did not know where or when. Among other things, the agent mentioned that the operation would be commanded by an American general named Eisenhower, that it had been given the code name Operation Flame, and that it looked to be a major undertaking. The agent actually got the code name wrong: the proposed landing operation was called Operation Torch. But the rest of his information turned out to be correct. The invasion he reported was to take place on the coast of French North Africa and would be significant in size and scope; its commander was Gen. Dwight D. Eisenhower.

In October 1942, German naval intelligence sent word that an Allied troop convoy had put to sea but could give no information regarding its destination. On November 7, agents in Spain observed a force of transports and warships steaming through the Strait of Gibraltar into the Mediterranean Sea. Members of the High Command, including Feldmarschall Keitel, could only guess at the convoy's destination—it might be headed for Sardinia, or Sicily, or Malta, or possibly North Africa. Feldmarschall Albert Kesselring, the overall commander of all German forces in the Mediterranean, could offer no opinion. The best he could do was suggest that it might be any one of the three objectives.

During the early hours of Sunday, November 8, 1942, all the guesswork and speculation came to an abrupt end. Three separate Allied landing forces came ashore on the North African coast that morning: at Casablanca, Oran, and Algiers. The troops were mostly American, although the Algiers landing force was made up of both British and American forces. All three landings took the defenders completely unawares. No one, including Feldmarschall Keitel, had any idea that a major amphibious operation was about to come ashore in French North Africa in spite of the information supplied to German intelligence.

The overwhelming success of Operation Torch came as a pleasant surprise to Allied planners. Elaborate deception schemes were mainly responsible for the operation's initial success. For months prior to the invasion, double agents had been leaking false information about Torch, fabricated but genuine-sounding stories that led some senior German officers to believe that the landings would take place in Dakar, in French West Africa. A tight security lid also restricted leaks of authentic data, which kept all "loose talk" to a minimum and made the fake stories of the double agents seem more believable. But Operation Torch also owed at least a small debt to the subtle but highly effective deception methods of Adm. Wilhelm Canaris.

Admiral Canaris's role in the success of Operation Torch was more a matter of omission than commission—he prevented an accurate report concerning the landings from reaching the High Command shortly before the invasion took place. Another German agent operating in Britain made the discovery that French North Africa, not Dakar, was the actual destination of the invasion force. He immediately sent his information across to Hamburg, the Abwehr's primary station for collecting information from Britain and the United States. The report was received by the station's commander, a Capt. Herbert Wichmann, who later stated that he forwarded it on to the attention of the German High Command under the highest priority. But no one at High Command ever saw any sign of Captain Wichmann's report or its warning. The landing force arrived at its destination undetected.

As head of the Abwehr, Admiral Canaris was asked to explain exactly what had happened to Captain Wichmann's communiqué. The admiral said simply that he had never seen it. Captain Wichmann insisted that he certainly had sent his report to Hamburg, but Admiral Canaris calmly repeated that it had not reached him. After the war, an Abwehr officer named Colonel Heinz remarked that Admiral Canaris deliberately downplayed or disregarded all intelligence information regarding Operation Torch. He had used the same methods of deception to keep Feldmarschall Erwin Rommel misinformed during his campaign against the British army in Libya. But instead of using misinformation to confuse German forces in North Africa, the admiral simply withheld information, confiscating the Wichmann report and preventing it from reaching Feldmarschall Keitel.[33]

Adolf Hitler was becoming increasingly angry with Admiral Canaris and his "inefficiency." Gen. Alfred Jodl, a member of Feldmarschall Keitel's staff, accused the admiral of being unstable. Hitler himself called him a fool. He certainly looked like one after Operation Torch. Approximately 110 transport and cargo ships, along with 200 warships, had sailed right through the Strait of Gibraltar and sneaked up on the North African coast, and Admiral Canaris, the officer in charge of military intelligence, claimed that he knew nothing about it.[34] No one suggested that the admiral's failure was anything more ominous than incompetence. Hitler and the High Command only knew that Canaris had fallen down on the job, with dire consequences.

Hitler and his generals had good reason for being unhappy with the admiral and his failure to give advance warning of the landings. The success of Operation Torch effectively sealed the fate of Feldmarschall Erwin Rommel's Afrika Korps, which was squeezed out of North Africa between the advancing British Eighth Army to the east and the Anglo-American forces to the west. Feldmarschall Rommel did give a good account of himself during the fighting that took place in the months following the landings. In February 1943, at Kasserine Pass, he surprised the green American troops with an unexpected attack and inflicted heavy casualties. But he knew that he could not hold out against the superior Allied forces for much longer. By the spring of 1943, all Axis forces in North Africa had either surrendered or withdrawn.

Admiral Canaris could be well satisfied that he had inflicted major damage upon Hitler by withholding vital information regarding Operation Torch. Losing North Africa to the Allies would prove to be the beginning of the end for Hitler and his regime. Members of the anti-Nazi resistance hoped that Hitler's generals might be persuaded to join them as a result of the German defeat in North Africa, on the basis of Hitler's inept leadership. Ulrich von Hassell wrote, "If the generals had it in mind to withhold their intervention until it was absolutely clear that the corporal [Hitler] is leading us into disaster, they have had their dreams fulfilled."[35] The anti-Hitler conspiracy was pressing for a coup and hoped that senior generals would fall in line behind them. Admiral Canaris, Ulrich von Hassell, Otto John, Gen. Hans Oster, and the other members could only hope that the coup would take place, and the atrocities would be brought to an end, before the Gestapo caught someone and forced them to talk under torture.

* * *

Helping fourteen Jews to escape Nazi Germany very nearly destroyed the anti-Nazi resistance, along with all of its members. "Dohnanyi's arrest dislocated the political structure of the conspiracy, and the unity of the numerous resistance groups began to crumble," Otto John wrote. "I was disillusioned and downcast."[36] Admiral Canaris was also downcast. He was frightened as well, not only for the future of the anti-Hitler conspiracy but also for his own future. It had become obvious by this time that the conspiracy's rescue efforts were too risky. In the wake of Operation 7 and Dr. Roeder's investigation, the main objective of the anti-Hitler resistance would have to be the elimination of Adolf Hitler himself. Removing Hitler was the only certain method for ending the Nazi regime, along with all of its aggressions and atrocities. Dietrich Bonhoeffer, using the language of a clergyman, made the comment, "Hitler is anti-Christ. Therefore we must go on with our work and eliminate him whether he be successful or not."[37] Admiral Canaris would never have used these particular words to express his opinion of Adolf Hitler—"anti-Christ" was not an expression that ever would have occurred to a career naval officer—but he would have agreed with Pastor Bonhoeffer's sentiments. The only way to rescue Germany, including the Jews and other non-Aryans in Germany and in all German-occupied countries, was to remove Hitler from power, either by coup d'état or assassination.

CHAPTER NINE

Authority and Opportunity

By the beginning of 1943, Adm. Wilhelm Canaris was almost totally exhausted, both physically and mentally. The worry and anxiety produced by Operation 7, along with Dr. Manfred Roeder's ruthless interrogation and prosecution, were the main causes of his condition. Both Hans von Dohnanyi and Dietrich Bonhoeffer were still in prison, and as von Dohnanyi pointed out, Dr. Roeder or some other investigator could very possibly begin another inquiry involving Operation 7 at any time. The anti-Nazi conspiracy was still in grave danger. Nobody was more aware of this than Admiral Canaris. The anti-Hitler movement had been saved by some persuasive talking, a lot of luck, and the timely intervention of Feldmarschall Wilhelm Keitel. But the admiral realized that the movement would not be nearly as fortunate if another cold-blooded official like Dr. Roeder, or possibly Roeder himself, decided to reopen the Operation 7 investigation—the anti-Nazi resistance could never be as lucky a second time. The entire matter left Admiral Canaris a nervous and physical wreck.

Friends could not help but notice the admiral's rundown condition and were dismayed by the sound of his voice—all of his worry and despair became evident every time he spoke. Not that he had very much to say; in his depression he spoke only when he thought it absolutely necessary. All the fatigue and strain he was suffering also showed in his face; he usually gave the impression of being tired and distracted. Admiral Canaris had acquired the nickname "Old Fox" for outthinking and outmaneuvering Reinhard Heydrich and any other Nazi official who threatened to interfere with any of his nefarious plans, enjoying the intrigue he was creating, and rescuing Jews and members of the Polish upper-class right under the noses of the Gestapo, the Sicherheitsdienst (SD), and the Schutzstaffel (SS). But now the Old Fox was too tired and depressed to do much except sit and worry. The crafty and calculating head of the Abwehr, who would do anything he thought feasible to undermine Adolf Hitler and the Nazis, was now almost unrecognizable.

In January 1943, an incident took place that showed exactly how tired and worn Admiral Canaris had become. German writer Franz Josef Furtwängler, who was also employed by the German Foreign Office at the time, approached the admiral with a request for help. Along with an associate named Hartmut Plaas, who had known the admiral before the war, Furtwängler told Canaris about a Jewish friend who suddenly found himself in a life-threatening situation: he would almost certainly be dead, probably by the end of the year, if he was not smuggled out of Nazi-occupied territory. This friend had legally emigrated from Germany to the Netherlands, where he had been living peacefully since 1938, but now suddenly found himself facing deportation to Poland. During the summer of 1942, the Nazi government had begun a major deportation program of individuals from the Netherlands and occupied France—Jews, Gypsies, political prisoners, and members of "inferior races," were being sent to concentration camps in eastern Poland, with Auschwitz designated as the primary extermination camp. Being sent to Poland would mean certain death at the hands of the SS in Auschwitz. Franz Furtwängler asked Admiral Canaris if he would save his friend from Auschwitz by disguising him as an Abwehr agent and smuggling him out of the Netherlands under the admiral's protection, as he had done several times before.

Admiral Canaris patiently listened to what Franz Furtwängler had to say and immediately turned down his request. He flatly stated that he would not be able to help. "The head of the Abwehr," Furtwängler would write, "admitted quite frankly that he was pretty well 'hemmed in.'" He went on to say that Heinrich Himmler "was on the verge of outright victory, and he, the admiral, no longer had the power to protect a person or 'requisition' him on behalf of his agencies."[1] Furtwängler admitted that the admiral's response inflicted a "shattering blow" to his plans, as well as to his opinion of the man himself. Canaris had come to the rescue of so many others in the past; Furtwängler expected him to rise to the occasion once again. He knew that the admiral had been directly responsible for secreting several hundred Jewish residents out of the Netherlands in the spring of 1941. He had given his unique brand of assistance to anyone who needed help, including Madame Szymańska and the Jewish refugees of Operation 7, and also encouraged any sympathetic Abwehr officers to come to the aid of any refugees in need of support.

But in January 1943, the Abwehr and Canaris were not what they once were. The Abwehr was in decline, as Admiral Canaris was fully aware. The SD and the SS were pushing the once-influential military intelligence service further into the background. There was no doubt in his mind that one of these two organizations would very shortly take control of the Abwehr and that he was "in the process of losing the last battle on behalf of Prussian military resistance to the National Socialist Revolution."[2] Admiral Canaris did not really know exactly what would happen to him when the Nazis took control of the Abwehr, but he had the feeling that it was not going to be very pleasant. He was in no condition to help any more Jews or anybody else, whether Furtwängler liked it or not. The way things were looking, Admiral Canaris was not even certain that he would be able to help himself.

* * *

In his diary entry for December 20, 1942, Ulrich von Hassell noted that German forces were fighting a losing battle on all fronts: at Stalingrad, where one and a half armies had been trapped by the Russians; throughout North Africa, where the Allied position had consolidated; and in Libya, where there had been "further retreats" by German forces. At home, the combined bombing campaign of the British and American air forces was systematically reducing German cities to fire-gutted ruins. The image of life inside Nazi Germany offered no encouragement either, at least not in von Hassell's view. "Throughout the whole world there is increasing activity against us," including in Spain, Portugal, and Turkey, throughout South America, and in most other neutral countries.

"Atrocities in Poland are exploited very dramatically in the House of Commons," he continued, also mentioning that any Italians who came to visit Germany were "shocked at our conditions of slavery and barbarism." Conditions inside Germany were not good and getting steadily worse. "There is increasing nervousness here at home arising out of anxiety over the outcome of the war and fear of domestic disturbances."[3]

This "nervousness" concerning the war was also having its effect on the SS, the SD, and the Gestapo, which were taking at least some of their anxieties out on Jews and other non-Aryans. Von Hassell was given a fairly horrific account of SS atrocities in Poland by his friend Dr. Max Frauendorfer, a member of the SS forces operating in Poland. Dr. Frauendorfer said that the SS campaign was "so terrible that he could not endure it. . . . Continual, indescribable mass murder of Jews." The SS sent patrols into Jewish districts after curfew to use automatic weapons on anyone they found out on the street. The situation seemed to be worsening as Germany's position in the war deteriorated.[4]

Dr. Frauendorfer was in a unique position to know about what was happening in Poland; he was a senior SS official in Poland and had access to all information regarding SS and SD activities. He was also a long-term Nazi and a party member in good standing, as well as a recipient of the Nazi Party's Golden Badge of Honor, a gold medal awarded by Adolf Hitler himself for outstanding service to the Nazi Party. But after witnessing what was taking place in Poland, he turned against both Hitler and the Nazi Party. He used his rank and authority to deliver a warning to von Hassell from a mutual friend: the Gestapo was keeping him under close observation and had probably increased its surveillance because of information received concerning Operation 7. "For that reason I would perhaps do well to keep out of sight," von Hassell wrote, "so that I can at least continue to work in some way."[5] He would do his best to avoid being seen with anyone suspicious or to do anything that might bring about his arrest at the hands of the Gestapo, but he would also continue to do whatever he could for the Schwarze Kapelle. Along with most members of the resistance, von Hassell was now convinced that the movement's first priority should be the overthrow of Hitler. In the months to come, as the war situation continued to deteriorate and the Nazi regime increased its campaign against Jews and other "undesirables," he would write about "the necessity of getting rid of Hitler."[6] And overthrowing Hitler and his government would almost certainly require the assistance of the British and the Americans.

* * *

"I reached Switzerland as the tide of war turned in November 1942," Allen Welsh Dulles recalled a few years after his arrival in that country.[7] The exact date was November 8, the same day that Operation Torch landed over fifty thousand troops on the beaches of North Africa. His residence was 23 Herrengasse, in Bern. As head of the Office of Strategic Services (OSS) in Bern, Dulles had a good many responsibilities. His tasks included collecting information concerning German troop movements, acquiring bombing reports on the Allied air offensive against Germany, and obtaining data on the highly secret V-1 flying bomb and V-2 rocket projects. Switzerland was a major center for espionage—making contact with spies, expatriates, and diplomats on both sides was a fairly simple matter. But supplying military intelligence to OSS headquarters in Washington, DC, was not Dulles's main job. "My first and most important was to find out what was going on in Germany," he said. Along with the bombing results and strategic information, "Washington wanted to know who in Germany were really opposed to the Hitler regime and whether they were actively at work to overthrow it."[8]

Dulles referred to Switzerland as an island of democracy in a sea of Nazi and fascist despotism. He also pointed out that it was "the only neutral country with a common land frontier with Germany," which made it the ideal location for finding out exactly what was happening inside Hitler's Third Reich as well as for broadcasting radio messages to the German public.[9] Dulles planned to begin a series of radio broadcasts for, as he put it, "the planting of deadly false rumors" along with the "enhancement of the free flow of accurate, open information in Europe."[10] Actually, Dulles really had in mind the broadcasting and distribution of propaganda. In one of his earliest telegrams to OSS headquarters in Washington, sent on December 6, 1942, he mentioned a "radio propaganda campaign" to supply German citizens with factual news releases concerning the fighting in

Russia and North Africa.[11] Dulles hoped that members of the anti-Nazi movement would be helpful with promoting his propaganda campaign, which was one of the main reasons he wanted to make contact with the German resistance.

One of Allen Dulles's earliest and most reliable contacts was Hans Bernd Gisevius. Gisevius's official position was vice consul at the German consulate in Zurich, but he had actually been sent to Switzerland by Admiral Canaris as an Abwehr agent. His real function was to make contact with Allied agents, especially with well-connected representatives such as Allen Dulles. This made Gisevius's job much easier, since Dulles had been sent to Switzerland to get in touch with Germans like Hans Gisevius, diplomats who had connections with the German underground. The two would do their best to make the most of their new acquaintance.

Hans Gisevius wrote that Dulles's house on the Herrengasse became "a virtual center of the European Resistance. Not only Germans, but Austrians, Hungarians, Italians, Rumanians, and Finns, not to mention the citizens of occupied countries, met there."[12] The house was situated adjacent a vineyard, which made it fairly easy for Dulles's secret visitors to come and go without being seen, especially at night. But Dulles's primary interest was in the German resistance and its activities. Gisevius would prove to be a major source of information regarding the anti-Hitler movement.

It took a while for Dulles and Gisevius to get to know and trust each other. Part of this hesitancy stemmed from circumstances: Germany and the United States were at war with each other, and, as Dulles stated, "a meeting between us was hardly according to the protocol."[13] Also, Hans Gisevius was not the friendliest or most outgoing person in the world; his personality tended to be reserved and formal and, at six feet, four inches in height, he looked down at the world both literally and figuratively. There were other problems as well. Gisevius often returned to Berlin. Making frequent trips between Berlin and Switzerland to meet with Dulles might stir up the suspicions of the Gestapo. Also, anything he said might not only endanger himself but also members of the anti-Nazi movement—the Gestapo might also be listening to his telephone conversations. But as Hans Gisevius and Allen Dulles became better acquainted, they began to lose their wariness as well as their concern for protocol. "It was only gradually, as mutual confidence was established," Dulles would later write, "that I began to get the first details of the organization and plans of the resistance movement."[14]

Hans Gisevius proved his value to the OSS station in Bern very shortly after Allen Dulles arrived in Switzerland. In February 1943, Gisevius returned to Switzerland from Berlin with some startling news: German deciphering services had succeeded in breaking one of the OSS codes. Gisevius had been given this information by Admiral Canaris, along with the evidence to back it up. "He took his little black notebook out of his pocket and pieced together the general contents of a considerable number of telegrams which had been sent from Bern to Washington," Dulles wrote. One of the telegrams concerned a group of high-ranking Italian officers who had turned against the Germans. This group included Field Marshal Galeazzo Ciano, who was also Benito Mussolini's son-in-law. The message was given directly to Adolf Hitler, who promptly forwarded it along to Mussolini "with his compliments." Ciano was removed from his post a few days later. Although Dulles later said that he was never able to discover "whether this was a coincidence or whether the cable was the cause," it can be safely assumed that Ciano's dismissal came as the direct result of the deciphered OSS message.[15]

Hans Gisevius's information allowed the OSS to turn the compromised code from a liability to an asset. After February 1943, "this code was used only for messages which we were quite willing or even anxious to have the Germans read, and over the months we discarded it entirely."[16] In other words, the broken code was used to feed German intelligence false but genuine-sounding information. As usual, Admiral Canaris had a direct hand in this highly effective bit of deception.

When Dulles was sent to Switzerland, his instructions were to find out everything possible about the anti-Hitler resistance. But he was not instructed to help any of the resistance members with their efforts to smuggle Jews or any other Nazi hostages out of Germany. Government bureaus in Washington, including the OSS, had been informed about the rescue operations—refugees who escaped occupied Europe disguised as Abwehr agents told their stories after they crossed the Atlantic.

Washington also knew about the concentration camps of eastern Europe. News of what was taking place in Auschwitz and other camps had been leaking out of Germany in spite of all attempts to keep these activities a secret. Reports had been spread by way of illegal radio broadcasts and eyewitness reports, as well as by rumor and secondhand information. An article in the March 1, 1942, edition of the *New York Times* carried the heading "Extinction Feared by Jews in Poland." The author of the piece stated that reports from "Underground Poland" predicted that "there will be no more Jews in Poland in five or six years" if "present conditions under Nazi rule continue." The reporter was Dr. Henry Shoskes; according to the news article, Dr. Shoskes was the "former general manager of the Central Cooperative Bank in Warsaw."[17]

High-ranking members of the Nazi government knew that word of the concentration camps had spread beyond Germany. Dr. Josef Goebbels, head of the Nazi propaganda ministry, wrote, "The question of Jewish persecution in Europe is being given top news priority by the English and the Americans. . . . At bottom, however, I believe both the English and the Americans are hoping that we are exterminating the Jewish riff-raff."[18]

Jewish leaders in Switzerland were determined to collect all the information possible regarding the Nazi extermination efforts that were being carried out. In July 1942, Swiss writer and reporter Benjamin Sagalowitz was attending a chess tournament in Lausanne when he received a message requesting him to return to Zurich on an urgent matter. "Benno" Sagalowitz had a reputation for being dependable and trustworthy and was also said to be acquainted with everyone in Switzerland worth knowing. The message was from someone named Isidor Koppelmann. He had no idea what the message was all about, had never heard of Isidor Koppelmann, and did not like being disturbed in the middle of the first major chess tournament in Switzerland since the beginning of the war—chess was Sagalowitz's great love, and he did not want to miss his chance to compete against some of Europe's greatest players. But after his telephone conversation with Koppelmann, who sounded annoyingly mysterious but also insisted that meeting with Sagalowitz in Zurich was a matter of life or death, he decided to take a train to Zurich the following morning. Before he left Lausanne, he persuaded the tournament organizer to reschedule his chess match.

Benno Sagalowitz and Isidor Koppelmann had their meeting in Zurich, as Koppelmann had requested. Koppelmann came right to the point. He took a note from his pocket and began to read: "I have received information from absolutely trustworthy sources that Hitler's headquarters is considering a plan to kill all remaining European Jews."[19] He went on to say that the person who gave him this information wanted Sagalowitz to deliver this information to the Western Allies, as well as to Jewish organizations in the United States—in this person's opinion, Sagalowitz was the most influential and trustworthy person for this vitally important assignment.

Sagalowitz was completely taken aback by what Koppelmann had to say. He wanted to know the name of the individual who supplied Koppelmann with this astonishing information and asked whether he would be allowed to mention his or her name when passing it along to contacts in Washington. Koppelmann said that the man absolutely refused to have his name mentioned; in fact, "he wanted your word of honor that his name will be kept out."[20] The man was not afraid for his own safety, he explained, but said there were others involved in gathering the data and also that he was protecting his own family. Sagalowitz could only agree to go along with the unknown informant's request.

Many years after the war ended, an article in the *New York Times* publicly disclosed that the intelligence regarding Hitler's decision was supplied by Eduard Schulte, "a mysterious German industrialist who also passed vital information about Hitler's war plans to the Allies." The article also stated that Schulte's "highly classified information came from Adm. Wilhelm Canaris, the chief of the Abwehr, the military intelligence branch of the high command of the German armed forces."[21] The admiral considered Schulte the person with the best chance of spreading and disseminating the data to sources outside Germany.

Admiral Canaris's report was reinforced by news that Heinrich Himmler had also mentioned Hitler's plan for exterminating all Jews throughout Europe. During the course of a dinner party, Reichsführer Himmler calmly spoke about Hitler's idea. Eduard Schulte heard about

Himmler's remarks, which confirmed what Admiral Canaris had said. He did not know if this information had already been passed along to Washington or not—if Admiral Canaris knew about Hitler's plans, it was possible that he had already sent a report out of Germany—but decided that he would send a report of his own to Washington. He traveled to Zurich, where he met with Isidor Koppelmann. Koppelmann met with Sagalowitz and read the message about Hitler's plan that Schulte had given him.

Benno Sagalowitz was not exactly sure what he should do with Schulte's information. He decided to pass it along to Gerhart Riegner, a thirty-year-old lawyer who was also a member of the World Jewish Congress, which was doing its best to protect European Jews from the Nazis, as well as to do whatever possible to oppose Hitler and his government. Although the organization was fairly small and did not have very much in the way of financial resources, it did have contacts in the United States, which was a major advantage. A few hours after his conversation with Eduard Schulte, Benno Sagalowitz telephoned Gerhart Riegner and arranged for a meeting the following day.

The two men met in Lausanne on August 1, where they talked at length—for at least five hours—about Hitler's plans and Himmler's dinner party remarks. They agreed that there was some doubt about the accuracy of the report they were discussing; even after all the information leaked to Washington and London since the beginning of the war, the stories about concentration camps and mass killings still seemed too lurid to be believed. But Riegner and Sagalowitz decided that it would be best to send the information regardless of their misgivings. Before forwarding their report to the Western Allies, they decided to have a talk with Isidor Koppelmann. Gerhart Riegner had not met Koppelmann, and Benno Sagalowitz wanted to confirm Koppelmann's information. A meeting was arranged between the three men—Riegner, Sagalowitz, and Koppelmann—on Monday, August 3.

Sagalowitz first wanted to make clear to Koppelmann that there was no question of doubting or disbelieving him. He and Gerhart Riegner just wanted to ask if he had any other information that might add to what he had already said about Hitler's intentions. Koppelmann replied that he had received information from several sources, all of whom were leading German businessmen; all indications pointed to some pending major campaign against the Jews that was already underway or would take place in the future. He referred to one of his informants as a "man I saw a few days ago." He went on to say, "Unless the Nazis are faced with some tangible, major threat, such as the arrest of hundreds of thousands of Germans living in America, they will not be impressed,"[22] meaning that objections and protests, no matter how strongly worded, would have no weight. Obviously Koppelmann had never heard of the US Constitution and Bill of Rights, which expressly forbid such arrests.

The meeting with Koppelmann satisfied both Sagalowitz and Riegner that everything they had been told about the plans for mass killings was true. Gerhart Riegner took the train back to Geneva, where he made appointments to visit both the British and American consulates. On August 8, he presented himself to the British vice consul, a Mr. Armstrong, to relay his information regarding Hitler's plans. He also asked Mr. Armstrong to inform the Foreign Office in London and to forward all information to Samuel Sidney Silverman, a member of both Parliament and the London branch of the World Jewish Congress. Mr. Armstrong said that he would carry out Riegner's requests.

Riegner had a similar conversation with the vice consul at the American legation, Howard Elting Jr. Vice Consul Elting was not inclined to believe Riegner's story, at least not at first. A tale about a Nazi plot to kill millions of Jews in concentration camps seemed too bizarre. But Riegner persisted, and the vice consul promised to send Riegner's information to the American legation in Bern. He advised Bern that Riegner would not have come to the US consulate with his story "if he did not seriously consider that the report may well contain at least an element of truth."[23] A senior official at the consulate asked Elting to write some sort of statement regarding Riegner and his report, which would be sent by telegram to Washington.

The American minister in Switzerland, Leland Harrison, did not share Howard Elting's enthusiasm for either Gerhart Riegner or his story. Harrison sent a message of his own along with Elting's report, advising Washington that Riegner's information was "war rumor inspired by fear."[24] Officials in the US State Department in Washington were more inclined to believe Leland Harrison, a trusted minister in the legation, over Gerhart Riegner, a civilian who could not even give the source of his information.

In London, Samuel Silverman took action regarding Riegner's report by mid-August. The Foreign Office had just as many doubts about the report as Leland Harrison and the US State Department; the credibility of the story was not helped when the Foreign Office did a background check on Riegner and could not find anything about him on file. But in spite of these uncertainties, Silverman sent a telegram to Rabbi Stephen Wise in New York to inform him of Riegner's story. Rabbi Wise was president of the American Jewish Congress and a founder of the World Jewish Congress, as well as a political ally of President Franklin D. Roosevelt. The message sent by Silverman, usually referred to as the "Riegner Telegram," arrived on August 29.

HAVE RECEIVED THROUGH FOREIGN OFFICE FOLLOWING MESSAGE FROM REIGNER GENEVA STOP RECEIVED ALARMING REPORT THAT IN FUHRERS HEADQUARTERS PLAN DISCUSSED AND UNDER CONSIDERATION ALL JEWS IN COUNTRIES OCCUPIED OR CONTROLLED GERMANY NUMBER 3-1/2 TO 4 MILLION SHOULD AFTER DEPORTATION AND CONCENTRATION IN EAST AT ONE BLOW EXTERMINATED TO RELIEVE ONCE FOR ALL JEWISH QUESTION IN EUROPE STOP ACTION REPORTED PLANNED FOR AUTUMN METHODS UNDER DISCUSSION INCLUDING PRUSSIC ACID STOP WE TRANSMIT ALL INFORMATION WITH ALL NECESSARY RESERVATION AS EXACTITUDE CANNOT BE CONFIRMED STOP INFORMANT STATED TO HAVE CLOSE CONNEXIONS WITH HIGHEST GERMAN AUTHORITIES AND HIS REPORTS GENERALLY RELIABLE STOP INFORM AND CONSULT NEW YORK STOP FOREIGN OFFICE [H]AS NO INFORMATION BEARING ON OR CONFIRMING STORY

SAMUEL SILVERMAN[25]

When he received this message, Rabbi Wise spoke with members of the Jewish community for several days before forwarding the telegram to Undersecretary of State Sumner Welles in Washington. The rabbi hoped that Undersecretary Welles would personally bring it to President Roosevelt's attention—besides having the authority to present the document, Welles was also a personal friend of the president. Instead, State Department officials decided that nothing should be done about it until its contents were confirmed. The phrases "exactitude cannot be confirmed" and "Foreign Office has no information bearing on or confirming story" did not inspire much confidence in the document or its source. In fact, no one in the State Department knew anything about the source of the information mentioned; also, there was no confirmation of the number of Jews being sent to eastern Europe or how many were being killed. There had been some reports that Jews were being deported from their homes but no official mention of mass executions. The very tone of the message left the State Department in doubt of its accuracy. On September 3, Undersecretary Welles telephoned Rabbi Wise and asked him not to make the telegram public until its contents could be verified. The rabbi agreed to cooperate with Welles and the State Department.

A week later, on September 10, Rabbi Wise went to Washington to discuss his growing anxiety concerning the Nazi extermination plan. He met with Vice President Henry Wallace and members of the US State Department to tell them about the details of the Riegner Telegram. During his visit to Washington, the rabbi did his best to keep as many officials as possible informed of the situation in eastern Europe, even though the information had still not been verified and he was speaking as a private citizen without any authority to mention such matters. But even though his comments were not authorized, he did manage to attract some attention. The assistant solicitor general, Oscar Cox, told the rabbi that his report might lead to the formation of a War Crimes Commission after the war. Also presidential advisor Myron Taylor contacted the Vatican to ask for papal support and also for suggestions regarding appropriate action from the Holy See that might persuade the Nazis to curtail their atrocities.

Although Rabbi Wise's activities were conducted with every good intention, there was no practical way to stop the Hitler regime from carrying out its campaign of mass killings. The White House issued a news release on October 7 promising that all criminals would be brought to justice at the end of the war. President Roosevelt stated, "I now declare it to be the intention of this Government that the successful close of the war shall include provision for the surrender to the United Nations of war criminals."[26] The Vatican replied that it had heard unconfirmed reports of the activities of Nazi death squads in occupied countries but could offer no realistic suggestions for how to put an end to them; the only effective way to stop Nazi atrocities would be the military defeat of Nazi Germany.

When Gerhart Riegner sent his telegram, and when Stephen Wise went to Washington, both hoped for more than press releases and promises of justice after the war ended. Riegner, Wise, and Eduard Schulte expected a lot more from President Roosevelt and were disappointed that he could not do more to rescue Jews and other political and racial outcasts. But President Roosevelt had already accomplished a lot more than either Rabbi Wise or Gerhart Riegner or Eduard Schulte realized.

Nearly four hundred thousand Jews managed to get out of Germany, about three-quarters of the country's Jewish population, before the war began. About one-quarter of these, approximately 105,000, were allowed to enter the United States. The quota for German Jewish immigration was 25,957, which means that four times as many actually entered the country than the immigration quota allowed. One of the last groups of Jewish refugees to arrive in the United States landed in New York on December 26, 1941, aboard the Portuguese steamer *Serpa Pinto*. The ship carried 178 passengers, most of whom had Jewish surnames; the majority of the exiles were from France, Poland, Czechoslovakia, and Germany. Everyone on board knew very well that they were lucky to be entering the United States. Most of their friends and relatives were still in occupied Europe, where they faced a very harsh future at the hands of the Nazis.[27]

After the Wehrmacht overran France and the Low Countries in the spring of 1940, the Jewish populations there, along with any other individuals found objectionable by the Nazis, were trapped. Neither

Franklin D. Roosevelt, Winston Churchill, nor anyone other member of the Western Allies could do much to rescue them. The president allowed many more refugees to enter the United States than the quota system allowed, but some individuals, including Riegner and Schulte, thought that this was not good enough and that he should have done more. An American writer had this to say about the United States and American efforts to rescue Jewish refugees in occupied territory: "The Nazis were the murderers, but we were the all too passive accomplices."[28]

Critics have complained that the Allies should have done something decisive, or at least more aggressive, to stop the mass executions, including carrying out bombing raids against Auschwitz and other death camps. This seemingly simple solution was not very realistic, however. The British Royal Air Force was trained to carry out a campaign of night area bombing; British bombers would have destroyed not only Auschwitz but also much of the surrounding area. Area bombing would have wrecked part of the camp and its facilities but would also have killed many of the prisoners. The US Eighth Air Force had the ability to hit Auschwitz, and its crews were trained to bomb targets in daylight, but it was not able to carry out attacks in Poland during 1942 and 1943; fighter escorts did not have the range to cover American bombers as far as the German-Polish border. The Schweinfurt/Regensburg mission of August 1943—targeting the ball bearing works at Schweinfurt and the Messerschmitt factory at Regensburg—resulted in unacceptable losses—60 bombers out of 147 did not return to base, a loss ratio of 40 percent[29]—and neither target was nearly as far from the American bases in England as Auschwitz. Also German construction crews had a talent for repairing badly damaged facilities with incredible speed. Builders would have rebuilt Auschwitz within a very short period and had the camp operating again at full capacity. Bombing the death camps was not a practical solution for ending the mass executions.

President Roosevelt did not see any realistic way of ending the Nazi extermination campaign and destroying places like Auschwitz beyond winning the war. As far as the president was concerned, the primary goal of the Allied powers was still the military defeat of German forces— destroy the German army, overthrow Adolf Hitler and his government, and occupy Germany and all German-occupied territory. War criminals would be put on trial after the fighting was over. There was no alternative, at least not in his view: winning the war had top priority over war tribunals or rescue operations or anything else. As far as the president was concerned, any activities that did not directly contribute to the defeat of Germany on the battlefield were nothing but a distraction and a waste of time.

Also, the Nazis were changing their methods for carrying out the killings. German authorities, realizing that transporting Jews and political prisoners to camps in Poland was badly straining their already overtaxed rail system, were making other arrangements for mass executions. In March 1942, a Swiss attorney sarcastically asked Ulrich von Hassell why the Nazis did not just murder their victims at home, instead of wasting time and expense by shipping them to the East. Some German official must have had the same idea. In 1943, an increasing number of Jews and other prisoners were being executed in Germany. Allen Welsh Dulles reported that fifteen thousand Jews were arrested between January 26 and March 2, 1943, but were not sent to Auschwitz.[30] "They were brought to four centers including the Bohemian church and two of the main Gestapo prisons" in Berlin, "where the shooting of several hundred adults took place." It looked as though this method of committing the mass killings on a local basis, using local SS officers, would now be the rule throughout Germany and in German-occupied countries. Allen Dulles ended his telegram by concluding, "The new policy is to kill the Jews on the spot rather than deporting them to Poland for killing there."[31]

Riegner's telegram went straight from OSS headquarters to President Roosevelt's desk. But despite having been advised that the killings were now being done "on the spot" as well as at Auschwitz, the president could still do nothing to stop them. After France surrendered in June 1940, the continent of Europe became a vast prison for everyone trapped in German-occupied countries. Any attempt to rescue victims of Hitler and his government—Jews, political prisoners, or anyone else—became impossible for anyone outside the Third Reich. Franklin Roosevelt issued a condemnation of Nazi war crimes on December 8, 1942, which did receive news coverage in the United States. With authorization from the State Department, Stephen Wise released the contents of the Riegner Telegram in November 1942, which resulted in "widespread public outrage." In December, at least a dozen governments, including the United States and Great Britain, issued a "Declaration on Atrocities"; the declaration did not mention any plans for Allied rescue missions.[32] Adolf Hitler ignored all the statements and declarations. Ending the Nazi atrocities would take a lot more than just angry words. For all the publicity it created concerning Nazi war crimes, the Riegner Telegram did not have any actual impact on Hitler's campaign of mass murder.

Adm. Wilhelm Canaris accomplished something that President Franklin D. Roosevelt, Prime Minister Winston Churchill, and Gerhart Riegner were never able to achieve. He had both the power as head of the Abwehr and the opportunity to act against Hitler and his mass executions, and he took full advantage of both to intervene on behalf of Jews and other unfortunates. After the fall of France, hundreds of Jews escaped Nazi-occupied territory, and almost certain death, because of Admiral Canaris's intervention. In the spring of 1941, he was directly responsible for smuggling five hundred Jews out of the Netherlands, disguised as Abwehr agents, in Operation Aguilar. Operation 7 allowed more Jews to escape, even though the success of the operation brought suspicion down on the anti-Hitler opposition and led to the arrest of two of its members. Admiral Canaris continued to help Jews and other "undesirables" until his nervous temperament got the better of him, but he would continue to undermine the Nazi regime in other ways. Eduard Schulte, Stephen Wise, and Gerhart Riegner all did their best to rescue Jews from the Nazi Third Reich, but Adm. Wilhelm Canaris actually succeeded.

CHAPTER TEN

An Unexpected Ally

ADM. WILHELM CANARIS REGRETTED THAT HIS HEALTH PREVENTED him from organizing another rescue mission along the lines of Operation Aguilar or even Operation 7, but he was not about to give up his fight to undermine the Nazis or to overthrow Adolf Hitler. Although he did not agree with President Franklin D. Roosevelt's notion that the only way to end Nazi atrocities was to overwhelm the German army on the battlefield, he realized that bringing about Adolf Hitler's downfall would end the war along with the mass killings. The admiral also realized that there were more ways to bring Hitler down than defeating him on the battlefield.

The admiral kept in touch with the Allies through Hans Bernd Gisevius. Hans Gisevius had developed a close working relationship with Allen Dulles by this time; the two had frequent meetings in Bern and Zurich. During his first twelve months in Switzerland, Dulles learned a great deal about the German underground and its secrets, including the activities of Admiral Canaris. Most of this information stemmed from his conversations with Gisevius. He assigned a code name, Breakers, to the anti-Nazi movement, and also assigned code names and numbers to its members. Admiral Canaris was 649; Hans Gisevius was 512; Eduard Schulte was 643. Otto John was given a code name: Luke.

Dulles, at the beginning of January 1944—after settling into his job and his surroundings, and as the result of a good many meetings with Hans Gisevius and his successor, Eduard Waetjen—sent a telegram to Office of Strategic Services (OSS) headquarters in Washington, DC.

Hans Bernd Gisevius was an ally of Admiral Canaris in the anti-Nazi movement. This photo was taken after the war, during the Nuremberg Trials. *Source:* National Archives.

The purpose of the telegram was to advise Washington of what he had learned about the resistance during the past several months. "The German oppositional group called Breakers is composed of various intellectuals from certain military and Government circles," he began. "They have loose organization among themselves." He went on to report, "Breakers maintain their foreign contacts and communications through 649 organization," meaning the Abwehr, "and both our 512 [Gisevius] and Gorter [Waetjen] act as intermediaries here in Bern."[1]

Allen Dulles and Eduard Schulte first made contact in May 1943. A short time after their meeting, Dulles asked Schulte to write a report on conditions inside Nazi Germany, as well as on his recommendations concerning the rebuilding of Germany after the war. Dulles was impressed by what Schulte had to say in his statement, which was translated and sent off to Washington. Afterward, Dulles sent a telegram of his own to Washington, complimenting Schulte and his activities: "643 is believed to be a most valuable source," he said. "He is a prominent businessman who, we feel, can be depended upon to cooperate with us after G's [Germany's] collapse."[2]

Dulles kept in constant touch with the opposition, especially Hans Gisevius. During one of their earliest meetings, Gisevius stressed that the Allies should encourage the German resistance. "He said that it is very important that encouragement be offered to the effect that the negotiations with the United Nations for a durable peace could be instituted if the Nazi leaders were eliminated by the group resisting them," Dulles commented to Washington.[3] Gisevius and his fellow conspirators were disappointed that Washington would not give them any sort of backing or support. Another resistance member, Adam von Trott zu Solz, was so disappointed that he complained to Dulles about the Western Allies' lack of interest in the anti-Hitler movement. He protested that "the Anglo-Saxon countries are filled with bourgeois prejudice and pharisaic theorizing" and also found fault with the point of view "that Germany must suffer military defeat" instead of being transformed by revolution. The protest was blunt and outspoken. Although it did not mention Jews or political prisoners specifically, von Trott's criticism did argue that the Germans were "themselves an oppressed people [living] in an occupied country."[4] But as persuasive as it might have been, von Trott's argument was ignored in both London and Washington.

Dulles did not ignore von Trott's letter (he always referred to von Trott as "Trott"), but he did recommend that Washington completely disregard it, along with all of its comments. He did send "Trott's" message along to OSS headquarters, but he also added his own opinion regarding what von Trott had to say. Dulles began by advising Washington that he was sending the letter "solely because it may be of interest in connection with the program of psychological warfare." As far as he was concerned, there was no "serious organization" among the anti-Nazi resistance; as such, it should not expect "any encouragement from us or any dealing with us." In his opinion, the resistance was not worth any support or encouragement; the OSS would just be wasting its time and resources by helping the anti-Nazi conspiracy.[5]

A few weeks later, Allen Dulles sent another cable on the subject of the resistance to OSS headquarters. This time, he suggested that the "German sources"—Admiral Canaris and the other members of the German conspiracy—should be informed that the Western Allies did not want Adolf Hitler overthrown and replaced by another supreme ruler; they were in favor of leaving Hitler in power for a very practical reason.

At the end of January 1943, the entire German Sixth Army, all twenty-two of its divisions, surrendered to Soviet forces at Stalingrad, Germany's greatest disaster of the war to date. Hitler's mismanagement of the army, his refusal to allow it to retreat or break out of the city, is given as one of the main reasons for the German defeat. Dulles's recommended response to any inquiries from the anti-Hitler resistance was that Hitler should be allowed to remain in power: "Hitler was proving to be a great asset to us, and . . . there was not anything we could think of which would be more contributive to our military success than his keeping supreme command of the German armed forces." Keeping Hitler as Germany's military commander would probably lead to more Stalingrads and a quicker military defeat of Germany.[6]

On the other hand, Allen Dulles was in favor of Hitler's removal from political power—including by assassination. "I am still of the opinion that if Hitler were to disappear, the end of Germany would begin," he stated in the same telegram, "and for that reason his disappearance is favored my me." But in spite of his personal opinion that Hitler should be eliminated, his outlook regarding the resistance and its ambitions was the same as President Roosevelt's: nothing short of the complete military defeat of Nazi Germany would be acceptable. If the resistance did manage to assassinate Hitler, this would certainly be welcome. But Dulles did not think the opposition had the organization to accomplish anything as ambitious as this. Admiral Canaris and the other members of the anti-Nazi movement would be left on their own. He did not want to offer them any sort of encouragement.[7]

If the Allies had decided to come to the assistance of the anti-Hitler resistance, a special department might have been created for the support of the underground movement. Any such section would have been assigned a department head, along with a staff to run it, and might have been attached to the Special Operations Executive (SOE). The SOE was a British unit that had been specially formed to train and work with underground groups in German-occupied territory. This organization did an excellent job of keeping in touch with units of the French resistance, as well as helping them to carry out their underground war against German forces in occupied France. The clandestine underground war that was carried out by the French resistance has been described as a series of "stabbing attacks" against the enemy, designed to "weaken him strategically" as well as to confuse and demoralize him. It was very effective, especially in gathering information and carrying out sabotage operations against the Germans in the run-up to D-Day.[8]

Active backing of the German resistance would certainly have made the anti-Nazi movement more effective in its own war against Hitler, including in the rescue of Jews, Polish nationals, and political prisoners. Although Allen Dulles complained that the anti-Hitler resistance was not very well organized, it was as organized as the French resistance fighters, known as the *Maquis*, a very loosely affiliated band of guerillas who fought the Germans throughout the war. The SOE supplied these groups with weapons, explosives, and radio sets. Support from the Allies would certainly have helped the anti-Nazi resistance to carry out any number of planned tasks, from planting false information to assassinating Adolf Hitler to carrying out rescue efforts.

Dulles's refusal to have anything to do with the German resistance, as well as its efforts to rescue Jews and other prisoners, has been the subject of a great deal of speculation. "Perhaps he feared that the flight of new refugees to Switzerland would interfere with his espionage activities," was one opinion.[9] He avoided helping anyone escape Nazi Germany or any German-occupied country, including Poles like Madame Szymańska, well-connected people who might have been able to supply the OSS with useful details concerning the German war effort. Admiral Canaris's interest in rescuing Jews and political dissidents from the Nazis was based upon both moral and political grounds. Operation 7, Operation Aguilar, and his saving of Madame Szymańska were opportunities for him to undo at least some of the evil that the Nazis had produced and also to undermine Hitler and his government. Dulles had no desire to rescue Jews or any other refugees. Because ending Nazi atrocities would not directly help the war effort, neither Washington nor London had anything but a passing interest in any rescue activities.

* * *

The most publicized event of January 1943 was the Casablanca conference of January 14 through 24. The meeting was covered by news media throughout the world, including in Germany. President Franklin D. Roosevelt, Prime Minister Winston Churchill, and French generals Charles de Gaulle and Henri Giraud were the major participants at the conference. Topics discussed at length during the ten days included the anticipated D-Day invasion of western Europe, the bombing campaign against Germany and German-occupied countries, the French political situation in North Africa, and Allied military operations in Italy and the Mediterranean. But the best remembered, as well as the most controversial, decision made at Casablanca was announced by President Roosevelt at a news conference: the Allies would accept nothing short of unconditional surrender from Germany, Italy, or Japan.

"Unconditional surrender" was also the most disputed item introduced at Casablanca. Some agreed that leaving the Axis powers no alternative but to surrender outright, with no terms or concessions available, was the only feasible way to deal with the enemy. "To stop short of total military victory, to allow Germany any doubt of its total defeat," Dulles wrote, "would have been unthinkable at this point."[10] A British writer had this to say: "It was necessary for the Nazi regime and/or the German generals to surrender unconditionally in order to bring home to the German people that they had lost the War themselves."[11]

Not everyone shared this view on unconditional surrender. After the war, Foreign Secretary Ernest Bevin told the House of Commons, "It left us with a Germany without law, without a constitution, without a single person with whom we could deal."[12] Dulles admitted that the Nazis "were able to use unconditional surrender to prolong a totally hopeless war for many months."[13] A few weeks after the Casablanca conference, Propaganda Minister Josef Goebbels told a rally that the unconditional surrender policy meant that Germany was now committed to total war, which helped to unite the country. "Nazi and non-Nazi alike both lost some illusions and drew a little closer together," was one comment.[14] A woman living in Germany at the time agreed. "There's no alternative," she said. "We've got to fight to the bitter end."[15]

The unconditional surrender proclamation certainly did not help to shorten the war. Both the Allies and the anti-Hitler opposition would have been much better off if President Roosevelt had made a more diplomatic statement at Casablanca. Soviet Premier Joseph Stalin did not endorse unconditional surrender. In fact, he took just the opposite stand—Stalin made a radio broadcast declaring that he was not fighting the German people or the German nation; his enemies were "the Hitlerites."[16] President Roosevelt would have helped the Allied cause, as well as the anti-Hitler resistance and all of its intentions, much more if he had made a similar statement at Casablanca—something to the effect that he had no intention of destroying either Germany or the German population, only Adolf Hitler and his government. Such a statement coming from the president of the United States would have sent a positive message to Germany. But the president decided to stand by the unconditional surrender proclamation.

Admiral Canaris immediately recognized the significance of unconditional surrender. He knew that the no German general would accept this declaration and was extremely annoyed and disappointed by what he referred to as "the other side" for insisting upon it. After Stalingrad, the anti-Hitler movement held some hope that overthrowing the Nazi government might now be feasible, or at least more feasible than before. But the unconditional surrender announcement put an end to that possibility, at least in Admiral Canaris's view. "I believe that the other side have now disarmed us of the last weapon with which we could have ended it," he told his friend Gen. Erwin von Lahousen. "Unconditional surrender, no, our generals will not swallow that. Now I cannot see any solution."[17]

As far as Admiral Canaris was concerned, the unconditional surrender decision had no good points. Because he was so upset by it, the admiral decided that he must oppose it. Making contact with American delegates seemed to be the most effective way of accomplishing this. The British would not talk to him; they had made clear that they had no intention of making contact with the admiral or any member of the anti-Nazi movement. Through a friend who worked for the German War Office in Istanbul, Admiral Canaris managed to arrange a meeting with the US naval attaché in the same city, Cdr. George H. Earle, to discuss the issue.

George Howard Earle III had an extremely varied and colorful career. Born into a wealthy family, he was a graduate of Harvard University. After enlisting in the army in 1916, he was assigned to Gen. John "Black Jack" Pershing's troops during their hunt for Pancho Villa in Mexico that same year. During World War I, he transferred to the US Navy, where he commanded a submarine chaser; by the time the war ended, Commander Earle had been awarded the Navy Cross. After the war, he entered politics and was elected governor of Pennsylvania. Governor Earle supported Franklin D. Roosevelt's presidency in the 1930s, and the two became friends. The president appointed the former governor assistant naval attaché to Turkey in 1943; Earle's orders were to report to the president personally with any news from Turkey, not to go through the usual diplomatic channels. When Admiral Canaris began circulating word that he was looking to make contact with Americans with high-level connections, George H. Earle was suggested. Commander Earle had the necessary rank and authority to negotiate with the head of the Abwehr and also the ability to make contact with the president of the United States. An appointment was made for Admiral Canaris to meet the assistant US naval attaché at Commander Earle's hotel.

Actually, the meeting between the two was fairly casual and informal. One morning, Admiral Canaris simply turned up at Commander Earle's suite at the Park Hotel in Istanbul. He wore civilian clothes, not wanting to call attention to himself by wearing a German naval uniform, and introduced himself as "Admiral Wilhelm Canaris, chief of the Abwehr." The German admiral and the American lieutenant commander talked about the Casablanca conference, especially the unconditional surrender decision. "This means war to the end," the admiral said, "the destruction of Germany as a military power, and the emergence of Russia as the dominating force in Europe." The admiral then came to his main point and asked the question that had brought him to Istanbul: "Do you think

President Roosevelt really means 'unconditional surrender,'" he asked, and hinted at the possibility of shortening the war by a negotiated peace. "Perhaps you will take the matter up with your president?"[18]

George Earle did what Canaris asked and sent the admiral's suggestion off to President Roosevelt. The proposal was sent to Washington via the next diplomatic pouch to leave Istanbul. But President Roosevelt had no interest in rescinding the unconditional surrender provision and refused even to consider any sort of peace agreement that did not include Soviet Russia. Also, he still had no intention of making any sort of arrangement with Admiral Canaris or any other member of the German resistance.

Admiral Canaris was disappointed by the rejection but far from discouraged. As a matter of fact, the negative reply actually convinced him to expand his efforts to make contact with both British and American representatives in neutral countries—Switzerland, Sweden, and Spain. But he realized that he still had to be very careful in any dealings he might have with foreign emissaries, even in neutral countries. He was well aware that both the Schutzstaffel (SS) and the Sicherheitsdienst (SD) were still watching him and that one false move could prove fatal. Fortunately for him, he was still on friendly terms with Francisco Franco, so friendly, in fact, that Franco offered to mediate with any British and American delegates on the admiral's behalf. He also allowed a meeting between Admiral Canaris and the leaders of both British and American intelligence services to take place in a Spanish city. In the middle of 1943, a secret conference was arranged between Admiral Canaris, the head of the Abwehr; Gen. William J. Donovan, head of the OSS; and Gen. Stewart Menzies, chief of the British Secret Intelligence Service, in the town of Santander, on the northern coast of Spain.

At the meeting, Admiral Canaris told General Menzies and General Donovan all about his proposal, which contained the same three basic components as the plan he had discussed with George Earle: a cease-fire with the Western Allies, a continuation of the war against Soviet Russia, and the ending of all Nazi war crimes. Both Menzies and Donovan listened to what Admiral Canaris had to say and seemed greatly impressed with his ideas. An Abwehr officer, a member of the admiral's staff, summed up the opinion of everyone who attended the meeting. "Donovan, his British colleague, and C[anaris] reached agreement on the basis of C's proposal," he recalled. "It was my most exciting experience as a member of C's staff."[19]

When informed of the meeting at Santander, President Roosevelt did not share the excitement. He was as determined as ever to avoid all contact with Admiral Canaris, along with anyone associated with the anti-Nazi movement, and especially did not want anything to do with a separate peace treaty that would exclude Soviet Russia. The president feared that if any rumors of separate peace talks with Germany reached the pathologically suspicious Joseph Stalin, even if completely unsubstantiated, they might persuade Stalin to begin his own negotiations with Hitler without consulting either himself or Prime Minister Churchill. The president's fears were not without foundation—Russia had signed a separate peace during World War I. In March 1918, the new Bolshevik government made a treaty with Germany that ended Russia's participation in the conflict. The treaty allowed Germany to transfer hundreds of thousands of troops from Russia to the western front.

President Roosevelt was especially unhappy with General Donovan for meeting with Admiral Canaris in the first place, which violated all the rules of protocol. As far as he was concerned, General Donovan had seriously overstepped his authority by agreeing to talk to *any* German officer, let alone the chief of Hitler's military intelligence service. The president wanted to make his position perfectly clear to everyone, including the head of the OSS: the only acceptable conclusion to the fighting would come when German leaders accepted unconditional surrender, which would only take place when all German forces had been destroyed by the Allied powers—which included the Soviet Union.

Admiral Canaris never quite understood that the West would not accept any agreement that did not include Soviet Russia and was now firmly committed to the policy of unconditional surrender. But after the Santander meeting, he finally realized that the West would not be persuaded to accept any offer or proposal from the anti-Hitler movement, no matter how convincing or persuasive. This did not stop the admiral from carrying on with his campaign to overthrow Hitler and undermine his war effort, as well as to end all Nazi atrocities.

* * *

In July 1943, the anti-Nazi resistance received some wonderfully encouraging news—and from a totally unexpected source. Allied forces landed on the beaches of Sicily on July 9, which many senior officers on both sides, Allied and German, saw as an unmistakable sign that the collapse of Benito Mussolini and his Fascist regime could not be very far off. But even the most optimistic of Allied planners could not have guessed just how quickly Mussolini's fall from power would follow the Sicilian landings. On July 25, just over two weeks later, he was removed from power, replaced by Marshal Pietro Badoglio, and placed under arrest. With the change in regime also came a change in allegiance—the new Italian government formally changed sides early in September, abandoning the Tripartite Pact between Italy, Germany, and Japan and joining the Allies. There would still be a great deal of fighting in both Italy and Sicily during the coming months, but Mussolini and his Fascist regime had been overthrown.

This was the best news the anti-Hitler movement had heard in some time. "On the day Mussolini fell my brother and I were alone in the house in the evening," Otto John would remember after the war. "We heard the news on the B.B.C. My brother jumped up and threw his arms around me and said that it would be ludicrous if we could not do what the Italians had apparently succeeded in doing quite easily." A short time later, a friend dropped in with a bottle of champagne so that everyone could drink a toast to Marshal Badoglio.[20]

Admiral Canaris was in Venice when he heard the news. As a matter of fact, he was in a meeting with the head of Italian intelligence, Gen. Cesare Amé, to discuss Italy's role in the war. When word of Mussolini's overthrow was received, the admiral issued a communiqué to Berlin stating that Italy would continue to fight alongside Germany in spite of the change in regime, but he did so only to mislead Hitler. During a break in the proceedings, he took General Amé aside and said what he was really thinking. "Congratulations on your July 25," he told the general. "We could use one, too. Germany's one dream is to get rid of Hitler."[21] General Amé was completely taken aback by the admiral's declaration—he even pretended not to understand what the admiral had said at first—but was very glad to have a new and unexpected friend and ally, especially one with so much authority in Berlin.

Mussolini was not nearly as harsh as Hitler in his treatment of Jews, outcasts, and political outsiders. His government "did not sanction physical abuse of Jewish citizens, did not execute anyone in the internment camps established for Jews in southern Italy, and did not begin to send Jews to Nazi concentration camps until the German occupation in 1943."[22] There was no Italian equivalent of Auschwitz or Dachau. But Mussolini was a Fascist and an ally of Hitler; overthrowing Mussolini seemed to bring Germany one step closer to "getting rid of Hitler" and everything he stood for, including Auschwitz and Dachau. Admiral Canaris welcomed Mussolini's demise for this reason as much as for the fact that it served as an encouragement for the anti-Hitler movement.

But Nazi Germany was not Fascist Italy, and removing Adolf Hitler from power would present a far different set of problems than those faced in ousting Mussolini.

* * *

In the days and weeks after the disaster at Stalingrad, the public's opinion of Adolf Hitler began to deteriorate. Stalingrad finally made the German population realize that their country had no hope of winning the war and also forced senior military officers, as well as an increasing number of Nazi officials, to acknowledge the fact that "a great and terrible Nazi dream was destroyed."[23] And the blame for this loss was directed at the leader of the Nazi government, Adolf Hitler.

Evidence of this increasing anti-Hitler feeling was evident throughout the Third Reich. On April 20, everyone in Germany was ordered to put out flags in honor of Adolf Hitler's birthday, his fifty-fourth. The public obeyed the order, but many people only displayed flags to avoid getting in trouble with the Nazi authorities. "Never before has this been done with so little enthusiasm," Ulrich von Hassell noted.[24] When Hitler did not make a speech on January 30 to commemorate the tenth anniversary of his swearing in as chancellor in 1933, the omission did not go unnoticed. Public lack of confidence in Hitler did not go unnoticed either and was not being kept a secret, in spite of the Gestapo. Von Hassell was told a story about how the "Heil Hitler" greeting had fallen into disrepute. "It seems that one never says 'Heil Hitler' in the flak [antiaircraft] batteries," he said, "but as a joke someone did so recently to a non-commissioned officer. He replied, 'Don't ever let me hear that stinking greeting.'"[25]

The possibility of an Allied invasion of France had also become a regular topic of conversation. Most people were of the opinion that an invasion would definitely take place, in spite of all Nazi propaganda claims to the contrary, and that it would be successful. The only question on everyone's mind was when and where it would happen. Dwindling confidence in Germany's ability to win the war was also becoming evident in other countries. Otto John was visiting Lisbon to meet with a British representative during the summer of 1943; their topic of discussion was the anti-Nazi resistance. While they were talking, a group of British fighters flew overhead on their way to North Africa. "Did you see that?" the man asked. "The Portuguese are now allowing us to fly freely over their country because they are convinced that we are winning the war."[26]

He went on to give his explanation for why the Allies were paying so little attention to the anti-Nazi movement. "The German opposition must soon prove itself by doing something if it wishes to get a hearing in London," he said. The opposition *had* been "doing something," even though Otto John's British acquaintance did not know about it. Specifically, it had saved several hundred Jews from Nazi concentration camps in Operation Aguilar and in Operation 7 alone. The anti-Hitler movement had also been responsible for rescuing political prisoners and Polish nationalists from the death camps. Apparently Otto John's British contact had not been informed of these activities.[27]

It is surprising that the anti-Hitler underground's activities had not been reported to London, or at least had not reached Otto John's connection in the British government. Reports of the Nazi regime's campaign in Poland against Jews and other racially and politically unacceptable individuals were reaching both Britain and the United States and were also spreading throughout Germany. Ulrich von Hassell's friend Max Frauendorfer kept sending his revealing accounts of Nazi activities from Poland: "The SS in Poland carries on most shamefully," he said. "Countless Jews have been gassed in specially built chambers, at least 100,000." Von Hassell went on to report, "But the Polish intelligentsia, too, is being decimated, just as before."[28] Except for the occasional eyewitness report, such as Max Frauendorfer's, these reports from Poland were filtering into the country mainly through illegal radio sets. These accounts were then spread by word of mouth to sympathetic friends and family members. Although some people still refused to believe the reports, most people were shocked and sickened by the news of the death camps. Killing thousands of Jews and Poles was not only morally repugnant, this line of thinking went, but was also making the world at large think of Germany as a country of murderers and executioners. "It is Hitler's achievement that the German has become the most loathed animal in the whole world," Ulrich von Hassell reflected. Millions of others, including Adm. Wilhelm Canaris, shared his opinion.[29]

But even though Adolf Hitler was becoming increasingly unpopular, there was not very much that could be done to end his regime. It may have been possible to overthrow an unpopular dictator in Fascist Italy, but the situation in Nazi Germany was completely different. The Gestapo was everywhere, looking for any sign of treason or disloyalty. The state was brutally harsh with anyone caught taking part in anti-Nazi activities. In February 1943, Germany found out just how harsh the Nazi regime could be.

Members of an anti-Hitler movement at the University of Munich, who called themselves the White Rose, had been writing "Down with Hitler" on walls and passing out anti-Nazi leaflets for some time. The White Rose members were mainly students at the university; their leaflets were highly critical of both Hitler and the Nazis. One of them spoke out against the persecution of the Jews: "Since the conquest of Poland 300,000 Jews have been murdered, a crime against human dignity. . . . Germans encourage fascist criminals if no chord within them cries out at the sight of such deeds. An end in terror is preferable to terror without end."[30] Two leaders of the White Rose, siblings Hans and Sophie

Scholl, were caught in the act of distributing leaflets and reported to the Gestapo. After a brutal interrogation, which left Sophie with a broken leg, both she and her brother Hans were executed by guillotine.

It did not take long for news of the anti-Hitler movement, including the activities of the White Rose, to spread beyond Munich. Even the *New York Times* featured a story with the headline "Signs of Strain Seen in German Populace."[31] Even though many Germans agreed with the Scholls, no one wanted to support them if it meant being executed by the Gestapo. Heinrich Himmler requested a stay of execution, but his communiqué arrived several hours too late. The Gestapo was very happy that Reichsführer Himmler did not get his request, as the execution of the Scholls provided a highly effective object lesson for the German public: oppose the Nazi regime and face almost certain execution.

Besides attempting to stop, or at least postpone, the execution of Hans and Sophie Scholl, Heinrich Himmler had also been covering up Admiral Canaris's anti-Nazi activities for quite some time, at least since Operation 7. Franz Xaver Sonderegger, the Gestapo agent responsible for the arrest of Hans von Dohnanyi, had not lost interest in the admiral or his activities. He forwarded a detailed report to Reichsführer Himmler accusing the admiral of not only being the guiding force behind Operation 7 but also heading a conspiracy against Adolf Hitler and the entire National Socialist government. As soon as Himmler read Sonderegger's report, he realized that he was holding enough evidence against the admiral to hang him. But instead of ordering Admiral Canaris's arrest, as Sonderegger expected, Himmler sent the file back to Sonderegger with a perplexing handwritten note on the cover: "Kindly leave Canaris alone."[32] He was letting the entire matter drop.

Franz Sonderegger was told by several acquaintances that this was not the first time Himmler had blocked an investigation concerning the admiral—he had let Admiral Canaris off the hook on at least three previous occasions. In 1942, when an Abwehr officer named Nickolaus von Halem was arrested for taking part in an assassination attempt against Hitler, von Halem's Gestapo interrogators came to the conclusion that Admiral Canaris was the instigator of the plot. An investigation was opened to determine exactly what role the admiral had played in the assassination conspiracy. As soon as he found out about it, Reichs-führer Himmler immediately ordered the investigation stopped and also instructed the Gestapo to delete any and all references to Admiral Canaris in any of their reports. A second incident involved another Abwehr agent, Mumm von Schwarzen, who was also implicated in an attempt on Hitler's life. Himmler would not even consider allowing any sort of investigation into any Abwehr connections with the conspiracy—he stopped the inquiry before it could even get started. Himmler also put an end to a third inquiry. A court official by the name of Strassmann had organized a small anti-Nazi group; the group was discovered by the Gestapo, and Herr Strassmann was arrested. Hans von Dohnanyi—and by implication Admiral Canaris—was alleged to be a member of the organization. Once again, Reichsführer Himmler intervened; he refused to allow any sort of inquiry.

Walter Schellenberg, the SD's chief of foreign intelligence, had the same reaction from Himmler when he presented his own file of information on Admiral Canaris's subversive activities—"reports about his various betrayals," as Schellenberg himself put it. Himmler was not interested in Schellenberg's evidence any more than he had been in Franz Sonderegger's. "Leave the dossier with me," he said. "I will bring it to Hitler's attention when the right opportunity arises." The right opportunity never presented itself, or at least that is what Himmler led Schellenberg to believe. It eventually became evident that the *Reichsführer* never had any intention of showing the Canaris file to Hitler or anyone else.[33]

Himmler's refusal to act against Admiral Canaris startled both Franz Sonderegger and Walter Schellenberg. Their only feasible conclusion was that the admiral must have some sort of damning evidence of his own against Himmler. "I am certain that at some time or other Canaris must have got to know something incriminating against Himmler," Schellenberg later wrote.[34] No one, including Schellenberg, had any idea what sort of evidence that might be.

One suggestion was that the admiral had proof of Himmler's own plot to overthrow Adolf Hitler and replace him as head of state—to make himself Führer. This scheme dates from the Wehrmacht's failed offensive at Stalingrad, where about 147,000 German soldiers died and another 90,000 were taken prisoner. Himmler was realistic enough to see what Stalingrad, along with the defeats in North Africa by British and American troops, meant for Germany. He also feared that German troops would be chased right out of France after the anticipated invasion of northern France in the not very distant future. As far as Himmler was concerned, the only practical way of rescuing Germany from her predicament was to remove Adolf Hitler as head of the government. After the war, Dulles wrote that Himmler "had evinced an interest in conspiring against Hitler" as early as 1943—Dulles read reports of Himmler's attitude toward Adolf Hitler in captured German files marked "Top Secret."[35]

Stalingrad and North Africa made Himmler realize that Germany had no realistic chance of winning the war, which coincided with Admiral Canaris's point of view: both thought that Hitler was to blame for the country's impending military collapse. The *Reichsführer* had a plan to arrange an armistice with the Western Allies and actually made contact with the OSS in Sweden to discuss the subject. He also met with a member of the anti-Nazi movement, the Prussian finance minister Dr. Johannes Popitz, to discuss removing Hitler from power. Neither meeting accomplished anything. Himmler's OSS contacts would not even consider an armistice that excluded the Soviet Union. And the resistance did not trust Himmler—his plan to overthrow Hitler sounded like a trap. Neither side would have anything to do with his basic plan, which was to remove Hitler from power, take over the office of Führer himself, and negotiate an armistice. As far as both the Allies and the anti-Nazi resistance were concerned, Himmler did not represent any sort of improvement over Hitler—Hitler may have been a lunatic, but Himmler was regarded as a homicidal maniac and a tyrant.

Admiral Canaris knew all about Himmler's contact with both the OSS and Johannes Popitz. He realized that if either of these incidents was reported to Hitler, Heinrich Himmler would be arrested and executed. Both Franz Sonderegger and Walter Schellenberg were absolutely correct that the admiral did have a file of incriminating evidence against Reichsführer Himmler, even though neither one of them had any idea what it might contain. But Heinrich Himmler's protection of Admiral Canaris was not based upon fear.

Himmler *was* doing his best to keep any and all enemies away from the admiral. Feldmarschall Wilhelm Keitel was informed that "the old man should be left in peace," an order the *feldmarschall* took to heart.[36] He had recently received a report from Manfred Roeder, who had conducted an investigation into Admiral Canaris's involvement in Operation 7. Roeder's report addressed the possibility of criminal proceedings against the admiral on the grounds of incompetence. Feldmarschall Keitel received the report, thanked Roeder for the time he had taken to compile the document, and then proceeded to write his own personal report on the cover page. According to what the *feldmarschall* had to say about Manfred Roeder's evidence, Reichsführer Himmler never read Roeder's report and had no interest in its contents. As far as any reference to Operation 7, Feldmarschall Keitel went on to say that Himmler knew all about the operation. He wrote that Heinrich Himmler "had personally given Canaris his oral consent to Op. V7" (the official name for Operation 7).[37]

By this time, the evidence that Admiral Canaris held against Heinrich Himmler was mainly just a precaution—he did not trust the SD, the SS, or the Gestapo, with good reason. But Himmler had already changed his mind on the subject of death camps and the final solution, as the admiral was aware. Himmler had known all about Admiral Canaris's rescue efforts at least since Operation 7 and had not only looked the other way but given his consent to the operation. In Heinrich Himmler, Reichsführer and head of the SS, Admiral Canaris had found an unexpected ally.

CHAPTER ELEVEN

"Getting Rid of Hitler"

No one can say exactly how much influence Adm. Wilhelm Canaris had on Heinrich Himmler's change of opinion about death camps and mass executions. The two of them shared similar points of view on a number of vital issues: the conduct of the war, how it should be brought to an end, and the subject of Adolf Hitler and his dictatorship. They both agreed that Germany had absolutely no chance of winning the war, that an armistice should be negotiated with the British and Americans, and that Hitler should be removed as head of state. By the end of 1943, Himmler also shared Admiral Canaris's point of view regarding the extermination of Jews, although by that time most Jews and other political and racial prisoners had either gone into hiding or been relocated to the death camps of eastern Europe and were beyond Admiral Canaris's protective influence.

One of Himmler's biographers stated that the *Reichsführer* suffered from a conflict between his oath of obedience to Hitler and "an inner aversion to mass slaughter and genocide."[1] Himmler was convinced that the wholesale execution of Jews and Poles served no useful purpose—the mass murders would not help Germany win the war, would not further and would probably be counterproductive to any peace negotiations, and should be ended on moral grounds in spite of Hitler's directive. He consented to go along with Operation 7, in direct opposition to Hitler, which means that he had decided to oppose Hitler's order on mass murder by the time Operation 7 had been carried out. Admiral Canaris changed Himmler's mind regarding these killings more by example than by verbal argument. Instead of ordering Canaris's arrest, which Himmler was bound to do as a *Reichsführer* of the Third Reich, he agreed to allow the admiral to carry out his plan. He realized that if his part in Operation 7 had been discovered, Hitler would have ordered his immediate execution. Himmler might have changed his entire point of view because of his "inner aversion," but this aversion was encouraged and abetted by Adm. Wilhelm Canaris.

Admiral Canaris also had an influence on the German High Command, but in a more direct way: he kept Hitler and his commanders completely in the dark by deliberately misleading and misinforming them concerning British and American forces. The admiral was always on the lookout for any sort of deception that would confuse the High Command, using any subterfuge that would help to shorten the war and end its atrocities.

Another opportunity to mislead Hitler and his generals presented itself during the first weeks of 1944. On January 21, Admiral Canaris was ordered to report to the headquarters of Feldmarschall Albert Kesselring, commander of all German forces in the Mediterranean, to discuss possible Allied plans concerning an invasion of Italy. Feldmarschall Kesselring's intelligence evaluation staff had lost track of Allied warships spotted in the western Mediterranean and had received recent reports that a large concentration of enemy ships, including battleships, cruisers, and landing craft, were now in Naples harbor. It looked as though the enemy might be gathering forces for an amphibious landing in the near future. As head of the Abwehr, the admiral was called in to give his views on the likelihood of an Allied invasion on the coast of Italy.

Admiral Canaris lost no time in putting everyone's mind at rest. There was no danger of an Allied invasion, he said. He did not go into any details, but he told everyone present not to worry about any landing in Italy. A general on Feldmarschall Erwin Rommel's staff, Siegfried Westphal, wanted to know where the missing Allied warships had gone and where they might be lurking. "We are looking after them—don't you worry," the admiral answered.[2] His tone of voice, along with his entire manner, radiated confidence. Admiral Canaris reassured everyone that there was absolutely nothing to fear—the enemy had no plans to make any offensive moves, at least not in the near future.

At that very moment, while the admiral was reassuring the meeting that the enemy had absolutely no intention to invade, several hundred Allied ships were heading for the Italian coast. A few hours later, at dawn on January 22, 1944, about three hundred landing craft carrying thirty-two thousand British and American troops and thirty-two hundred vehicles came ashore at Anzio, about fifty miles behind the German lines on the southwestern coast of Italy.[3] Anzio was one of the largest amphibious operations of the war. It was also the beginning of a lethal battle of attrition that would go on until early June and end with the capture of Rome.

Admiral Canaris had misled the High Command again, just as he had done during the run-up to Operation Torch in November 1942. But whereas the admiral got away with misleading the generals concerning Operation Torch, he would not be as lucky this time. Adolf Hitler was already more than annoyed with Admiral Canaris because of his previous failures, including Operation Torch, and his "defeatism" concerning the fighting in Russia. Also, Abwehr agents in neutral countries—Switzerland, Turkey, and Portugal—had been defecting to the Allies, which reflected on Admiral Canaris and gave Hitler another complaint against him. Hitler decided to do something about the "little admiral" and his inefficiency. The Anzio deception would turn out to be Admiral Canaris's last act as chief of the Abwehr.

The person who approached Hitler with the idea of removing Admiral Canaris was Reichsführer Heinrich Himmler. After a fiasco on the scale of Anzio, Himmler realized that he could not go on covering up for the admiral—continuing would only bring suspicion upon them both. Hitler listened to what Himmler had to say and agreed with him. On February 18, 1944, Hitler signed a decree that not only dismissed Admiral Canaris as head of the Abwehr but also dissolved the Abwehr itself. The decree was short and to the point:

1. A uniform German intelligence service is to be established.

2. I put the Reichsführer-SS [Himmler] in charge of this German intelligence service; and

3. Insofar as this affects the military intelligence and counterespionage service, the Reichsführer-SS and the chief of the OKW [German High Command] are to take the necessary steps after due consultation.[4]

Reichsführer Himmler was only the titular head of the newly formed organization. Ernst Kaltenbrunner, Reinhard Heydrich's replacement as head of the Sicherheitsdienst (SD), was actually in charge of the "uniform German intelligence service."

Himmler arranged that Admiral Canaris's removal should be carried out as quietly as possible, in a very discreet and low-key manner. If the *Reichsführer* had not interceded, Canaris's removal from office would not have been nearly as respectful and considerate. As a sort of consolation prize, the admiral was appointed director of the Economic Warfare Department, which was basically a dead-end bureaucratic job that consisted mainly of overseeing clerks and other bureaucrats. His new appointment took Canaris miles away from Berlin, both literally and figuratively. He would be working from Burg Lauenstein, a secluded fourteenth-century castle in Franconia. The castle's commandant—Burg Lauenstein was an Abwehr facility used for microfilming secret documents and creating forged passports—was instructed to keep the admiral as comfortable as possible but not to allow him any contact at all with any intelligence activities. Admiral Canaris accepted his new assignment, which was clearly a drastic demotion, without a word. He lived a quiet life in an out-of-the-way corner of Germany with his wife and his dachshunds, waiting to see what the future held in store for him.

Most accounts of the admiral's reassignment to Franconia insist that it marked the end of his career. Some romantically state that the Old Fox ended his reign over the Abwehr and left his lair on Tirpitz Ufer for an obscure post in the hinterlands. Otto John was more straightforward in his reaction to the admiral's reassignment. "Canaris was appointed head of the Special Staff for Economic Warfare," he noted, adding with a note of disappointment, "a position in which he could do nothing for the conspiracy."[5] William L. Shirer's assessment of Admiral Canaris's fate was even gloomier: "With the assumption of this empty title the 'little admiral' faded out of German history."[6] But actually, Admiral Canaris's transfer from Berlin to Burg Lauenstein was probably the best thing that could have happened to the anti-Nazi resistance and Allied intelligence: from Franconia he was able to maintain contact with the Allies with no fear of being observed by the Gestapo or the SD. Beginning in February 1944, the admiral simply moved his base of activities from Tirpitz Ufer to Burg Lauenstein.

After Admiral Canaris had been removed as chief of intelligence, Ernst Kaltenbrunner and the SD left him alone. He had been shipped off to the wilds of Franconia, safely out the way; Kaltenbrunner paid no attention to him and suspected nothing regarding his activities. He was not considered worthy of surveillance by the SD. This total lack of interest by Kaltenbrunner left the admiral free to carry out his personal campaign against Hitler and the Nazis without fear of detection. Being in charge of a department within the government bureaucracy, even though the Economic Warfare Department was small and insignificant, gave him the authority to travel anywhere within the Third Reich. This included trips to Berlin. The admiral carried on doing everything he had been doing while he was head of the Abwehr, including keeping in touch with the Allies as well as with his fellow conspirators in the anti-Hitler movement, without either the SD or the Gestapo suspecting anything.

Admiral Canaris apparently began contacting the Allies from Burg Lauenstein as early as February 1944—as soon as he had been relieved of his job as chief of intelligence. No one is exactly sure how he managed to stay in touch, although it was probably through his contacts in Spain. No matter how he did it, the admiral sent a good many reports and a great deal of priceless information throughout the buildup to D-Day and beyond. This might be the reason, or at least one reason, that Admiral Canaris left his post at the Abwehr so quietly. He was able to carry on with his resistance work from Franconia without any problems or complications; for all intents and purposes, he might just as well have stayed at Tirpitz Ufer.

The impending invasion was on everyone's mind, including members of the anti-Nazi movement. "The situation is marked by the increasingly nervous expectation of 'invasion' on the part of both friend and foe. Will it really come?" wrote Ulrich von Hassell at the end of May 1944, adding, "Hitler and his henchmen see the failure of the invasion as the only real chance left to them."[7] Political prisoners and other outcasts also waited for the invasion. "Invasion fever is mounting daily throughout the country," Anne Frank noted in her diary. "The papers are full of invasion news and are driving everyone insane with such statements as: 'In the event of a British landing in Holland, the Germans will do what they can to defend the county, even flooding it, if necessary.'"[8]

Because he was no longer head of the Abwehr and could not smuggle refugees out of occupied territory disguised as Abwehr agents, Admiral Canaris could only continue with his plan to rescue victims of the Nazi regime by helping the coming Allied invasion to succeed. He supplied Gen. Dwight D. Eisenhower's Supreme Headquarters, Allied Expeditionary Force (SHAEF) with updated reports of German defenses on the coast of France. Supplying the Allies with information that would make it easier for British and American troops to get ashore on D-Day would enable these troops to overrun the German-occupied countries and eventually capture the concentration camps—at least that was the admiral's hope. His main concern would now be to supply the British and Americans with as much useful information about German activities and strategy as possible; he would now perform his rescue operations by indirect means.

The admiral also tried his best to convert Gen. Erwin Rommel, who had not yet been promoted to field marshal, to his own point of view regarding "undesirables" and other concentration camp inmates. He had compiled a list of Schutzstaffel (SS) atrocities committed throughout eastern Europe and gave a copy to Rommel. The dossier, meant to be an indictment against Hitler and the Nazis, had no effect at all on Rommel. The general was "hardly sympathetic" toward anything Admiral Canaris had to say, according to one of Canaris's biographers; he was "so keen on his desert war that he had no time to be shocked by mass murder and racial extermination."[9]

Admiral Canaris was annoyed by Rommel's lack of sympathy. "You, Rommel of the Army," he said, "will one day be held responsible for what is happening behind the lines." But the general did not agree with him. "That's not behind my front—not my concern at all," he replied. "I'm a fighting man." Rommel would eventually change his mind about Hitler, but his disillusion would stem from Hitler's failures as a military leader and not rest on moral or ethical grounds.[10]

The admiral's activities after being shipped off to Burg Lauenstein still remain hazy and mysterious. He managed to keep in touch with his fellow conspirators in the resistance and remained as active as ever in his campaign to undermine Hitler and the Nazis. During the weeks and months leading up to D-Day, Admiral Canaris kept SHAEF supplied with invaluable reports on German defenses in Normandy. An American colonel attached to SHAEF's intelligence department found out just how valuable Admiral Canaris had become to Allied intelligence in the spring of 1944.

The American colonel in question was James O. Curtis, the only American intelligence evaluator in SHAEF. The other three members of the department—Col. E. J. Foord, Col. Eric Birley, and Maj. John Austin—were British. The main task of an intelligence evaluator was to read each and every intelligence report received by SHAEF—amounting to many thousands during the period leading up to the invasion—to determine which were genuine and which were unreliable or sometimes blatantly fraudulent. Colonel Curtis was on very friendly terms with his British colleagues, but he had the feeling that they were not telling him everything, especially about the sources of the information being received.

SHAEF had its own system of grading information based on its authenticity and reliability. The highest-quality reports were classified A-1; the lowest were F-6. As soon as he joined the evaluation unit, Colonel Curtis noticed that a surprising number of reports were being graded A-1. A great deal of this A-1 material seemed too accurate and detailed to be true, at least to Colonel Curtis's way of thinking. He refused to believe that all the reports received by SHAEF were as accurate as his British colleagues seemed to think. The three British officers were reluctant to divulge the source of many of these reports. Colonel Curtis insisted that he would be unwilling to pass the questionable information along to American planners at SHAEF unless he knew something about its source.

Colonel Foord, the head of the department, finally decided to let the American in on their little secret. He took Colonel Curtis "quietly on one side [Curtis here inserted, 'Just two in the room'] and said that the source was Canaris personally." This disclosure was to be considered top secret, Colonel Curtis was warned. "The only reason that I am telling you this is that we want you to regard this information as being priceless and copper-bottomed." Colonel Foord went on to explain that only a select few high-ranking individuals—President Franklin Roosevelt, Prime Minister Winston Churchill, General Eisenhower—knew anything at all about Admiral Canaris's connection with SHAEF. Colonel Curtis was taken completely by surprise by what Colonel Foord told him. "I was, at first, afraid to go to sleep in case I talked in my sleep," he said.[11]

"I first heard the name Canaris in February 1944," Colonel Curtis wrote—more evidence that the transfer to Burg Lauenstein did not interfere with the admiral's anti-Nazi activities at all. "His most important service was to give us substantially the complete order of battle plans for the German Army, together with the plans they had worked out for coping with the invasion."[12] Delivering the order of battle was one of Admiral Canaris's major achievements for Allied intelligence. Receiving the Wehrmacht's listing of men and divisions was an enormous help for SHAEF intelligence. Piecing together that much information would have taken SHAEF a great deal of time and effort, if it managed to do so at all; instead it put that energy to use on other projects. No one was exactly certain how he sent his information from Franconia to Supreme Headquarters, although it was probably via contacts in Spain. No matter how he managed to do it, Admiral Canaris kept on sending his reports on German activities in France. Even though he was no longer in a position to carry out rescue missions, the admiral was still doing his best to overthrow Adolf Hitler, even from exile. His plan was to let Allied troops take over his rescue attempts after they came ashore in Normandy.

American troops on Utah Beach, Normandy, after coming ashore on D-Day. Admiral Canaris sent the Allies the order of battle of the German army, along with other information regarding German defenses in Normandy. *Source*: US Navy.

* * *

The prospect of "getting rid of Hitler" was becoming more and more urgent among the members of the anti-Hitler conspiracy, with assassination the favored method of eliminating him. "The state is deteriorating more and more into an immoral and bankrupt existence under the leadership of an irresponsible gambler who can scarcely be called mentally normal and who is surrounded by riffraff," Ulrich von Hassell wrote. "And thus we roll on toward disaster."[13] In the eyes of the anti-Nazi resistance, Adolf Hitler was mentally incompetent at best and was probably a full-blown lunatic. The members of the anti-Hitler movement were not the only people in Germany who thought of Hitler in that way. A joke making the rounds at the time concerns a young fellow recently conscripted into the German army. He tells his superior that he would like to be assigned to Adolf Hitler's headquarters. "Are you crazy?" the officer asks. "Is that one of the requirements?" the young conscript replies.[14]

During the months between the spring of 1943 and the spring of 1944, this negative opinion of Hitler did not improve; if anything, it worsened. German cities were being systematically destroyed by British and American bombers on a daily basis; reports of atrocities committed by SS death squads kept coming from the East, and any hope of Germany winning the war was diminishing with each passing week. Throughout Germany, it was becoming increasingly evident that the situation was not going to improve as long as Adolf Hitler remained head of the government. The only certain way of bringing the war and all of its horrors to an end would be to rid the country of Hitler. The surest way of accomplishing that task was assassination. By 1944, members of the conspiracy were convinced that killing Hitler was the only way to rid the country of the Nazis and everything they represented.

By the early part of 1944, at least eight attempts had been made since the war began. The first assassination attempt was made on the evening of November 8, 1939, at the Bürgerbraükeller in Munich, where Hitler was scheduled to give a speech. A bomb had been placed behind the speaker's platform by Georg Elser, only recently released from Dachau concentration camp, where he had been detained for having communist sympathies. Hitler was scheduled to make a lengthy address but left the beer hall much sooner than expected. When the time bomb exploded at about 9:30 p.m., Hitler had already left the building. The British secret service was blamed for the incident.

Hitler managed to escape all the other attempts on his life as well, mainly because of bad luck on the part of the conspirators. About a month after France surrendered in June 1940, a group of German officers conspired to shoot Hitler while he attended a victory parade in Paris. The plan came to nothing when Hitler cancelled the parade. The same thing happened nearly a year later, in May 1941, when another group of officers planned to kill Hitler at a parade. Once again, the parade was called off. A few months after this, an attempt failed when the would-be assassins were prevented from getting close enough to Hitler to shoot him. In March 1943, another group of conspirators planned to blow Hitler's airplane out of the sky over Minsk. A bomb with an acid detonator was secretly placed aboard the aircraft, but the acid froze in the cold Russian air, and the bomb did not explode. A week later, a bomb was planted among a display of captured Russian weapons at an armory in Berlin; Hitler was planning to make a tour of the exhibition. But Hitler seemed to sense that something was wrong and left the exhibition after only a few minutes. An officer hurried off to the nearest washroom and ripped the fuse out of the bomb before it went off. Another attempt failed when the explosives to be used in the assassination detonated prematurely. The most recent plot had involved Capt. Axel von dem Bussche, who planned to kill Hitler with a bomb during an inspection of new uniforms. When the uniforms were blown up in an air raid, the opportunity was lost.

Not everyone connected with the anti-Nazi movement agreed that Hitler should be killed. Several members of the movement objected on religious grounds—killing Hitler, or anyone else, violated the Ten Commandments. Feldmarschall Erwin Rommel, who eventually sympathized with the movement but never joined it, also did not approve of any proposed assassination plot. Although he did agree that Hitler should be removed from power, his was a soldier's solution: one of his Panzer units would take Hitler prisoner and transport him to Berlin, where he would be put on trial for crimes against Germany and against humanity. "He should be tried by the people who elected him," as Feldmarschall Rommel phrased it.[15]

But in spite of any misgivings, killing Hitler was the only certain way of ending the Nazi regime and putting a stop to the war. When Hitler finally committed suicide in April 1945, both the government and the Nazi Party collapsed—Hitler *was* the party as well as the regime. Count Claus von Stauffenberg pointed out that assassinating Hitler would not only stop the slaughter on the eastern front but also put an end to the atrocities being committed in places like Auschwitz and Dachau. He agreed that the only way to rid the country of Adolf Hitler was to kill him, not arrest him.

Admiral Canaris was well aware of the assassination plots, but he was not directly involved in any of them. He knew what was going on but let others manage the details. The Abwehr sabotage branch helped to make the acid fuses that froze aboard Hitler's plane over Russia, and according to one source, Admiral Canaris "himself took fuses of this type in his aircraft when he flew to Smolensk."[16] This same writer also commented that although Admiral Canaris knew about the assassination attempts against Hitler, "he did not want to be too much in the picture" concerning them.[17]

But even though Admiral Canaris kept his distance from Axel von dem Bussche and the other would-be assassins, he still managed to keep in touch with Allied intelligence from his exile in Franconia and did supply SHAEF with vital information. Gen. Sir Francis "Freddie" Guingand, Field Marshall Bernard Law Montgomery's chief of staff, was informed after the war that Admiral Canaris passed along top-level German command decisions to British intelligence "not once, but several times." All of the reports he sent were of high quality and extremely valuable. "I distinctly remember being told that Canaris was the source of some of our most secret intelligence," he recalled.[18] The admiral was using his unique position as head of the Economic Warfare Department, along with his ability to travel anywhere he wanted, to gather material and pass it along to British intelligence or to SHAEF.

Just about everything that Admiral Canaris did in the spring of 1944 remains a mystery, but he certainly was active during this time. It is known that he made contact with Gen. Sir Stewart Menzies, head of the British Secret Intelligence Service, MI6, at the end of May—a message from Admiral Canaris to General Menzies was smuggled from northern France to England. No one is absolutely certain what the message contained. It might have been another attempt to arrange an armistice between Germany and the West, or it might have been something else, information directly connected to the invasion. At around the same time, Admiral Canaris himself was seen in Paris—he was positively identified by the mother superior of a Paris convent. The admiral met with another member of the MI6 network at the convent, which British intelligence used as its primary center of operations in Paris. General Menzies was informed of this meeting, which might have been another peace feeler, provided more data on German defenses in France, or both.

Admiral Canaris, determined to do his best to end the war, was willing to do everything in his power to help the coming invasion succeed. He was well aware that the war would go on indefinitely if the Allied landings failed, possibly for several more years, and that its outcome would be unpredictable. A Nazi victory was out of the question. "To him, a victory for Hitler meant the end of Christian civilization, and of Western culture in Europe, and possibly in the world," said Allen W. Dulles of the attitude of another anti-Nazi conspirator, Hans Bernd Gisevius. Admiral Canaris shared the same viewpoint. "He proposed to prevent it," meaning a Nazi victory, and "he wanted the Allies to hurry. . . . He wanted to prevent Hitler from carrying on the fight 'to the bitter end.'"[19] The crimes of Hitler and his government also had to be stopped. Admiral Canaris could see that the most effective method for him to put an end to the Nazi regime would be through deception and subterfuge—to supply the Allied intelligence services with as much up-to-date information on German forces in northern France as could be smuggled across the channel to England.

* * *

Count Claus Philipp Maria Schenk Graf von Stauffenberg did not have Admiral Canaris's guile, his contacts, or his patience. But Colonel von Stauffenberg did have his own simple and straightforward idea for getting rid of the Nazis and ending the war: kill Hitler. He could see that if Hitler was assassinated, the Nazi government would collapse, and the war would be over by the end of summer. The only problem was that Hitler seemed to have a charmed life. Von Stauffenberg knew that several attempts had already been made to assassinate Hitler and that every one of them had failed, for one reason or another. He also did not have very much faith or confidence in the officers who had planned the previous attempts, including the senior officers. "Since the generals have so far done nothing," he said, "the colonels must now go into action."[20] If Hitler was ever going to be eliminated, it seemed to Colonel von Stauffenberg, someone with more enthusiasm, and possibly more courage, should take the lead in the conspiracy. And the person he had in mind for the job was himself.

The thirty-six-year-old colonel was the descendent of generals and German nobility, with a genealogical line that could be traced back to the thirteenth century. He was a professional soldier who had served with distinction in Poland, France, and North Africa, even though he had begun to rebel against Hitler and the Nazis during the early months of the war. Although Hans Bernd Gisevius said that Colonel von Stauffenberg "shifted to the rebel side only after Stalingrad,"[21] the colonel actually began to have thoughts of removing Hitler because of the atrocities committed against Jews, Poles, and political "undesirables" by the SS in 1939. By the early part of 1943, von Stauffenberg had determined to assassinate Hitler. During a discussion of the most effective way to change Hitler's method of leadership, von Stauffenberg offered his own solution with a terse, two-word response: "Kill him."[22]

But before he was able to carry out any plan to kill Hitler, Colonel von Stauffenberg was very nearly killed himself. On April 7, 1943, shortly after joining the 10th Panzer Division in North Africa, his automobile was attacked by an enemy fighter. The fighter's machine-gun and cannon fire struck the vehicle and also hit the colonel, costing him his left eye, his right arm, and the fourth and fifth fingers of his left hand. He was taken to the military hospital in Carthage in critical condition and was not expected to live. But to the surprise of his doctors, he recovered to the point where he could be transferred to a hospital in Germany.

In Germany, Colonel von Stauffenberg continued to recover and regain his strength. He was taught how to use the fingers on his left hand and also had an artificial hand attached. Although he had not fully recovered from his injuries, the colonel dedicated himself to overthrowing the Nazi regime—to say that he threw himself into the task would not be an overstatement. While Admiral Canaris worked against Hitler from the shadows, Colonel von Stauffenberg took a more direct approach. His plan, code-named Walküre (Valkyrie), was to kill Hitler, abolish the Nazi Party, eliminate the concentration camps, take control of the government, and negotiate an armistice. In the words of a co-conspirator, the colonel had become a "soldier, politician, tyrannicide, [and] savior of his fatherland," as well as the redeemer of its honor. The same writer stated that von Stauffenberg was also determined to administer "just punishment to the Nazis and Gestapo murderers" who had killed millions of civilians and shattered the reputation of Germany in the eyes of the world.[23] But before any of these things could be accomplished, Adolf Hitler would have to be killed. Eliminating Hitler would now be his top priority.

* * *

The anti-Nazi resistance made contact with Allen W. Dulles several times during the early part of 1944. Hans Bernd Gisevius and Eduard Waetjen both visited him in Bern regarding "a deal between the German opposition group and the Western Allies." Admiral Canaris was mentioned by name during the discussion. During the course of the conversation, the two conspirators discussed the determination of their group, which the Office of Strategic Services (OSS) had given the code name Breakers, to oust Hitler and the Nazis. But there was more to this particular visit than just talking about overthrowing Hitler. In a memo to Secretary of State Cordell Hull, OSS Assistant Director G. Edward Buxton made this extraordinary statement: "The group stated that the German generals now commanding in the West—particularly Rundstedt and Falkenhausen—would be ready to cease resistance and aid Allied landings once the Nazis had been ousted."[24] The memo went on to state, "The group was reportedly ready to help Allied units get into Germany if the Allies agreed that the Wehrmacht should continue to hold the Russian front," although "Rommel cannot be counted on for cooperation."[25] Except for Feldmarschall Rommel, German generals would be willing to come to the aid of Allied forces in their offensive against Germany once Hitler had been removed from power.

It was a startling declaration. Secretary of State Hull probably read the memo several times, not believing what he was reading. But Assistant Secretary Buxton was not altogether reassured about "the group" and their planned assistance of Allied forces after D-Day. For one thing, he advised Cordell Hull that although the anti-Hitler resistance might have been willing and eager to attempt a coup, they "did not guarantee success"—implying that their plan should not be taken too seriously. Buxton went on to report that Allen Dulles also had his doubts as to whether or not the anti-Hitler movement "would have the determination to act effectively at the appropriate time" or—a vital point—would be "sensitive to the problem of Soviet relations." Joseph Stalin was as wary as ever regarding the Western Allies contacting the anti-Hitler movement and especially suspicious about their making a separate peace with the Germans.[26]

But the OSS, as well as the US government, could have offered encouragement to the anti-Nazi resistance without even mentioning an armistice. On July 6, 1944, Deputy Prime Minister Clement Attlee addressed the House of Commons on the subject of a coup in Germany. He told the Commons that if the German people really wanted "a return to a regime based on respect for international law and for the rights of the individual, they must understand that no one will believe them until they have themselves taken active steps to rid themselves of their present regime."[27] A week later, Winston Churchill addressed the Commons on the same subject, saying, "It would certainly be a very well-advised step on the part of the Germans to overthrow Hitler and the Nazis."[28] These statements did not go unnoticed by the German resistance. Dulles informed OSS headquarters in Washington that "Attlee's statement, made recently during a debate in the House of Commons, seems to have made a great impression on German groups."[29] But the statement made absolutely no impression in Washington. The Roosevelt administration still refused to make any sort of speech or proclamation supporting the German resistance in its attempts to overthrow the Nazi regime.

When Hans Bernd Gisevius first heard about Operation Valkyrie in May 1944, he was discouraged that it was also based on the "Western plan"—the Valkyrie plotters would only consider surrendering to the Western Allies and refused to have any dealings at all with the Russians. From Switzerland, Hans Gisevius made a special effort to persuade his fellow conspirators that the "Western plan" was totally impractical. Dulles recalled that Gisevius "told me that he had already sent word back to Germany that it was useless to hope that we"—the British and Americans—"would break faith with our Russian allies."[30] The message was reluctantly accepted by the members of the anti-Hitler resistance, who were finally beginning to understand that their plan for dealing only with the West had absolutely no hope of succeeding.

Dulles did his best to convince the American government to issue a statement along the lines of Attlee's and Churchill's words of support, a speech that would encourage the German population to rise against Hitler. "I urged that a similar statement be made from America," Dulles would later write. He was totally convinced that any attempt to overthrow Hitler, "whether or not successful," would help to shorten the war.[31]

President Roosevelt continued to stand by his declaration that the only acceptable end to Hitler and his regime would come as the result of force of arms—the invasion of the Continent, followed by the military defeat of all German armed forces. There would be no broadcast in support of the German resistance from Washington, DC.

CHAPTER TWELVE

The Bitter End

"'THIS IS D-DAY,' THE BBC ANNOUNCED AT TWELVE. THIS IS *THE* DAY. The invasion has begun!" Anne Frank made this entry in her diary on Tuesday, June 6, 1944. Some residents of the Annex in Amsterdam thought that the invasion was only a preliminary landing, "like the one two years ago in Dieppe," but Anne felt certain that this was the "real" invasion.[1]

The BBC made the D-Day announcement in several languages, including English, German, French, and Dutch. The official announcement from Gen. Dwight D. Eisenhower's headquarters was broadcast at about 9:30 a.m.: "Under the command of General Eisenhower, Allied naval forces, supported by strong air forces, began landing Allied armies this morning on the northern coast of France."[2] Anne wrote that the news filled everyone with fresh courage and went on to say, "The best part of the invasion is that I have the feeling that friends are on the way." The Nazis "have oppressed us for so long that the thought of friends and salvation means everything to us! Now it's not just the Jews, but Holland and all of occupied Europe."[3]

All over the German-occupied Continent, fugitives from the Nazi regime—Jews, political dissidents, and anyone who owned a radio—heard the news. In cellars and attics and hidden alcoves throughout France, Belgium, Luxemburg, and Holland, people listened to reports on illegal receivers, risking harsh imprisonment if caught. Some could not bring themselves to believe what they were hearing and decided to wait for other, more updated reports before allowing themselves to accept the news as true. In far-off Burg Lauenstein, Adm. Wilhelm Canaris also heard the broadcasts and could feel satisfied that he had done his part in making the invasion a reality.

After listening to the radio reports, a good many of those who had gone into hiding drew maps of northern France to track the advance of the Allied forces. They were fully aware of what the retreat of German forces from their country would mean for their friends and families, as well as for themselves. "Great news of the invasion," Anne wrote on June 9. "The Allies have taken Bayeux, a village on the coast of France, and are now fighting for Caen." Everyone realized that D-Day did not mean the end of the war or the end of Nazi rule, but it gave them hope that the end would not be far off. "The excitement has died down somewhat; still, we're all hoping that the war will finally be over by the end of the year."[4]

Among the broadcasts that were made on the morning of June 6 was a message from General Eisenhower. "People of Western Europe," he began, "a landing was made this morning on the coast of France by members of the Allied Expeditionary Force." He made a point of mentioning that the landings took place "in conjunction with our great Russian allies." The message was addressed to the "citizens of France," "all patriots, young and old," and advised everyone, including members of the French resistance, "Follow the instructions you have received." General Eisenhower referred to the Normandy landings as the "initial assault," implying that there would be a second landing in the near future. It was a stirring speech, ending with "I call upon all who love freedom to stand with us. Keep your faith staunch—our arms are resolute—together we shall achieve victory."[5]

General Eisenhower made no mention of the anti-Nazi resistance in any part of his address. He could very easily have urged the German resistance to rise up against Adolf Hitler and his government, just as Winston Churchill had done. He addressed the French resistance; he could also have spoken a few words to the anti-Hitler movement. Any words of encouragement from the supreme commander of the Allied forces would have been welcome, especially since the long-awaited invasion of France had just taken place. But no such words of encouragement came from General Eisenhower or any other American general or public official. In any event, the anti-Nazi conspiracy had its own plans for over-throwing Hitler, as the world would very shortly discover.

* * *

"There is a possibility that a dramatic event may take place up north, if Breakers courier is to be trusted." Allen W. Dulles telegraphed this message from Bern, Switzerland, to the Office of Strategic Services (OSS) headquarters in Washington, DC, on July 12, 1944.[6] Three days earlier, he had sent another telegram to Washington on the same subject: "The next few weeks are believed by Breakers to represent the final opportunity to start action to prove the desire of the German people themselves to overthrow Hitler and his organization and to set up a respectable government." The "dramatic event" and "final opportunity" mentioned in the two telegrams referred to Operation Valkyrie, Col. Claus von Stauffenberg's plan to assassinate Hitler and overthrow the Nazi government. Dulles did not know any of the Valkyrie details. He only knew that "something spectacular" would be taking place up north in Germany very soon, at least according to the anti-Hitler movement.[7]

Operation Valkyrie was carried out on the afternoon of July 20, 1944, when Colonel von Stauffenberg attempted to kill Hitler at his headquarters in East Prussia. The colonel carried a bomb, hidden inside a briefcase, into a strategy meeting with Hitler and members of his staff. When he was inside the headquarters, von Stauffenberg set the ten-minute time fuse, slid the briefcase under the conference table, and waited for his chance to leave the building. While Hitler and his senior officers were engrossed in a situation map of the Russian front, the colonel slipped out of the room unnoticed.

Just after Colonel von Stauffenberg left, Col. Heinz Brandt entered the conference room and occupied the space at the table a few feet away from Hitler. As the colonel moved to get a better view of the map, he accidentally kicked Colonel von Stauffenberg's briefcase. He tried to push it out of the way with his foot, but it was too heavy—the bomb inside it weighed several pounds. Colonel Brandt reached down with one hand and moved the case, placing it on the far side of a heavy wooden table support. The support stood between the bomb and Hitler, who was standing at the center of the table.

The bomb went off between 12:40 and 12:50 p.m. Colonel von Stauffenberg was a short distance away from the explosion and saw the results. He said that the building looked as though it had been hit by a 155-mm howitzer shell. Debris shot high into the air. The massive conference table had been destroyed, along with everything else in the room. Colonel von Stauffenberg was absolutely certain that no one could have survived the blast, but he had no idea that his plan had gone completely wrong. Everyone in the room suffered injuries, ranging from slight to severe, and three of the officers were killed outright, but Hitler was not dead. He had been injured, but not severely—his eardrums had burst, his trousers had been blown off his legs, which had been burned and lacerated by the explosion, and his right arm had been paralyzed. Although badly shaken, he was still very much alive.

After the initial shock wore off, Hitler's thoughts turned to the cause of the explosion. At first, he thought that a single Allied fighter-bomber might have eluded the antiaircraft defenses and scored a direct hit on the building. One of the officers thought that laborers somehow managed to plant a bomb underneath the building's floor—the blast left a deep crater in the floor, giving the impression that the explosion might have come from below. But when investigators began to piece together all the evidence, what had actually happened soon became apparent.

Hitler was determined to round up every person who had any connection at all, no matter how slight, with the plot to kill him. The Gestapo carried out Hitler's orders with brutal efficiency. According to one historian, "The barbarism of the Nazis toward their own fellow Germans reached its zenith."[8] Four hundred special investigators, including Franz Sonderegger, were given instructions to question anyone suspicious. Hundreds of German officers were tried and convicted for participation in the failed assassination attempt. A source on the subject states that under one thousand were arrested in connection with the July 20 plot, and under two hundred were executed.[9] That means that about 20 percent of all those arrested were executed; many were tortured beforehand.

Admiral Canaris was not involved in the plot. A few hours after the bomb had exploded, Colonel von Stauffenberg telephoned the admiral to inform him that Hitler was dead, killed by a bomb. Admiral Canaris knew enough of the Gestapo and its methods to realize that his telephone line had been tapped and that his conversation with von Stauffenberg was being overheard and recorded—a suspicion that turned out to be true. "Dead? For God's sake, who did it? The Russians?" he said for the benefit of the wiretappers.[10] He later also sent a telegram to Hitler, congratulating him on his miraculous escape from the assassination attempt.

By the end of July 20, Colonel von Stauffenberg had been arrested; he was shot by a firing squad early on the morning of July 21. Admiral Canaris realized that he was in grave danger himself but kept hoping against hope that he might be overlooked by the Gestapo. But the special investigation team approached one of the senior officers in the Secret Intelligence Service, Col. Georg Hansen, and subjected him to the mental and physical stresses of one of their special interrogations. Under the pressure of this examination, Colonel Hansen named Admiral Canaris as one of the conspirators. He implicated the admiral not only as a member of the July 20 plot but also as one of the leaders of the anti-Hitler resistance. "I regard Canaris as the spiritual instigator of the revolutionary movement that led to July 20," he informed his interrogators in a written statement. "Canaris made an important personal contribution to this by maintaining the requisite contacts abroad." Colonel Hansen then made an unexpected revelation, something that took the Gestapo completely by surprise. "Canaris was at pains to get people who did not agree with the National Socialist regime out of the country. These included numerous Jews, persons with religious affiliations, etc." Franz Sonderegger finally had the testimony he was looking for against Admiral Canaris.[11]

On the following day, July 23, the admiral was arrested by his old acquaintance Walter Schellenberg. As a matter of fact, Schellenberg did not want to arrest Canaris and threatened to complain to Heinrich Himmler if he was forced to do so. But he was bluntly informed that Himmler was not in charge of the investigation; Ernst Kaltenbrunner had been given that assignment. Schellenberg had no choice but to comply. When he arrived at Canaris's house, the admiral did not seem surprised to see his old colleague. "Somehow I felt that it would be you," he said.[12]

Admiral Canaris asked Schellenberg if the investigators had any evidence in writing "from that fool Colonel Hansen." Schellenberg admitted that Hansen had given evidence against him. The admiral realized that this put him in a very awkward, and possibly lethal, position. "You must promise me faithfully that within the next three days you will get me the opportunity to talk to Himmler personally," he said. Schellenberg promised and was as good as his word. He spoke with Himmler the following day; Himmler agreed to speak with Canaris.[13]

No record exists of the meeting between Himmler and the admiral, but whatever Canaris said certainly had its desired effect. Instead of being sent off to the Gestapo prison in Berlin, Canaris was driven to the Frontier Police College in the town of Fürstenburg, which was a good deal less terrifying than being shut up in the cells of the secret police. At Fürstenburg, he was treated with some degree of respect, at least by Gestapo standards. He was not subjected to torture or duress, although he was cross-examined thoroughly. His interrogators did their best to prove that Admiral Canaris had been involved in the July 20 plot, even if he did not have an active role in it. Franz Sonderegger was brought in to help with the questioning.

Other members of the anti-Hitler conspiracy were also questioned by the Gestapo, including Hans von Dohnanyi, Dietrich Bonhoeffer, and Josef Müller, another member of the anti-Nazi resistance who had contacted British intelligence and asked for cooperation with their movement to replace Hitler. Hans Oster was also arrested; his interrogation was handled by Sonderegger personally. Over the course of these questionings, evidence that Wilhelm Canaris had information regarding the assassination plot began to accumulate, piece by piece. By the end of August, enough proof had been assembled to allow the Gestapo to transfer Canaris from Fürstenburg to the Gestapo prison at Prinz Albrecht Strasse in Berlin. Not even Heinrich Himmler could help him now that the secret police had him in custody in the most feared building in Berlin.

* * *

One conspirator who managed to escape the Gestapo was Otto John, who was able to get out of Germany. He left the country simply by taking the regular Lufthansa flight from Berlin to Madrid—because he was an employee of Lufthansa, his departure did not arouse suspicion. Shortly after he arrived in Spain, John discussed the failed July 20 plot with an old friend. The man was absolutely appalled by the ineptness of the plotters. "A dagger's the right way to murder a man like Hitler," he scolded. "If one of you had the courage to do that, the *coup* would have succeeded. What you did was wrong and too late."

"Confounded" by this reaction, John tried to explain the reason that a bomb was used instead of a dagger or a revolver. "Stauffenberg had only his left hand and only three sound fingers on that," he said. "He couldn't have held a dagger or even a revolver properly. In addition, he had only one eye. He had to try a bomb. It was the only possibility for him." But the explanation only made the man even angrier and more agitated. "Stauffenberg was a cripple?" he asked in disbelief. Otto John "just nodded dumbly" in reply. "And there was no other officer with sound eyes and hands? You allowed a cripple to attack with a bomb?! Shame on you!" This time, John could think of nothing to say in response.[14]

News that a group of German conspirators nearly succeeded in killing Adolf Hitler received a variety of reactions throughout the world. Otto John's Spanish friend was angry that the plot had failed. Jews and political dissidents in occupied Europe were encouraged by the fact that somebody had at least made an effort to do away with Hitler. "Great news!" Anne Frank wrote in her diary on Friday, July 21, 1944. "An assassination attempt has been made on Hitler's life, and for once not by Jewish Communists or English capitalists, but by a German general who's not only a count but young as well."[15]

In Britain and the United States, the failed coup was mainly treated as a routine news item. Winston Churchill did mention the failed coup in the House of Commons, but his remarks were anything but elated or encouraging. "The highest personalities in the German Reich are murdering each other or trying to" was all he had to say about the incident.[16] News headlines in Britain and the United States mentioned that Hitler had escaped an assassination plot, but their accounts tended to be routine and straightforward. "And what came from Washington and London?" Allen W. Dulles asked rhetorically. "The attempt on Hitler's life was dismissed as no consequence."[17]

There were even those who expressed relief that the assassination attempt had not succeeded. A report from US Army counterintelligence stated that the failure of the coup was the best thing that could have happened. "If the plot of 20 July 1944 had succeeded it would have undoubtedly saved the lives of thousands of Allied soldiers," the report admits, before going on to say that "the total defeat of Germany seems a far better guarantee for world security than might have been created by a peaceful entry of Allied armies into Germany in July or August 1944." Killing Hitler might very well have produced a situation very similar to what happened in November 1918, according to the report. The assassination would probably have been followed quickly by the surrender of Germany, while German forces were still in the field. Another "stab-in-the-back" legend might have been created if the July 20 coup attempt had not miscarried. "Many Germans might have believed the German Army was not really defeated and that the surrender was only brought about because a clique of traitors sold the country out to the Allies." In other words, if Colonel von Stauffenberg's bomb plot had succeeded, Hitler "would have been the great martyr. It would have been said, 'If the Fuehrer had not been murdered we would have won after all.' Such an attitude on the part of a people not really convinced that the war was lost might easily have given rise to still another nationalistic movement, perhaps still another war."[18]

A coup of any sort would have given the Germans an alibi for a Fourth Reich and another war. "We may expect to hear between now and the next German war the claim that Germany was not defeated in the field in this war, but that it was cheated out of the war by the disloyalty of a small group of traitorous generals."[19]

There were those outside US Army counterintelligence and the OSS who agreed with this outlook. Anne Frank was optimistic about the assassination attempt itself but had absolutely no confidence in the outcome of any successful coup. "This is the best proof we've had so far that many officers and generals are fed up with the war and would like to see

Hitler sink into a bottomless pit," she wrote, "so that they can establish a military dictatorship, make peace with the Allies, rearm themselves and, after a few decades, start a new war." She went on to reflect, "Perhaps Providence is deliberately biding its time getting rid of Hitler, since it's much easier, and cheaper, for the Allies to let the impeccable Germans kill each other off."[20]

Anne Frank would not live long enough to see whether or not her prediction would come true. The remarks she made in her diary concerning the assassination attempt, which were dated July 21, 1944, would be her next-to-last entry. On August 4, she and the others hiding in the Annex were arrested by the Schutzstaffel (SS) and the Dutch Security Police and taken to prison in Amsterdam; from there Anne was moved to Auschwitz and then to the concentration camp at Bergen-Belsen. She died of typhus in late February or early March 1945. Bergen-Belsen was captured by British troops on April 12, 1945.

* * *

Now that Admiral Canaris had been taken into custody by the Gestapo, he was no longer in the protective orbit of Heinrich Himmler. But even though Himmler was not in a position to shield or defend the admiral, he did use his considerable influence to release Jews and other prisoners from concentration camps in Germany. The admiral may have been in a Gestapo prison cell in Berlin, but his influence on Himmler was still evident. It was as though Himmler were carrying on where Admiral Canaris had left off. He did not have the means or the method to smuggle prisoners out of the country disguised as intelligence agents, the way Admiral Canaris had done. And he was deathly afraid of Adolf Hitler. But as *Reichsführer-SS*, he was one of the most powerful and influential men in Nazi Germany. He used his status to release several thousand Jews and others from the camps in Germany.

At the beginning of August 1944, Himmler was asked by Dr. Felix Kersten to support a plan to release about twenty thousand Jews from concentration camps—to send them over the border to Switzerland, where they would then be sent on to the South of France. Dr. Kersten was Himmler's personal physical therapist, as well as his confidant. As it turned out, Himmler had already heard something about this plan and refused to be involved. He was not against the concept but did not want to do anything that might turn Hitler against him either. At one point he told Dr. Kersten that Hitler would have him shot dead for any such activities.

About four months later, at the end of November, Dr. Kersten came to see Heinrich Himmler again, for the same purpose—he wanted to discuss sending interned Jews to Switzerland. He did not mention the number of inmates he had in mind. Himmler once again said that he knew about "the affair" that Dr. Kersten had in mind and once again refused to support the plan. Dr. Kersten was just as persistent as Heinrich Himmler: he tried again a few days later. "I spoke to Himmler again today about releasing the Jews," he wrote on December 2, 1944. This time, the *Reichsführer* was not quite as adamant as he had been before. "He was hesitant, but did not actually refuse," Dr. Kersten said. Himmler wanted to know exactly how many Jews he wanted to release. "Twenty thousand, men and women," he replied.

Himmler could not believe what he was hearing. "Good God, I can't do that," he said. "Do you realize that you are giving [Josef] Goebbels enough rope for the Führer to hang me?" This would not be the last time that Himmler would express his almost morbid fear of what might happen to him if Hitler ever discovered what he was up to.

Dr. Kersten seemed to have expected this sort of response and was prepared to try a different tack. He made "an appeal to his Germanic humanity" and lowered the number of Jews to be released—instead of twenty thousand, Dr. Kersten suggested twelve thousand. Himmler was not all that enthusiastic about this arrangement either—he was afraid that the "world press" might find out about the story—but he agreed to think it over. The *Reichsführer* did just that and allowed himself to be persuaded: he authorized the release of twenty-seven hundred Jews.[21] According to a British writer, not only Jews were released. Himmler also saved the lives of "1,000 Dutch women, 1,500 French women, 500 Polish women, and 400 Belgians, provided he could obtain asylum for them in Sweden, and 2,700 Jews to be transported to Switzerland."[22]

Admiral Canaris, no longer in a position to carry out any rescue operations himself, would have been glad to know that Reichsführer Himmler had saved so many captives of the Nazi regime from certain death. The admiral was being kept under close observation, confined to a cell measuring eight feet by five feet, in the cellar of Gestapo headquarters in Berlin. He never received any information concerning the outside world. He was not even allowed to converse with his fellow prisoners, although he did manage the occasional word with some of the inmates, including Hans Oster. The guards kept his cell doors open at all times, and the lights were left on all day and all night. The diet of the prisoners was as meagre and unpleasant as the rest of their existence. "For breakfast and supper there was a mug of coffee substitute and two slices of bread and jam; at midday some soup."[23]

Admiral Canaris was regularly interrogated by Gestapo agents who specialized in either tricking or intimidating their prisoners into telling them what they wanted to know. But the admiral had a few tricks of his own and always managed to avoid giving a straight answer. He sometimes pretended to be a stupid old man and acted as though he did not understand the question. Another ploy was to answer a question that his interrogators did not ask; his rambling, sometimes incoherent response would have nothing to do with the subject under discussion. By an ingenious combination of acting, doubletalk, and sometimes just sidestepping the question, Admiral Canaris thwarted every attempt on the part of his interrogators to find out what he knew about the July 20 plot or the anti-Nazi resistance. One of his biographers noted, "For months, Canaris baffled them with one ruse after another. His skill in acting a part, his cunning imagination, the ease with which he affected naïve stupidity and then emerged into the most subtle reasoning disarmed the security agents who interrogated him."[24] But the admiral was much too important a prisoner to leave alone. The interrogators may have been frustrated, but they were not about to give up. They always had more questions and always kept coming back.

* * *

The World Jewish Congress (WJC) in New York received some unsettling information from inside Germany during the winter of 1944–1945. Adolf Hitler had ordered all concentration camps destroyed as the Allied forces advanced eastward toward places like Bergen-Belsen and Buchenwald. Hitler did not intend to let the camps to fall into the hands of the enemy; he wanted them blown up—along with all of their inmates and all of the guards. There had been previous attempts to intervene on behalf of concentration camp inmates and bring some sort of relief, including efforts to get food parcels and medical aid to the prisoners. Every attempt ended in frustration; the Nazi regime was not about to cooperate. But Hitler's order rendered the situation suddenly desperate. Another effort had to be made, and as quickly as possible. Admiral Canaris was no longer in any position to help; in his current situation, he could not even help himself. Leading figures of the WJC turned to Dr. Felix Kersten for assistance.

One of the WJC's leaders, Hillel Storch, flew to Stockholm in February 1945, where he met Dr. Kersten. The main topic of discussion was if Dr. Kersten would be willing to speak with Heinrich Himmler regarding Hitler's order to destroy the camps and, specifically, if he would ask Himmler to rescind the order. Dr. Kersten very willingly agreed to do his best.

Discussions between Dr. Kersten and Himmler began on March 5, 1945, at Hartzwalde, Dr. Kersten's estate about forty-five miles northwest of Berlin. The *Reichsführer* was "in a highly nervous condition," Dr. Kersten remembered; negotiations were "difficult and stormy." The talks "lasted for days and had dramatic moments." One of the dramatic moments came when Himmler declared, "If National Socialist Germany is going to be destroyed, then her enemies and the criminals in concentration camps shall not have the satisfaction of emerging from our ruin as triumphant conquerors. They shall share in the downfall." He went on to say that these were Hitler's direct orders, and he "must see to it that they [were] carried out to the letter."[25]

But Dr. Kersten refused to be put off by such flare-ups and continued to argue against the killing of concentration camp prisoners. Sounding very much like Admiral Canaris, he later wrote, "I succeeded in convincing Himmler that this final outburst of large-scale slaughter was quite senseless, and, in the name of humanity, persuaded him that he should fail to carry out the order in question."[26] And at the end of all the arguing and shouting, the two reached an agreement consisting of four points:

1. Heinrich Himmler would refuse to obey Adolf Hitler's order to destroy all concentration camps and kill all prisoners.

2. As Allied forces approached the vicinity of the camps, a white flag was to be shown, and the facilities were to be handed over "in an orderly manner."

3. Jews were to receive the same treatment as other prisoners.

4. The camps were not to be evacuated. Prisoners were to be left where they were and would be allowed to receive food parcels.[27]

"This was the first decisive step which averted danger from the Jewish prisoners and at the same time saved the lives of thousands of prisoners of various nationalities," Dr. Kersten said. Heinrich Himmler signed the document as *Reichsführer-SS*. Dr. Kersten countersigned the agreement and added "in the name of humanity." After looking at the signature, Himmler stared at Dr. Kersten for a moment, nodded his head, and handed the doctor his copy without saying a word. Dr. Kersten put the agreement in his pocket and left the room before Himmler had the chance to change his mind.[28]

Walter Schellenberg had been in constant contact with Himmler on the subject of the concentration camps and was well aware that the *Reichsführer* had overturned Hitler's directive. Schellenberg informed Jean-Marie Musy, who had been president of Switzerland in the 1920s, of Himmler's decision and asked him to pass this information along to General Eisenhower as quickly as possible. Three days later, Musy informed Schellenberg that Washington, DC, had received the news, presumably by way of General Eisenhower's headquarters, and had "reacted favorably" to the information.[29]

Throughout the month of March, the two continued to negotiate and talk about the release of other prisoners—Dr. Kersten referred to this process as making a deal. The main problem during these talks was Heinrich Himmler's constant changes of mind—sometimes he would be more than willing to come to an agreement, but at other times he was argumentative and difficult. The way Dr. Kersten saw it, the *Reichsführer* was living in a state of "constant fear of Hitler and those around him." Even though it was obvious that German forces would not be able to hold out much longer and that the war would be over in a matter of weeks, at best, Himmler was still afraid that Hitler would somehow find out about his talks with Dr. Kersten—especially the four-part agreement that nullified Hitler's order to destroy the concentration camps. "He is constantly swearing me to the strictest secrecy," Dr. Kersten wrote. "His worst worry is that the document would fall into the hands of 'the jackals of the press'" and become public. The doctor promised that no living soul would ever find out anything about the document or its contents, which seemed to put the *Reichsführer*'s mind at ease.[30]

The two kept talking and negotiating the release of other prisoners being held captive by the Nazis. Another item on Dr. Kersten's agenda was the freeing of French women interned at Ravensbrück. He did not think that Himmler would have any objections to this idea since France was no longer under German occupation. But this time, Himmler refused to go along with Dr. Kersten—he wanted to keep at least some of the women at Ravensbrück "in order to have a hold over France." Some "strong discussions" followed Himmler's decision, and Dr. Kersten once again managed to change the *Reichsführer*'s mind; he agreed that eight hundred French women would be released and sent to neutral Sweden.[31]

During the same week, Himmler and Dr. Kersten also talked about the release of Jewish inmates from Bergen-Belsen. The camp was being ravaged by an outbreak of typhus, which had killed many of its inmates (including Anne Frank). Dr. Kersten stressed that the camp should not be allowed to become a plague center that might eventually lead to the infection of the rest of Germany. Himmler approved the release. "They are all to receive South American passports and permission to enter

Sweden," Dr. Kersten wrote. Admiral Canaris had used the same method to smuggle Jews out of occupied countries and into Switzerland.[32]

As the talks went on, Himmler seemed to become friendlier and more agreeable toward both Dr. Kersten and his suggestions. When Dr. Kersten brought up the subject of freeing "certain categories of Jews" and sending them to Sweden and Switzerland, Himmler approved. "Himmler was very open with me and promised to go thoroughly into the question of releases," Dr. Kersten noted. The *Reichsführer*'s only misgiving concerned supplying transport for the prisoners. At this point in the war, the German army did not have enough vehicles to move its own troops, let alone hundreds of concentration camp inmates. Himmler insisted that either Switzerland or Sweden take responsibility for transporting the prisoners. Apart from this consideration, the inmates were free to leave Germany as soon as arrangements could be made.[33]

On the same day, Heinrich Himmler also issued an order forbidding "any sort of cruelty to Jewish prisoners" in concentration camps. A week later, he went a step further. On March 24, he sent "detailed instructions" to all camp commanders regarding the humane treatment of all inmates. Specifically, he warned that "every camp commandant would be held responsible for every Jewish prisoner's death" and would be required to make "an exact report on the circumstances." But the *Reichsführer* also made a point of informing Dr. Kersten that every one of his concessions would be withdrawn if one word of his actions somehow found its way into the "world press." His main concern was that news of his meeting with Dr. Kersten would be seen as "a sign of weakness on Germany's part."[34]

Heinrich Himmler's motive in releasing the concentration camp victims had been a topic of discussion since the last days of the war. According to Baldur von Schirach, leader of the Nazi Youth movement, Himmler only agreed to Dr. Kersten's proposals to "redeem himself with his good treatment of the Jews."[35] Himmler was all too aware that the end of the war was now terrifyingly close at hand and that he would almost certainly be tried as a war criminal when the fighting ended. But there was a lot more behind the *Reichsführer*'s activities than just making himself look good in the eyes of a war crimes tribunal. He had protected

Admiral Canaris's rescue efforts as far back as Operation Aguilar in 1943, when the outcome of the war was still an unanswered question.

Although a dedicated Nazi, Himmler did have misgivings regarding the wholesale slaughter of Jews and other "undesirables." This is why he did not prosecute Admiral Canaris for his rescue efforts. He failed to report Operation Aguilar and other rescue operations at great risk to himself—he was fully aware that he would have been summarily executed if Hitler discovered that he had covered up for Admiral Canaris. Redeeming himself was only a partial motive for cooperating with Dr. Kersten.

* * *

In the middle of March, Heinrich Himmler made another remarkable decision: he agreed to meet with a member of the World Jewish Congress to discuss the release of Jewish prisoners from concentration camps. The meeting was suggested by Felix Kersten. Himmler rejected the idea at first—"I can never receive a Jew," he said. "If the Führer were to hear of it, I would be shot dead on the spot." But Dr. Kersten argued that Himmler would be able to keep the meeting a secret and that Hitler would never find out about it—Himmler could hold the meeting at Dr. Kersten's estate and decide who would be informed of the gathering. Reichsführer Himmler listened to what Dr. Kersten had to say and agreed to see a World Jewish Congress representative at Hartzwalde.[36]

The WJC member that Dr. Kersten had in mind for the meeting with Himmler was Hillel Storch. Storch agreed to meet with the *Reichsführer*, but only if Dr. Kersten agreed to come with him. Dr. Kersten was more than willing to go along with this request—after all, the meeting was his idea. But at the last minute Hillel Storch announced that he would not be able to go. Norbert Masur, director of the WJC's Swedish branch, agreed to go instead.

Norbert Masur and Dr. Kersten were flown from Stockholm to Berlin on the afternoon of April 19, 1945; they were the only two passengers on board the aircraft. Dr. Kersten wrote that he did not see any German or Allied airplanes in the sky during the four-hour flight. This is not surprising: by the middle of April, the German Luftwaffe had ceased to exist, having been shot out of the sky by the Royal Air Force and the US Army Air Force. The flight arrived at Tempelhof airport during the late afternoon and was met by a half dozen smartly uniformed police. The policemen snapped to attention and shouted, "Heil Hitler!" Masur removed his hat and politely replied, "Good morning."[37]

Norbert Masur and Dr. Kersten met with Heinrich Himmler and SS-Brigadeführer Walter Schellenberg at Hartzwalde two days after arriving in Berlin. Reichsführer Himmler seemed pleasant enough and agreed to do everything possible for Masur. "I want to bury the hatchet between us and the Jews," he said. Dr. Kersten had been informed that a new commandant had been assigned to the Bergen-Belsen camp and also that the Red Cross had been allowed to visit the camp at Theresienstadt. The talks opened on this encouraging note, but the conversation soon took what the doctor would later describe as "a dangerous turn."[38]

Himmler declared that the Jews were "an alien element" in Germany. Shortly after the Nazis came to power, he had attempted to start an emigration program to relocate the Jews in other countries. But, he explained with some annoyance, none of the countries that "pretended to be so friendly towards the Jews" would accept them. The British demanded that all Jews who entered the British Isles bring at least £1,000 with them—a considerable amount of money in the 1930s, much more than most people could afford. Since the invasion of Russia in June 1941, the Jews of eastern Europe had created another kind of problem. "These European Jews aid the partisans and help the underground movements" on the Russian front, Himmler said. "They also fire on us from their ghettos and are carriers of epidemics such as typhus."[39]

The *Reichsführer* next went on to defend the concentration camps. He insisted that they should actually be called "training camps," because they were not just prisons. Along with imprisoned Jews and political detainees, he explained, criminals were also being rehabilitated in the camps. Himmler also claimed that the camps were responsible for lowering Germany's crime rate—in 1941, the country "had the lowest criminal rate in many years." Norbert Masur interrupted Himmler, saying that countless horrific crimes had been committed inside the concentration camps; he did not mention their nature but declared that they were unspeakable. "I concede that this has happened occasionally," Himmler admitted, "but I have also punished the persons responsible." He was referring to the commandant at Buchenwald, a Standardenführer Koch, who had been shot for the ill treatment of prisoners by Reichsführer Himmler's direct order.[40]

The conversation went on for about three-quarters of an hour before Masur finally said that although the *Reichsführer's* account "had been very interesting it was not in any way conducive toward changing the situation."[41] He asked Himmler to release all the Jews, but the *Reichsführer* responded by mentioning what had happened when the Bergen-Belsen and the Buchenwald camps had been handed over to American troops. According to his version of the story, "The advancing American tanks suddenly opened fire and set the camp hospital aflame." The fire very quickly spread until the entire building was burning. Many of the patients died in the fire. "The corpses were then photographed and more propaganda against us was provided." Reichsführer Himmler went on to complain that the newspapers also used the release of twenty-seven hundred Jews to Switzerland as the basis of a "personal campaign" against him, insisting that he had only released them to provide evidence for his defense at a war crimes trial. "Newspapers abroad have started a campaign against me which is no encouragement to me to continue handing over the camps."[42]

Dr. Kersten convinced the *Reichsführer* that he must stand by the principles set down in their "March agreement." Himmler replied that he would set a figure of a thousand to be released. He was as good as his word, authorizing the release of a thousand Jewish women from the Ravensbrück camp. But he also insisted upon one stipulation: the women would be listed as Poles, not Jews, to get around Adolf Hitler's directive against the release of Jewish prisoners.[43]

The talks went on until 5:00 a.m., according to Dr. Kersten. Walter Schellenberg remembers the time as 4:30 a.m. The agreement reached at Hartzwalde consisted of two main points: "that no more Jews would be killed; and that the remaining Jews—and their numbers were very uncertain—should remain in the camps and under no circumstances be evacuated."[44] Dr. Kersten also mentioned preventing the indiscriminate shooting of "political prisoners"—non-Jews—as the Allied armies approached.[45]

After the conversation finally wound down in the early morning of April 22, the men said their good-byes and went their separate ways. Dr. Kersten drove back to Berlin with Norbert Masur. Masur had been given a special pass for leaving the country by Reichsführer Himmler; Himmler did not want Masur to have any problems at the airport.

* * *

Heinrich Himmler was not completely reformed as a Nazi. He may have wanted to put an end to the persecution of the Jews, but he still thought they were an alien element in German society and also defended the existence of concentration camps. Himmler also agreed to release more inmates from the camps but made a point of letting Norbert Masur know his opinion of the Jews, especially German Jews, and of the "Jewish question." Admiral Canaris certainly had a profound effect on the *Reichsführer*, as well as on uncovering his long-buried sense of humanity. But the admiral was not able to overcome all of Himmler's prejudices and could do nothing to help him overcome his fear of Adolf Hitler.

CHAPTER THIRTEEN

Father of the Persecuted

DURING THE EARLY SPRING OF 1945, ALLIED FORCES FINALLY REACHED the borders of Germany and began their drive to overrun the country. Gen. Dwight D. Eisenhower described this offensive as an "Allied avalanche" that inflicted "a series of losses and defeats of staggering proportions."[1] On March 7, the US First Army crossed the Rhine "with dry feet" at Remagen over the captured Ludendorff Bridge; one of Germany's traditional defensive barriers had been penetrated. Less than three weeks later, Soviet troops attacked Königsberg, a Prussian city that the Soviet Union captured, annexed, and renamed Kaliningrad. By mid-April, over three hundred thousand German troops had been taken prisoner in the Ruhr pocket. By this time, German industry could no longer supply the Wehrmacht with the weapons and matériel needed to carry on with the war. While Heinrich Himmler and Norbert Masur were negotiating the release of prisoners from the concentration camps, Allied troops were closing in on those same camps. The Allies were invading the country in overwhelming numbers. As writer and historian William L. Shirer put it, "The war had come home to Germany."[2]

President Franklin D. Roosevelt died of a cerebral hemorrhage on April 12, 1945, and did not see the Allied advance or the final collapse of Nazi Germany. But if he had lived until the close of the war, he would have been well satisfied by its outcome. By the end of April, the German army had been completely overpowered. After the war, the country would be occupied by the Allied forces for years to come. President Roosevelt would have been assured that no German politician could ever claim that

Germany had been stabbed in the back by traitors, like Adolf Hitler had done in the 1930s. There would be no twenty-year armistice this time and no Fourth Reich in the 1960s. Roosevelt had done what he had set out to accomplish.

As the Allied forces pushed their way deeper into Germany, they began to come across the concentration camps. Most soldiers had never heard the phrase "concentration camp." Those who had heard something about them had thought they were just large prison compounds, along the lines of prisoner of war stockades. Nobody was prepared for what they actually found. "We just got orders that morning to get moving," recalled Sgt. Henry de Jarnette of the US 42nd Division. "I saw a sign on the side of the road that said 'Dachau,' but it didn't mean anything to me—just another town ahead."[3]

As soon as they entered the town, Sergeant de Jarnette and the rest of the 42nd Division realized that Dachau was like no other place they had ever seen. They first encountered a train surrounded by "little objects lying on the ground." As they came closer, the GIs could see that the "little objects" were actually corpses. They soon met the survivors of the camp, who did not seem much better off than the dead. "It was a day that young men vomited and cried at the sight and smell" of Dachau, Sergeant de Jarnette recalled. "Being hugged and kissed by walking skeletons. Death wherever we looked. We couldn't believe what we were seeing—the inhumanity of man to man, the torture, disease, starvation."[4]

Journalist Edward R. Murrow had a similar reaction to the camp at Buchenwald. He broadcast a description of what he saw inside the camp: men too weak from hunger to get out of bed; corpses stacked like so much cordwood; hundreds of children barely alive on the verge of starvation. Murrow ended his broadcast by asking his listeners to believe what he had told them about Buchenwald. "I reported what I saw and heard, but only part of it. For most of it, I have no words."[5] Newspaper reporters also visited the camps. When American troops arrived at Dachau, Marguerite Higgins of the New York *Herald Tribune* wrote, "the liberation was a frenzied scene. Inmates of the camp hugged and embraced the American troops, kissed the ground before them and carried them shoulder high around the place."[6]

General Eisenhower did not visit Dachau, but he did see what he described as the "horror camp" at Ohrdruf Nord, near the town of Gotha. "I visited every nook and cranny of the place," he wrote, and remembered of what he saw, "I have never at any other time experienced an equal sense of shock." Some members of the general's group were not able to go through with the complete inspection of the camp. Later that same day, General Eisenhower sent messages to both Washington, DC, and London urging the British and American governments to send reporters to the camps and write stories about what they saw of "Nazi brutality."[7]

Most daily reports and weekly summaries submitted by American and British army units covered only military subjects and tended to be self-consciously laconic. The US 42nd Division's official report on the capture of Dachau was typical of these statements; direct and straightforward, it said only, "Early in afternoon, the concentration camp Dachau surrendered to General Linden." But the unit's senior intelligence officer submitted his own report, a sixty-eight-page account that included

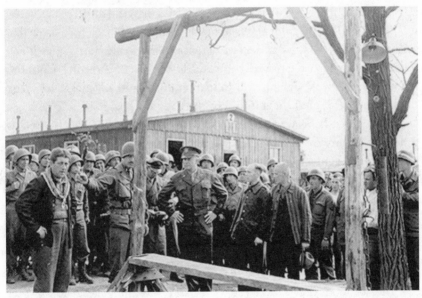

General Eisenhower visits the "horror camp" at Ohrdruf Nord. He urged news reporters to write stories about the camps and what they saw there. *Source:* National Archives.

photos of Dachau along with interviews with camp survivors. "Dachau and death were synonymous," said the report, which was anything but detached and unemotional. The headline of the April 29, 1945, issue of the *45th Division News* summed up the feeling of the men who liberated the camp: "We Have Seen Dachau. Now We Know What We Are Fighting For."[8]

Adm. Wilhelm Canaris knew what he was fighting for, as well. Perhaps even more importantly, he also knew what he was fighting against. By smuggling Jews out of Nazi-occupied territory disguised as Abwehr agents, the admiral prevented several hundred of them from ending up in camps like Dachau. He had been fighting Adolf Hitler and the Nazis for years. Sending Jews to Switzerland and Spain was one way of carrying out that fight. And he influenced Heinrich Himmler to free several thousand more.

One bit of good news that made the rounds came on February 3, 1945: Judge Roland Freisler of the People's Court had been killed in a daylight air raid. Judge Freisler, known as the Hanging Judge, has been referred to as "a vile, vituperative maniac."[9] Unmerciful and vindictive, he was the presiding judge at the trial of Hans and Sophie Scholl, as well as at many other trials for anti-Nazi activities. The same bomb that killed Judge Freisler also destroyed the records of one of Admiral Canaris's fellow conspirators, Fabian von Schlabrendorff, and saved his life. Von Schlabrendorff joined the admiral in the cells at Gestapo headquarters.

Even though he was forbidden to talk to anyone, either his fellow prisoners or any of the guards, Admiral Canaris still managed to keep informed of events. His usual method of finding out what he wanted to know was to trick his guards into telling him bits of information, in spite of themselves and their orders. "I suppose by now we are pushing the Russians back to the Vistula," he would say to one of the Schutzstaffel (SS) men.

"Ach, what nonsense," would come the sneering reply. "They are approaching the Oder."[10]

The air raid that killed Judge Roland Freisler gave Adolf Hitler second thoughts about keeping prisoners at Gestapo headquarters in Berlin. He decided to move them out of Berlin for safekeeping—a dead prisoner would be of no use to the Gestapo or anyone else. On February 7, 1945, Admiral Canaris was transferred to the concentration camp at Flossenbürg, about a mile from the Czechoslovak border and far from the flight paths of enemy bombers. Hans Oster was also sent to Flossenbürg along with his lawyer friend Dr. Josef Müller from Munich, Fabian von Schlabrendorff, and other former members of German intelligence. Prisoners with no connection to the intelligence service, including theologian Dietrich Bonhoeffer, were kept in other areas of the camp, away from Canaris and Oster.

Admiral Canaris occupied Cell 22. The occupant of Cell 21, next door to the admiral, was Lt. Col. Mathiesen Lunding, who had been the director of Danish military intelligence. The two had known each other earlier in the war. Colonel Lunding had been assigned to the Abwehr detachment in Copenhagen. He was arrested in August 1943, when the Danish resistance began to revolt against occupying German forces— the Gestapo suspected Lunding of sympathizing with the resistance. Admiral Canaris protested Colonel Lunding's arrest but was ignored. Colonel Lunding was placed in the custody of the Gestapo and sent to Flossenbürg in July 1944. The admiral and the Danish intelligence officer recognized each other and began communicating by means of a unique tapping code, which was the only method possible at Flossenbürg. Messages were usually tapped out at night, when the guards were fewer and not as watchful.

After his arrival at Flossenbürg, Admiral Canaris continued to be questioned. Security officers asked him how much he knew about the July 20 bomb plot, as well as what connection he might have had with other treasonable activities. The routine was basically the same as it had been at Gestapo headquarters. And the admiral's own routine, answering the questions with vague statements and half-truths, worked just as well for him at Flossenbürg as it had in Berlin. The officers asked their questions; the admiral told his interrogators absolutely nothing, in a series of well-thought-out, meaningless sentences.

At night, while the rest of the camp was quiet, Admiral Canaris and Colonel Lunding kept in touch with each other. Sometimes they

Admiral Canaris spent his last days in Flossenbürg concentration camp, where he was executed in April 1945. *Source:* US Army.

compared notes. The alphabet of their simple code was divided into five groups; the letter *J* was omitted.

1 2 3 4 5

A F L Q V

B G M R W

C H N S X

D I O T Y

E K P U Z

The first tap indicated the line; the second tap gave the letter on that line.

Throughout February and March, the interrogation of Admiral Canaris continued. A special Gestapo commissioner came to the camp to confront the admiral with some supposedly new evidence. Colonel

Lunding watched through the tiny window that faced the courtyard as the Gestapo commissioner, who was much taller than Admiral Canaris, spoke in loud, threatening tones and punctuated his remarks with intimidating gestures. The admiral responded to the threats and bombast in a normal, conversational voice. As the two walked around the courtyard, the commissioner's voice became louder and angrier, while Admiral Canaris remained calm and composed. The special Gestapo interrogator had no more success with the admiral than any of his predecessors. He returned to Berlin without having learned anything about Admiral Canaris's involvement in anti-Nazi activities.

Admiral Canaris's morale remained high in spite of everything. He had succeeded in sidestepping and evading every attempt by his captors to trap or intimidate him. He knew that the war could not go on for much longer. All the prisoners were well aware that American units were not far away and headed toward Flossenbürg. From his communications in code with the admiral, Colonel Lunding was under the impression that "his neighbor had not lost hope of escaping the Gestapo noose."[11]

But Admiral Canaris did not know about a discovery by an officer in the Wehrmacht that would change everything. The find was made in the town of Zossen, about twenty miles south of Berlin. An army general named Walter Buhle had come upon several binders inside a safe at Camp Zepplin in Zossen, the headquarters of the Army General Staff. Inside the binders were many pages of Admiral Canaris's diary, in the admiral's own handwriting. They recorded, in great detail, activities of the anti-Nazi movement from the 1930s onward. The contents effectively gave the Gestapo everything they had been looking for and condemned Admiral Canaris to the gallows.

No one knows exactly why Wilhelm Canaris kept such a detailed account—he gave dates, names, and the particulars of just about every action of the anti-Hitler resistance—for so many years. Possibly it was to record the activities of the resistance for future historians, or maybe it was to set down an official record of the corruption of Adolf Hitler and the Nazis, told from the point of view of Hitler's own chief of intelligence. Whatever the reason, the diaries have been one of the great mysteries of Admiral Canaris's often enigmatic life.

General Buhle quickly informed the Gestapo of what he had found at Zossen—he personally handed the Canaris file to the head of the security service directly responsible for the safety of Adolf Hitler. Early in April, probably April 4, the security head then gave the diaries to SS-Obergruppenführer Ernst Kaltenbrunner, who reported their existence directly to Hitler.

Adolf Hitler read some of the entries, especially concentrating on passages marked by Obergruppenführer Kaltenbrunner. After going through Admiral Canaris's comments and observations, Hitler ordered that the prisoners at Flossenbürg be dealt with in the manner reserved for all traitors and enemies of the Reich: given a quick trial and then hung. He issued this order on the afternoon of April 5. Admiral Canaris, Hans Oster, Dietrich Bonhoeffer, Dr. Josef Müller, Fabian von Schlabrendorff, and two others were to be disposed of, once and for all, for numerous crimes against the Fatherland. The hangings were to be carried out as quickly as possible, after a short and meaningless trial.

Dr. Müller was supposed to have been executed first, on April 8, three days after Hitler issued his order. "The last act is about to begin," a guard shouted at him. "You will be hanged right after Canaris and Oster." But Admiral Canaris and Hans Oster had not yet had their trials for treason, and Josef Müller was not hanged—he was taken from his cell to the gallows but was left standing there. After a while, the SS guards took him back to his cell, then back to the gallows a second time. Finally, he was told, "We'll have to forget you for today," and was led back to his cell again.[12]

While Josef Müller was going through this ordeal, Admiral Canaris and Hans Oster were living a nightmare of their own. After being tried, found guilty, and sentenced to death, the admiral was interrogated under torture. Hitler's order of April 5 finally allowed the SS to do what it had been wanting to do. After the brutal interrogation, he was brought back to his cell in a badly battered and roughed-up state, bruised and bleeding. He sent a message in code to Mathiesen Lunding: "That . . . will . . . have . . . been . . . the . . . last . . . I . . . think . . . badly . . . mishandled . . . nose . . . broken." He went on to say, "I die for my Fatherland. I have a clear conscience. I only did my duty to my country when I tried to oppose the criminal folly of Hitler leading Germany to destruction." Admiral Canaris asked Colonel Lunding, if he managed to survive his stay at Flossenbürg, to visit his wife and two daughters.[13]

During the early hours of April 9, a Gestapo official came to Fabian von Schlabrendorff's cell and asked if he was Dietrich Bonhoeffer. Later in the morning, the same man returned and repeated the question. An SS guard asked a surprised Josef Müller if *he* was Dietrich Bonhoeffer. Shortly afterward, sometime after daybreak, a perplexed guard came to remove Müller's handcuffs. "I don't know what's going on," he said. "I was told you were the leading criminal and now we don't know what to do with you."[14]

It had been a bizarre and frightening night. Müller heard the guards shouting out cell numbers, including Number 22—Admiral Canaris's cell—and then, "Out! Out!" Colonel Lunding heard the admiral's shackles fall to the floor and also heard the order, "Clothes off!" Through a crack in his cell door, he saw Admiral Canaris and Hans Oster being led away to the gallows with Karl Sack, a former army judge who had been implicated in the July 20 plot; Theodor Strünck, another Abwehr officer arrested for treason; and a Captain Gehre, who had been arrested by the Gestapo for treason.[15]

Dr. Müller did not witness Admiral Canaris's execution, but he heard that the admiral took half an hour to die. Fabian von Schlabrendorff was also told by one of the guards that the admiral died slowly and horribly. An iron collar had been placed around his neck before the execution began, and a noose was placed over the collar. This was done to prolong his agony or, as one of the guards put it, "to give him a foretaste of death."[16] He was hanged with the iron collar still in place, taken down while he was still alive, and then hanged again. The second time, he was left hanging until he was dead. Fabian von Schlabrendorff was later informed that the men who carried out the execution were rewarded with extra rations of sausage and whisky.

The bodies of the prisoners were burned on a huge bonfire. Josef Müller remembers someone speaking in English through his cell window sometime after the executions had been carried out. Several British agents were also being held at Flossenbürg, including two officers with the last name Churchill: Lt. Col. John Churchill and Capt. Peter Churchill. The Gestapo thought the two agents might have some future value: the two officers, the Gestapo reasoned, must be related to the prime minister and could possibly be held as hostages at some point. The man in the window asked Dr. Müller, "Are you one of those top officials to be hanged?"

The doctor answered, "I think so."

The man did not think that Dr. Müller was going to be executed. "Your friends have been executed already," the man explained, "and are now being burned behind their cells."[17] Dr. Müller had apparently been lost in some sort of bureaucratic shuffle, along with Fabian von Schlabrendorff.

Dr. Müller had smelled the smoke from the bonfire and seen bits of ash floating through the bars of his window like snowflakes. It took a moment or two before he realized that the grey flakes were the cremated remains of Admiral Canaris, Hans Oster, and the others hanged earlier in the day. The wind was blowing in the direction of his cell, and the ashes kept blowing through the window and settling on and all around him. Dr. Müller recalled nearly fainting when he understood what was happening.

Adm. Wilhelm Canaris, head of the Abwehr, was finally dead. The Sicherheitsdienst, the Schutzstaffel, and the Gestapo had all been doing their best to dispose of the little admiral—either hang him or have him buried alive in some concentration camp—for the past several years. On April 9, 1945, they achieved what they had been trying to accomplish for so long. Dr. Müller could hardly believe that Admiral Canaris, who had outsmarted and outmaneuvered the Nazi regime so many times, was actually gone. He had smuggled several hundred Jews and other outcasts out of Nazi-occupied territory right past the Gestapo. He had also sent military information to the Allies and done everything possible to prevent Adolf Hitler from winning the war. And with a great deal of cunning and an equal amount of good luck, along with the assistance of Heinrich Himmler, the admiral had managed to avoid detection.

But his luck ran out on July 20, 1944, when he was implicated in the failed Hitler assassination plot. Although he got away with all of his activities against Hitler and the Nazis, he was hanged because of a conspiracy in which he had played no active part. He would have been satisfied that at least his death did not help the Nazis; by the time he was hanged at Flossenbürg, the war was nearly over, and the concentration camps were being liberated.

Exactly two weeks after Admiral Canaris was hanged, members of the 358th and 359th US Infantry Regiments arrived at Flossenbürg and liberated the camp. About two thousand prisoners were still there and being forced to evacuate by their SS guards. When they saw the American troops, the guards panicked and began shooting the prisoners. About two hundred of the inmates were killed. The Americans opened fire on the Germans as they fled into the woods, killing about one hundred of the SS guards. Dr. Josef Müller was among the inmates who survived their captivity in Flossenbürg.

A week after Flossenbürg was liberated and three weeks after Admiral Canaris was hanged, Adolf Hitler committed suicide in his Berlin Chancellery. He shot himself on April 30. His bride, the former Eva Braun, swallowed poison. Seven days later, during the early hours of May 7, Germany surrendered unconditionally to the Allied powers, and the Third Reich ceased to exist. The end came too late to save the inmates who died in the concentration camps, but the mass murders had finally come to an end. Admiral Canaris had done his part in bringing the Nazi regime to its end, as well as in saving hundreds of political and religious pariahs from Flossenbürg and other camps.

The admiral's unlikely ally in saving concentration camp inmates, SS-Reichsführer Heinrich Himmler, managed to evade capture until the end of May. Following the surrender of all German forces, the *Reichsführer* and eleven other SS officers tried to pass through the British and American lines on their way to Bavaria. In an attempt to outwit any patrols that might be encountered along the way, he had shaved his moustache, wore a patch over one eye, and carried the identification of a sergeant in the Geheime Feldpolizei (secret field police) named Heinrich Hitzinger. But in spite of his disguise, Reichsführer Himmler was arrested, along with his companions, at a British checkpoint and taken to a camp near Bremen—the Geheime Feldpolizei were as notorious as the SS, and its members were arrested on sight. During interrogation,

Himmler inexplicably decided to identify himself to his guards: "Ich bin der Reichsführer-SS."[18]

As soon as they realized that their prisoner was one of the leading figures of the Nazi regime and the head of the SS, the soldiers sent for a British intelligence officer to question him. Col. Michael Murphy was called in to do the interrogation. While the colonel was driving to the checkpoint, the soldiers ordered Himmler to undress. They quickly discovered two small containers in his uniform and concluded that these contained poison—other prisoners had committed suicide recently by biting into similar vials. Following this search, and the confiscation of the two vials, the *Reichsführer* was given a British army uniform. He wore this uniform to another interrogation, conducted at Second Army Headquarters outside Lüneburg. The questioning was to be conducted by Colonel Murphy, but Himmler was subjected to another body search before the questioning began. The *Reichsführer* had another vial concealed between his teeth; he bit into it before his guards could prevent him. In spite of all efforts to keep him alive, he died in about fifteen minutes. Heinrich Himmler's body was buried in an unmarked grave on Lüneburg Heath.

Admiral Canaris has no grave, but he does have a memorial plaque in Flossenbürg. The plaque's inscription reads, "Im Widerstand gegen Diktatur und Terror gaben ihr Leben für Freiheit Recht und Menschenwürde [In resistance against dictator and terror they gave their lives for freedom and mankind]." Beneath the inscription are the names of the others who were hanged on April 9, 1945: Dietrich Bonhoeffer, Hans Oster, and the others executed that day. (Hans von Dohnanyi was also executed, probably also on April 9, but at the Orianienburg/Sachsenhausen concentration camp.) Above the names and the description is a Roman cross with the note "2 TIM.1.7." The Bible verse from the second book of Timothy, chapter 1, verse 7, reads, "For God did not give us a spirit of timidity, but the spirit of power and love and self-control."[19]

One of Admiral Canaris's biographers called him the "father of the persecuted."[20] This may sound romantic and starry-eyed, but the description does have more than just a kernel of truth in it. The admiral put his life in jeopardy, along with the lives of his colleagues in the resistance, every time he did something to protect or help the persecuted. Whenever he provided Abwehr identification documents to any of the Nazi regime's victims, which allowed them to travel out of German-occupied territory, he knew that he was risking his life. Admiral Canaris was dedicated to undermining the Nazis by using any method that was open to him, including by helping the targets of their bigotries and prejudices. As it was, his activities in the anti-Hitler movement ultimately did cost him his life.

Over the years, the German resistance to Hitler and his government has been either downplayed or totally forgotten. The resistance was "fragmented and ultimately ineffective," according to an account written nearly fifty years after the war ended.[21] The anti-Hitler movement was certainly fragmented, especially when compared with the highly organized resistance groups in other countries, including in France and the Netherlands. A women connected with the German underground declared, "Don't talk about *Widerstand* [resistance]," meaning an organized and structured opposition movement. "We did not think of ourselves as being part of a *Widerstand*. We merely thought somehow to survive in dignity."[22] Not all members of the anti-Nazi movement survived, but they did make a difference in reinstating integrity and human rights in Germany.

The same reporter who called the anti-Hitler movement "fragmented" and "ineffective" also commented on the conspirators who carried out the July 20, 1944, plot to kill Hitler. "For years after, many Germans did not know what to make of the deed," he wrote. "Were these unsung heroes, or were they traitors?"[23] The anti-Nazi resistance might have lacked the organization of the French resistance movement, but it was certainly not ineffective. Admiral Canaris managed to send vital information regarding German secret weapons to the Allies, along with data on Wehrmacht defenses in Normandy.[24] And Madame Halina Szymańska would not have thought of Admiral Canaris as either ineffective or a traitor. Neither would any of those who escaped from German captivity as part of Operation Aguilar or Operation 7, all of whom outlived the admiral by many years.

NOTES

CHAPTER ONE: ORDERS FROM THE FÜHRER

1. Roger Manvell and Heinrich Frankel, *The Canaris Conspiracy: The Secret Resistance to Hitler in the German Army* (New York: David McKay Co., 1969), p. 233.

2. Richard Bassett, *Hitler's Spy Chief* (New York: Pegasus Books, 2011), p. 14. This is an excerpt from a letter to the author.

3. Manvell and Frankel, *The Canaris Conspiracy*, pp. 102, 234.

4. Karl Heinz Abshagen, *Canaris*, tr. Alan Houghton Brodrick (London: Hutchinson, 1956), p. 19.

5. Report by the captain of the *Bremen*, November 12, 1908. From Heinz Höhne, *Canaris: Hitler's Master Spy* (New York: Cooper Square Press, 1979), p. 15.

6. Details of Wilhelm Canaris's early naval career are from Ian Colvin, *Chief of Intelligence* (London: Victor Gollancz, 1951); Höhne, *Canaris*; Abshagen, *Canaris*; Andre Brissaud, *Canaris* (New York: Grosset & Dunlap, 1974).

7. Erich Raeder, *Der Kreuzerkeig in ausländischen Gewässern* (Berlin: E. S. Mittler, 1922), p. 371.

8. Diary of Albert Hopmann, in Höhne, *Canaris*, p. 20.

9. Raeder, *Der Kreuzerkeieg*, p. 142.

10. Ibid., p. 387.

11. Ibid., p. 393.

12. The story of the *Dresden's* action off Más a Tierra is mainly from Raeder, *Der Kreuzerkeieg*, pp. 395–405.

13. Colvin, *Chief of Intelligence*, p. 19.

14. Höhne, *Canaris*, p. 42.

15. Colvin, *Chief of Intelligence*, p. 19.

16. Details of Lieutenant Canaris's activities are from Otto Gessler, *Reichswehrpolitik in der Weimarer Zeit* (Stuttgart: Deutsche Verlags-Anstalt, 1958), pp. 135–50.

17. Höhne, *Canaris*, p. 86.

18. Letter dated January 15, 1924, is from Wilhelm Canaris's personal file; from Höhne, *Canaris*, p. 87.

19. Höhne, *Canaris*, p. 87.

20. William L. Shirer, *The Rise and Fall of the Third Reich: A History of Nazi Germany* (New York: Simon & Schuster, 1960), p. 61.

21. Heinz Kiel, *Canaris zwischen den Fronten: Aufstieg und Untergang des Chefs der deutschen Spionageabwehr 1914–1945* (Bremerhaven: Hermann Verlag (1950), p. 11. Heinz Kiel wrote that Hitler and Canaris had a meeting in Munich in 1920 but does not supply any references.

22. Adolf Hitler, *Mein Kampf*, tr. Ralph Manheim (Boston: Houghton Mifflin, 1999), pp. 464, 632.

23. Ibid., p. 123.

24. "Judenstern," *Nation*, December 17, 2010, www.globalecho.org/408/judenstern.

CHAPTER TWO: CHANGES OF REGIME, CHANGES OF FORTUNE

1. Heinz Höhne, *Canaris: Hitler's Master Spy* (New York: Cooper Square Press, 1979), p. 114.

2. William L. Shirer, *The Rise and Fall of the Third Reich: A History of Nazi Germany* (New York: Simon & Schuster, 1960), pp. 141–42.

3. Jost Dülffer, *Weimar, Hitler, und die Marine: Reichspolitik und Flottenbau, 1920–1939* (Düsseldorf: Droste, 1973), p. 122.

4. Shirer, *The Rise and Fall*, p. 116.

5. Ibid., p. 187.

6. From a letter by Dr. Werner Best, in Höhne, *Canaris*, p. 133.

CHAPTER THREE: TURNING AGAINST HITLER

1. William L. Shirer, *Berlin Diary: The Journal of a Foreign Correspondent, 1934–1941* (New York: Alfred A. Knopf, 1941), p. 32.

2. Ibid., p. 32.

3. Adolf Hitler, *Mein Kampf*, tr. Ralph Manheim (Boston: Houghton Mifflin, 1999), p. 651.

4. Shirer, *Berlin Diary*, p. 31.

5. From a letter dated March 19, 1935, in Heinz Höhne, *Canaris: Hitler's Master Spy* (New York: Cooper Square Press, 1979), p. 185.

6. Shirer, *Berlin Diary*, p. 36.

7. Ibid., p. 40.

8. Ladislas Farago, *The Game of the Foxes* (New York: Bantam Books, 1973), p. 10.

9. Heinrich Fraenkel and Roger Manvell, *The Canaris Conspiracy* (London: William Heinemann, 1969), pp. 190, 240.

10. From an address by Admiral Canaris in March 1938, in Höhne, *Canaris*, p. 213.

11. Shirer, *Berlin Diary*, p. 91.

12. Ian Colvin, *Chief of Intelligence* (London: Victor Gollancz, 1951), p. 43.

13. Otto John, *Twice through the Lines*, tr. Richard Barry (New York: Harper & Row, 1972), p. 37.

14. Ibid.

15. *New York Times*, November 11, 1938.

16. Klaus-Jürgen Müller, *Das Heer und Hitler: Armee und nationalsozialistisches Regime 1933–1940* (Stuttgart: Deutsche Verlags-Anstalt, 1969), p. 386.

17. Richard Bassett, *Hitler's Spy Chief* (New York: Pegasus Books, 2011), pp. 13–14.

CHAPTER FOUR: CHEATING THE GESTAPO

1. The original German version of Hitler's speech at the Berghof is in *Akten zur Deutchen Auswärtigen Politik*, Series D, Vol. VII, p. 167. Heinz Höhne, *Canaris: Hitler's Master Spy* (New York: Cooper Square Press, 1979), p. 346, offers an incomplete translation of the speech. It is given in a full translation in Louis P. Lochner, *What about Germany?* (New York: Dodd, Mead & Co., 1942), pp. 1–4. The Nuremberg Tribunal later identified the document as L-3 or Exhibit USA-28. In his book *Hitler and the Armenian Genocide* (Cambridge, MA: Zoryan Institute, 1985), Dr. Kevork B. Bardakjian says that the L-3 document probably originates in the notes secretly taken by Wilhelm Canaris during the meeting of August 22, 1939.

2. *Akten*, pp. 171–72; Höhne, *Canaris*, p. 347; Lochner, *What about Germany?*, pp. 1–4.

3. *Akten*, pp. 171–72; Höhne, *Canaris*, p. 348.

4. Ulrich von Hassell, *The Von Hassell Diaries: The Story of the Forces against Hitler inside Germany, 1938–1944* (Boulder, CO: Westview Press, 1994), p. 68.

5. Hans Bernd Gisevius, *To the Bitter End* (London: Jonathan Cape, 1948), p. 373.

6. Ian Colvin, *Chief of Intelligence* (London: Victor Gollancz, 1951), p. 95.

7. Von Hassell, *The Von Hassell Diaries*, p. 75.

8. *Akten*, pp. 171–72; Höhne, *Canaris*, p. 347; Lochner, *What about Germany?*, pp. 1–4.

9. Helmut Krausnick, "Hitler und die Morde in Polen," *Vierteljahreshelfte für Zeitgeschichte*, April 1963. Translated in Höhne, *Canaris*, p. 363.

10. Höhne, *Canaris*, p. 364; Ladislas Farago, *The Game of the Foxes* (New York: David McKay, 1971), pp. 194–95. The original German version is in Helmuth Groscurth, *Tagebücher eines Abwehroffiziers 1938–1940: Mit weiteren Dokumenten zur Militäropposition gegen Hitler*, ed. Helmut Krausnick and Harold C. Deutsch, with the assistance of Hildegard von Kotze. Quellen und Darstellung zur Zeitgeschichte 19 (Stuttgart: Deutsche Verlags-Anstalt, 1970), p. 594.

11. Colvin, *Chief of Intelligence*, p. 89.

12. Ibid., p. 89.

13. Ibid., p. 89.

14. Ibid., p. 90.

15. "Halina Szymańska—Life," primidi.com, www.primidi.com/halina_szymańska/life.

16. Nigel West, *MI6: British Secret Intelligence Service Operations, 1909–45* (New York: Random House, 1983), pp. xiv, 117.

17. "Halina Szymańska—Life."

18. Colvin, *Chief of Intelligence*, p. 91.

19. Ibid.

20. "Halina Szymańska—Life."

21. Allen Welsh Dulles, *Germany's Underground: The Anti-Nazi Resistance* (New York: Da Capo Press, 2000), p. 75.

22. Karl Heinz Abshagen, *Canaris*, tr. Alan Houghton Brodrick (London: Hutchinson, 1956), p. 150.

23. Abshagen, *Canaris*, p. 150.

24. "Hitler's Jewish Armed Forces," *Cosmic Logic*, March 11, 2017, https://cosmiclogic .wordpress.com/2017/03/11/hitlers-jewish-armed-forces.

25. "How Chabad's Beloved Rebbe Was Saved," *Atlanta Jewish Times*, October 12, 2012, https://www.atlantajewishtimes.com/how-chabads-beloved-rebbe-was-saved -from-the-nazis-by-the-nazis.

26. Abshagen, *Canaris*, p. 150.

27. Robert Gerwarth, *Hitler's Hangman: The Life of Heydrich* (New Haven, CT: Yale University Press, 2011), p. 61.

CHAPTER FIVE: OPENING A SPANISH DOOR

1. John Gunther, *Inside Europe* (New York: Harper & Brothers, 1940), p. xvi.

2. R.V. Jones, *Most Secret War* (London: Wordsworth Editions, 1998), p. 68.

3. R.V. Jones, *Reflections on Intelligence* (London: Heinemann, 1989), p. 275.

4. Jones, *Most Secret War*, p. 70.

5. R. V. Jones, "Scientific Intelligence," *Journal of the Royal United Services Institute*, August 1947.

6. Anthony Cave Brown, *Bodyguard of Lies* (New York: Harper & Row, 1975), p. 220.

7. Andrew Knighton, "Early in WW2 the British Received a Dossier of Nazi Military Secrets & Why Britain Almost Ignored It," War History Online, April 3, 2018, https:// www.warhistoryonline.com/world-war-ii/oslo-report-german-scientist-nazi.html.

8. Ibid.

9. John Waller, *The Unseen War in Europe* (New York: Random House, 1996), p. 152.

10. Karl Heinz Abshagen, *Canaris*, tr. Alan Houghton Brodrick (London: Hutchinson, 1956), p. 115.

11. Ian Colvin, *Chief of Intelligence* (London: Victor Gollancz, 1951), p. 149.

12. Ulrich von Hassell, *The Von Hassell Diaries: The Story of the Forces against Hitler inside Germany, 1938–1944* (Boulder, CO: Westview Press, 1994), p. 159.

13. Colvin, *Chief of Intelligence*, p. 151.

14. Von Hassell, *The Von Hassell Diaries*, p. 156.

15. Ibid., p. 159.

16. Colvin, *Chief of Intelligence*, p. 152.

17. Ibid., p. 155.

18. Letter from Dr. Stefan Heyden, dated November 3, 2008, in Richard Bassett, *Hitler's Spy Chief* (New York: Pegasus Books, 2011), pp. 13–14.

19. Gena Olan, "Franco's Spain and the Jewish Rescue Effort during World War Two" (thesis submitted in partial fulfillment of the requirements for graduation with distinction, Duke University, April 2013).

20. "Was Franco the 'Good' Fascist?," *Jewish Chronicle*, November 23, 2015.

21. Olan, "Franco's Spain," p. 53.

22. Ibid.

23. Aharon Lapid, "The Truth about Franco and the Jews," *Jewish Press*, June 25, 2008.

24. Olan, "Franco's Spain," p. 52.

25. Ibid., p. 54.

26. "General Franco Gave List of Spanish Jews to Nazis," *The Guardian*, June 20, 2010.
27. Ibid.
28. Von Hassell, *The Von Hassell Diaries*, p. 152.
29. Ibid., p. 150.
30. Ibid., p. 151.
31. "Amateur Diplomat Sought Nazi Pact," *BBC News*, August 30, 2008, http://news .bbc.co.uk/2/hi/uk_news/7589251.stm. Ulrich von Hassel visited James Lonsdale-Bryans in Switzerland, not Italy, as the report states.
32. Von Hassell, *The Von Hassell Diaries*, p. 116.
33. Ibid., p. 117.
34. Ibid., pp. 116–17.
35. Ibid., pp. 117–18.
36. Ibid., p. 118.
37. Cave Brown, *Bodyguard of Lies*, p. 228.
38. E. L. Woodward and Rohan Butler, eds., *Documents on British Foreign Policy, 1919–1939* (London: Her Majesty's Stationers Office, 1949), p. 2:688.

CHAPTER SIX: SUSPICIONS AND BRUTALITIES

1. Heinz Höhne, *Canaris: Hitler's Master Spy*, tr. J. Maxwell Brownjohn (New York: Cooper Square Press, 1979), p. 456.
2. Max Hastings, *Inferno: The World at War, 1939–1945* (New York: Alfred A. Knopf, 2011), p. 145.
3. Ulrich von Hassell, *The Von Hassell Diaries: The Story of the Forces against Hitler inside Germany, 1938–1944* (Boulder, CO: Westview Press, 1994), p. 207.
4. Höhne, *Canaris*, pp. 461–62.
5. Helmut Krausnick et al., *Anatomy of the SS State*, tr. Richard Barry, Marian Jackson, and Dorothy Long (London: Collins, 1968), p. 526.
6. Ibid.
7. Karl Bartz, *The Downfall of the German Secret Service* (London: William Kimber & Co., 1956), pp. 75–76.
8. "German Nazi Abwehr Officer Who Saved Jews," Passport-collector.com, January 6, 2018, www.passport-collector.com/german-nazi-officer.
9. Ibid.
10. Ibid.
11. Ibid.
12. Fabian von Schlabrendorff, *The Secret War against Hitler*, tr. Hilda Simon (New York: Pitman Publishing, 1965), p. 169.
13. "German Nazi Abwehr Officer Who Saved Jews."
14. Ibid.
15. Hans Bernd Gisevius, *To the Bitter End*, tr. Richard and Clara Winston (Cambridge, MA: Houghton, Mifflin, 1947), p. 101.
16. Otto John, *Twice through the Lines*, tr. Richard Barry (New York: Harper & Row, 1972), p. 71.
17. Ibid.

18. Ibid., p. 68.

19. Ibid., p. 71.

20. Ibid.

21. Ibid., p. 72.

22. Ibid., p. 73.

23. Ibid.

24. Ibid., p. 72.

25. Ibid., p. 74.

26. Joseph E. Persico, *Roosevelt's Secret War: FDR and World War II Espionage* (New York: Random House, 2001), p. 218.

27. Eva Fogelman, *Conscience and Courage: Rescuers of the Jews during the Holocaust* (New York: Doubleday, 1994), p. 47.

28. Michael L. Fullilove, *Rendezvous with Destiny* (New York: Penguin Press, 2013), p. 19.

CHAPTER SEVEN: A DIPLOMAT, AN ASSASSINATION, AND A PESTILENT PRIEST

1. National Archives, Record Group 226, Box 12.

2. Ibid.

3. National Archives, Record Group 226, Box 9.

4. Ibid.

5. Ibid.

6. Louis L. Snyder, *Encyclopedia of the Third Reich* (New York: Marlow & Co., 1976), p. 72.

7. Walter Schellenberg, *The Labyrinth: Memoirs of Walter Schellenberg, Hitler's Chief of Counterintelligence*, tr. Louis Hagen (New York: Da Capo Press, 2000), p. 351.

8. Ibid., p. 355.

9. Ian Colvin, *Chief of Intelligence* (London: Victor Gollancz, 1951), p. 187.

10. Schellenberg, *The Labyrinth*, p. 353.

11. Ibid., p. 352.

12. Ulrich von Hassell, *The Von Hassell Diaries: The Story of the Forces against Hitler inside Germany, 1938–1944* (Boulder, CO: Westview Press, 1994), p. 256–57.

13. Schellenberg, *The Labyrinth*, p. 353.

14. Charles Wighton, *Heydrich: Hitler's Most Evil Henchman* (London: Chilton Books, 1962), p. 327.

15. Peter Longerich, *Heinrich Himmler: A Life* (New York: Oxford University Press 2012), p. 508.

16. Wighton, *Heydrich*, p. 214. The complete text of the Madagascar Plan can be found at "The Nazis & the Jews: The Madagascar Plan (July 3, 1940)," Jewish Virtual Library, www.jewishvirtuallibrary.org/the-madagascar-plan-2.

17. Wighton, *Heydrich*, p. 214.

18. Callum MacDonald, *The Killing of Obergruppenführer Reinhard Heydrich* (New York: Free Press, 1989), pp. 175–76.

19. Statistics on the destruction of Lidice in Lt. Col. Eddy Bauer et al., *Illustrated World War II Encyclopedia* (Westport, CT: H. S. Stuttmann, 1966), p. 5:688.
20. Details of Reinhard Heydrich's funeral are from Wighton, *Heydrich*, and MacDonald, *The Killing of Obergruppenführer Reinhard Heydrich*.
21. Dietrich Bonhoeffer, *Conspiracy and Imprisonment, 1940–1945*, ed. Mark S. Brocker, tr. Lisa E. Dahill with Douglas W. Stott. Dietrich Bonhoeffer Works 16 (New York: Fortress Press, 2006), pp. 311–12. Also in Eric Metaxis, *Bonhoeffer: Pastor, Martyr, Prophet, Spy* (Nashville, TN: Thomas Nelson, 2010), p. 401.
22. Bonhoeffer, *Conspiracy and Imprisonment*, p. 313. Also Metaxis, *Bonhoeffer*, p. 401.
23. Metaxis, *Bonhoeffer*, p. 402.
24. Bonhoeffer, *Conspiracy and Imprisonment*, pp. 347–48. Also Metaxis, *Bonhoeffer*, p. 403.
25. Bonhoeffer, *Conspiracy and Imprisonment*, p. 349. Also Metaxis, *Bonhoeffer*, p. 40.

CHAPTER EIGHT: A HAZARDOUS OPERATION

1. Peter Padfield, *Himmler: Reichsfuhrer-SS* (New York: Henry Holt, 1990), p. 417.
2. Ulrich von Hassell, *The Von Hassell Diaries: The Story of the Forces against Hitler inside Germany, 1938–1944* (Boulder, CO: Westview Press, 1994), p. 261.
3. Ibid., pp. 246–47.
4. Ibid., p. 274.
5. Richard Bassett, *Hitler's Spy Chief* (New York: Pegasus Books, 2011), p. 14.
6. Eric Metaxis, *Bonhoeffer: Pastor, Martyr, Prophet, Spy* (Nashville, TN: Thomas Nelson, 2010), p. 389.
7. *The Righteous among the Nations: The Dohnanyi Family*, from the Vad Vashem, World Holocaust Reembrace Center, website.
8. Ibid.
9. Otto John, *Twice through the Lines*, tr. Richard Barry (New York: Harper & Row, 1972), p. 110.
10. Ibid.
11. Ibid., p. 112.
12. Ibid., p. 115.
13. Von Hassell, *The Von Hassell Diaries*, p. 299.
14. John, *Twice through the Lines*, p. 112.
15. Von Hassell, *The Von Hassell Diaries*, p. 300.
16. John, *Twice through the Lines*, p. 113.
17. Ibid., pp. 113–14.
18. Mary Bosanquet, *The Life and Death of Dietrich Bonhoeffer* (New York: Harper & Row, 1968), pp. 247–48.
19. John, *Twice through the Lines*, p. 115.
20. Ibid.
21. Anthony Cave Brown, *Bodyguard of Lies* (New York: Harper & Row, 1975), p. 337.
22. John, *Twice through the Lines*, p. 115.
23. Von Hassell, *The Von Hassell Diaries*, p. 309.
24. John, *Twice through the Lines*, p. 116.

25. Ibid.
26. Fabian von Schlabrendorff, *The Secret War against Hitler*, tr. Hilda Simon (New York: Pitman Publishing, 1965), p. 169.
27. Ibid., pp. 169–70.
28. Joachim C. Fest, *Plotting Hitler's Death: The Story of the German Resistance*, tr. Bruce Little (New York: Metropolitan Books, 1996), pp. 223–24.
29. "Baron Axel von dem Bussche, 73; Joined Officers' Plot to Kill Hitler," obituary in *New York Times*, January 30, 1993.
30. Anne Frank, *The Diary of a Young Girl: The Definitive Edition*, tr. Susan Massotty (New York: Bantam Books, 1997), pp. 54–55.
31. Louise Ridley, "The Holocaust's Forgotten Victims: The 5 Million Non-Jewish People Killed by the Nazis," *HuffPost UK*, January 27, 2015, updated December 6, 2017, https://www.huffingtonpost.com/2015/01/27.
32. Karen Silverstrim, "Overlooked Millions: Non-Jewish Victims of the Holocaust" (MA thesis, University of Central Arkansas, 1997).
33. I discovered Admiral Canaris's role in the Operation Torch deception while researching *Righteous Deception: German Officers against Hitler* (Conshohocken, PA: Books, 2001).
34. The numbers regarding the Operation Torch invasion force are from Dwight D. Eisenhower, *Crusade in Europe* (Garden City, NY: Doubleday, 1948), p. 90.
35. Von Hassell, *The Von Hassell Diaries*, p. 281.
36. John, *Twice through the Lines*, p. 119.
37. John W. Wheeler-Bennett, *The Nemesis of Power: The German Army in Politics, 1918–1945* (London: Macmillan & Co., 1964), p. 556.

CHAPTER NINE: AUTHORITY AND OPPORTUNITY

1. Franz Josef Furtwängler's quote is from his *Männer, die ich sah und kannte* ("Men I saw and knew") in Heinz Höhne, *Canaris: Hitler's Master Spy*, tr. J. Maxwell Brownjohn (New York: Cooper Square Press, 1999), p. 488.
2. Ibid.
3. Ulrich von Hassell, *The Von Hassell Diaries: The Story of the Forces against Hitler inside Germany, 1938–1944* (Boulder, CO: Westview Press, 1994), pp. 276–78.
4. Ibid., pp. 277–78.
5. Ibid., p. 277.
6. Ibid., p. 306.
7. Allen Welsh Dulles, *Germany's Underground: The Anti-Nazi Resistance* (New York: Da Capo Press, 2000), p. 125.
8. Ibid., p. xi.
9. Ibid., p. 125.
10. Ibid.
11. Neal H. Petersen, ed., *From Hitler's Doorstep: The Wartime Intelligence Reports of Allen Dulles, 1942–1945* (University Park, PA: Pennsylvania State University Press, 1996), pp. 22–24.
12. Hans Bernd Gisevius, *To the Bitter End*, tr. Richard and Clara Winston (Cambridge, MA: Houghton, Mifflin, 1947), p. 101.

13. Dulles, *Germany's Underground*, p. 128.

14. Ibid., p. 130.

15. Ibid., pp. 130–31.

16. Ibid., p. 131.

17. *New York Times*, March 1, 1942. This article was written by Dr. Henry Shoskes, who became the Hebrew Immigrant Aid Society overseas representative after the war.

18. Josef Goebbles, *The Goebbles Diaries*, ed. Louis P. Lochner (Garden city, NY: Doubleday, 1948), p. 241.

19. Walter Laquer and Richard Breitman, *Breaking the Silence* (New York: Simon & Schuster, 1986), p. 129.

20. Ibid.

21. "Unsung 'Good German': Fame Comes at Last," *New York Times*, November 9, 1983.

22. Laquer and Breitman, *Breaking the Silence*, p. 144.

23. Ibid., p. 145.

24. Ibid., p. 149.

25. "The Riegner Telegram," United States Holocaust Memorial Museum, Holocaust Encyclopedia, https://encyclopedia.ushmm.org/content/en/article/the-riegner-telegram.

26. "Franklin Roosevelt Administration: Statement on War Crimes, October 7, 1942," Jewish Virtual Library, https://www.jewishvirtuallibrary.org/president-roosevelt-statement.

27. Joseph E. Persico, *Roosevelt's Secret War: FDR and World War II Espionage* (New York: Random House, 2001), pp. 229–30. Also William J. Vanden Heuvel, "America and the Holocaust," *American Heritage*, July–August 1999.

28. David S. Wyman, *The Abandonment of the Jews: America and the Holocaust, 1941–1945* (New York: Pantheon Books, 1984), p. ix.

29. Roger A. Freeman, *The Mighty Eighth: A History of the U.S. Eighth Air Force* (Garden City, NY: Doubleday, 1970), pp. 67–69.

30. Peter Grose, *Gentleman Spy: The Life of Allen Dulles* (Boston: Houghton Mifflin, 1994), p. 174.

31. Petersen, *From Hitler's Doorstep*, p, 51.

32. "The Riegner Telegram."

CHAPTER TEN: AN UNEXPECTED ALLY

1. National Archives, Record Group 226, Entry 146, Box 235.

2. Walter Laquer and Richard Breitman, *Breaking the Silence* (New York: Simon & Schuster, 1986), p. 171.

3. National Archives, Record Group 226, Entry 134, Box 307.

4. Allen Welsh Dulles, *Germany's Underground: The Anti-Nazi Resistance* (New York: Da Capo Press, 2000), pp. 131–33.

5. National Archives, Record Group 226, Entry 146, Box 235.

6. National Archives, Record Group 226, Entry 144, Box 307.

7. Ibid.

8. M. R. D. Foot, *S.O.E. in France* (London: HMSO, 1966), p. 12.

9. Neal H. Petersen, ed., *From Hitler's Doorstep: The Wartime Intelligence Reports of Allen Dulles, 1942–1945* (University Park, PA: Pennsylvania State University Press, 1996), p. 570.

10. Dulles, *Germany's Underground*, p. 133.

11. John W. Wheeler-Bennett, *The Nemesis of Power: The German Army in Politics, 1918–1945* (London: Macmillan, 1964), p. 559.

12. Ernest Bevin, *House of Commons Debate*, July 21, 1949.

13. Dulles, *Germany's Underground*, p. 133.

14. Neal Ascherson, "Inside the Reich: Germany, 1940–1944," episode 16 of *The World at War* (New York: Time-Life, 1974).

15. Ibid.

16. William L. Shirer, *The Rise and Fall of the Third Reich: A History of Nazi Germany* (New York: Simon & Schuster, 1960), p. 934.

17. Ian Colvin, *Master Spy* (New York: McGraw-Hill, 1951), p. 193.

18. George H. Earle, "F.D.R.'s Tragic Mistake," *Confidential Magazine*, August 1958.

19. Heinz Höhne, *Canaris: Hitler's Master Spy*, tr. J. Maxwell Brownjohn (New York: Cooper Square Press, 1999), p. 486.

20. Otto John, *Twice through the Lines*, tr. Richard Barry (New York: Harper & Row, 1972), p. 119.

21. Höhne, *Canaris*, p. 531.

22. "Scholars Reconsidering Italy's Treatment of Jews in Nazi Era," *New York Times*, November 4, 2010.

23. Shirer, *The Rise and Fall*, p. 934.

24. Ulrich von Hassell, *The Von Hassell Diaries: The Story of the Forces against Hitler inside Germany, 1938–1944* (Boulder, CO: Westview Press, 1994), p. 297.

25. Ibid., p. 294.

26. John, *Twice through the Lines*, p. 99.

27. Ibid.

28. Von Hassell, *The Von Hassell Diaries*, p. 307.

29. Ibid., p. 303.

30. Margie Burns, "Sophie Scholl and the White Rose," International Raoul Wallenberg Foundation, https://www.raoulwallenberg.net/holocaust/articles-20/sophie-scholl-white-rose.

31. *New York Times*, April 13, 1943.

32. Höhne, *Canaris*, p. 508.

33. Walter Schellenberg, *The Labyrinth: Memoirs of Walter Schellenberg, Hitler's Chief of Counterintelligence*, tr. Louis Hagen (New York: Da Capo Press, 2000), p. 355.

34. Ibid., pp. 355–56.

35. Dulles, *Germany's Underground*.

36. Höhne, *Canaris*, p. 529.

37. Ibid. Höhne cites a deposition by Walter Huppenkothen, who was a member of the SD, from July 12, 1950.

CHAPTER ELEVEN: "GETTING RID OF HITLER"

1. Peter Padfield, *Himmler: Reichsführer-SS* (New York: Henry Holt, 1990), pp. 119–20.

2. Heinz Höhne, *Canaris: Hitler's Master Spy*, tr. J. Maxwell Brownjohn (New York: Cooper Square Press, 1999), p. 539.

3. Clayton Laurie, *Anzio* (Washington, DC: United States Army Center of Military History, 1994), p. 9.

4. Reinhard Gehlen, *The Service: The Memoirs of General Reinhard Gehlen*, tr. David Irving (New York: Popular Library, 1972), p. 94.

5. Otto John, *Twice through the Lines*, tr. Richard Barry (New York: Harper & Row, 1972), p. 136.

6. William L. Shirer, *The Rise and Fall of the Third Reich: A History of Nazi Germany* (New York: Simon & Schuster, 1960), p. 1026.

7. Ulrich von Hassell, *The Von Hassell Diaries: The Story of the Forces against Hitler inside Germany, 1938–1944* (Boulder, CO: Westview Press, 1994), p. 343.

8. Anne Frank, *The Diary of a Young Girl: The Definitive Edition*, tr. Susan Massotty (New York: Bantam Books, 1997), p. 177.

9. Ian Colvin, *Master Spy* (New York: McGraw-Hill, 1951), p. 160.

10. Ibid.

11. Anthony Cave Brown, *Bodyguard of Lies* (New York: Harper & Row, 1975), p. 665.

12. Ibid.

13. Von Hassell, *The Von Hassell Diaries*, p. 303.

14. Ibid.

15. Hans Speidel, *Invasion 1944* (Chicago: Henry Regnery, 1950), p. 66.

16. Colvin, *Master Spy*, p. 190.

17. Ibid.

18. Cave Brown, *Bodyguard of Lies*, pp. 665–66.

19. Hans Bernd Gisevius, *Valkyrie: An Insider's Account of the Plot to Kill Hitler*, tr. Richard and Clara Winston (Cambridge, MA: Da Capo Press, 2009), p. xiv.

20. Joachim Kramarz, *Stauffenberg: The Life and Death of an Officer*, tr. R. H. Barry (London: Andre Deutsch, 1967), p. 122.

21. Gisevius, *Valkyrie*, p. 139.

22. Joachim C. Fest, *Plotting Hitler's Death: The Story of the German Resistance*, tr. Bruce Little (New York: Metropolitan Books, 1996), p. 217.

23. Gisevius, *Valkyrie*, p. 139.

24. National Archives, Record Group 226, Entry 146, Box 234, Folder 3294.

25. Ibid.

26. Ibid.

27. "German People (Peace Terms) Commons, July 6, 1944," at "Mr Clement Attlee, 1883–October 8, 1967, Summary information for Mr Clement Attlee," UK Parliament, https://api.parliament.uk/historic-hansard/people/mr-clement-attlee/1944.

28. Winston S. Churchill, *The Dawn of Liberation: War Speeches by the Right Hon. Winston S. Churchill*, comp. Charles Eade (London: Cassell, 1945), p. 204.

29. National Archives, Record Group 226, Entry 146, Box 235, Folder 3296.

30. Allen Welsh Dulles, *Germany's Underground: The Anti-Nazi Resistance* (New York: Da Capo Press, 2000), p. 134.

31. Ibid., p. 141.

Chapter Twelve: The Bitter End

1. Anne Frank, *The Diary of a Young Girl: The Definitive Edition*, tr. Susan Massotty (New York: Bantam Books, 1997), p. 306.

2. *Stars and Stripes*, June 6, 1944.

3. Frank, *The Diary of a Young Girl*, pp. 306–8.

4. Ibid., pp. 308–9.

5. "Eisenhower's Address to Western Europe," American Veterans Center, https: //americanveteranscenter.org/avc-media/magazine/avq/issue-vi-springsummer-2009/d -day-65-years-later-eisenhowers-broadcast-to-western-europe-june-6-1944. This is the full text of the address:

> People of Western Europe: A landing was made this morning on the coast of France by troops of the Allied Expeditionary Force. This landing is part of the concerted United Nations' plan for the liberation of Europe, made in conjunc-tion with our great Russian allies.
>
> I have this message for all of you. Although the initial assault may not have been made in your own country, the hour of your liberation is approaching.
>
> All patriots, men and women, young and old, have a part to play in the achievement of final victory. To members of resistance movements, I say, "Follow the instructions you have received." To patriots who are not members of organized resistance groups, I say, "Continue your passive resistance, but do not needlessly endanger your lives until I give you the signal to rise and strike the enemy. The day will come when I shall need your united strength." Until that day, I call on you for the hard task of discipline and restraint.
>
> Citizens of France! I am proud to have again under my command the gallant Forces of France. Fighting beside their Allies, they will play a worthy part in the liberation of their Homeland.
>
> Because the initial landing has been made on the soil of your country, I repeat to you with even greater emphasis my message to the peoples of other occupied countries in Western Europe. Follow the instructions of your leaders. A premature uprising of all Frenchmen may prevent you from being of maximum help to your country in the critical hour. Be patient. Prepare!
>
> As Supreme Commander of the Allied Expeditionary Force, there is imposed on me the duty and responsibility of taking all measures necessary to the prosecution of the war. Prompt and willing obedience to the orders that I shall issue is essential.
>
> Effective civil administration of France must be provided by Frenchmen. All persons must continue in their present duties unless otherwise instructed. Those who have made common cause with the enemy and so betrayed their

country will be removed. As France is liberated from her oppressors, you yourselves will choose your representatives, and the government under which you wish to live.

In the course of this campaign for the final defeat of the enemy you may sustain further loss and damage. Tragic though they may be, they are part of the price of victory. I assure you that I shall do all in my power to mitigate your hardships. I know that I can count on your steadfastness now, no less than in the past. The heroic deeds of Frenchmen who have continued the struggle against the Nazis and their Vichy satellites, in France and throughout the French Empire, have been an example and an inspiration to all of us.

This landing is but the opening phase of the campaign in Western Europe. Great battles lie ahead. I call upon all who love freedom to stand with us. Keep your faith staunch—our arms are resolute—together we shall achieve victory.

6. National Archives, Record Group 226, Entry 99, Box 14, Folder 58a.

7. National Archives, Record Group 226, Entry 146, Box 235, Folder 3296.

8. William L. Shirer, *The Rise and Fall of the Third Reich: A History of Nazi Germany* (New York: Simon & Schuster, 1960), p. 1069.

9. Peter Hoffmann, *The History of the German Resistance, 1933–1945*, tr. Richard Barry (Cambridge, MA: MIT Press, 1977).

10. Karl Heinz Abshagen, *Canaris*, tr. Alan Houghton Brodrick (London: Hutchinson, 1956), p. 242.

11. Heinz Hohne, *Canaris: Hitler's Master Spy*, tr. J. Maxwell Brownjohn (New York: Cooper Square Press, 1999), p. 570.

12. Walter Schellenberg, *The Labyrinth: Memoirs of Walter Schellenberg, Hitler's Chief of Counterintelligence*, tr. Louis Hagen (New York: Da Capo Press, 2000), p. 357.

13. Ibid., p. 358.

14. Otto John, *Twice through the Lines*, tr. Richard Barry (New York: Harper & Row, 1972), pp. 153–54.

15. Frank, *The Diary of a Young Girl*, p. 329.

16. John, *Twice through the Lines*, p. 356.

17. Allen Welsh Dulles, *Germany's Underground: The Anti-Nazi Resistance* (New York: Da Capo Press, 2000), p. 172.

18. National Archives, Record Group 165, Entry 179, Box 702.

19. National Archives, Record Group 226, Entry 190, Microfilm Roll 52, Frames 21–22.

20. Frank, *The Diary of a Young Girl*, p. 329.

21. Felix Kersten, *The Kersten Memoirs, 1940–1945*, tr. Constantine Fitzgibbon and James Oliver (New York: Macmillan, 1957), pp. 203–5.

22. H. R. Trevor-Roper, "The Strange Case of Himmler's Doctor Felix Kersten and Count Bernadotte: Another Mystery of Nazi Times," *Commentary*, April 1957.

23. Eberhard Bethge, *Dietrich Bonhoeffer*, tr. Erich Mossbacher (London: Collins, 1970), p. 810.

24. Ian Colvin, *Chief of Intelligence* (London: Victor Gollancz, 1951), p. 242.
25. Kersten, *The Kersten Memoirs*, p. 277.
26. Ibid.
27. Ibid.
28. Ibid.
29. Schellenberg, *The Labyrinth*, p. 380.
30. Kersten, *The Kersten Memoirs*, p. 278.
31. Ibid., p. 238.
32. Ibid., pp. 276–79.
33. Ibid., p. 280.
34. Ibid.
35. Peter Padfield, *Himmler: Reichsführer-SS* (New York: Henry Holt, 1990), p. 577.
36. Kersten, *The Kersten Memoirs*, p. 281.
37. Ibid., p. 283.
38. Ibid., p. 287.
39. Ibid., pp. 286–87.
40. Ibid., p. 287.
41. Schellenberg, *The Labyrinth*, p. 393.
42. Kersten, *The Kersten Memoirs*, p. 288.
43. Ibid., p. 289.
44. Schellenberg, *The Labyrinth*, p. 393.
45. Kersten, *The Kersten Memoirs*, p. 290.

CHAPTER THIRTEEN: FATHER OF THE PERSECUTED

1. Dwight D. Eisenhower, *Crusade in Europe* (Garden City, NY: Doubleday, 1948), p. 405.
2. William L. Shirer, *The Rise and Fall of the Third Reich: A History of Nazi Germany* (New York: Simon & Schuster, 1960), p. 1085.
3. Leslie Milk and Jeremy Milk, "Witness to the Holocaust," *American Legion Magazine*, August 1994.
4. Ibid.
5. "Buchenwald: Report from Edward R. Murrow, April 16, 1945," Jewish Virtual Library, https://www.jewishvirtuallibrary.org/report-from-edward-r-murrow-on-buchenwald.
6. Samuel Hynes et al., comp., *Reporting World War II* (New York: Library of America, 1995), pt. 2, p. 720.
7. Eisenhower, *Crusade in Europe*, pp. 408–9.
8. Milk and Milk, "Witness to the Holocaust."
9. Shirer, *The Rise and Fall*, p. 1070.
10. Ian Colvin, *Chief of Intelligence* (London: Victor Gollancz, 1951), p. 241.
11. Andre Brissaud, *Canaris* (New York: Grosset & Dunlap, 1974), p. 329.
12. John Toland, *The Last 100 Days* (New York: Bantam, 1967), p. 401.
13. Colvin, *Chief of Intelligence*, p. 248.
14. Toland, *The Last 100 Days*, p. 404.

15. Ibid.

16. Colvin, *Chief of Intelligence*, p. 249.

17. Toland, *The Last 100 Days*, p. 404.

18. Peter Padfield, *Himmler: Reichsführer-SS* (New York: Henry Holt, 1990), p. 610.

19. Inscription is from a photo in the author's collection. Bible verse is from the Revised Standard Version.

20. Ian Colvin, *Master Spy* (New York: McGraw-Hill, 1951), p. 255.

21. Craig R. Whitney, "Who Resisted Hitler? Germans Can't Unite," *New York Times*, July 24, 1994.

22. Klemens von Klemperer, *German Resistance against Hitler: The Search for Allies Abroad, 1938–1945* (Oxford, UK: Clarendon Press, 1992), p. 1.

23. Whitney, "Who Resisted Hitler?"

24. My book *Righteous Deception* gives a detailed account of how Admiral Canaris and the anti-Nazi movement misinformed Hitler's intelligence services regarding the time and place of D-Day.

INDEX

Bell, George, 122–25
Berlin (ship), 22–24
Blomberg, Werner von, 41, 46, 50
Bonhoeffer, Dietrich, 122–25, 128
Brauchitsch, Walter von, 54, 59
Bremen (ship), 6–8
Bürkner, Leopold, 111–12

Canaris, Amelie, 5–6
Canaris, Erika, 24
Canaris, Karl, 4–6
Canaris, Wilhelm: agrees with
　Hitler and Nazis, 26–28;
　appalled by German-Soviet
　treaty, 57; appointed Abwehr
　director, 38–39; arrested, 205–6;
　aware of assassination plots
　against Hitler, 193–94; begins
　to turn away from Hitler,
　46–52; changes Himmler's
　opinion of death camps, 183;
　convinced that invasion of
　Russia would be disastrous,
　89; decides to work against
　Nazis in secret, 51; delivers
　accurate information on D-Day
　landings to Allies, 189–90;

diary discovered, 227; escapes
captivity, 15–16; executed,
229–31; gives Hitler's plans
to invade Poland to Britain
and France, 53–56; happy that
Nazis are elected, 35–37; helps
Dietrich Bonhoeffer, 123–25;
helps Halina Szymanska escape
to Switzerland, 61–65; helps
Jews escape to Spain, 80–82;
hinders transfer of Jews to
concentration camps, 127–28;
holds secret information against
Reinhard Heydrich, 68–69;
horrified by mass executions in
Poland, 58–59; interrogated by
Gestapo, 211; keeps in touch
with Allies, 165; learns of
D-Day, 202; meets Heydrich,
23–24; memorial plaque in
Flossenbürg, 232; misinforms
Hitler of fighting in Poland,
60–61; misleads Hitler
regarding Anzio invasion, 184–
85; officer during World War
I, 9–15; Operation Pastorius,
xii–xiii, 1–2; and Operation